HARRY WAUGH'S WINE DIARY

HARRY WAUGH'S WINE DIARY

1982-1986

The Wine Appreciation Guild
San Francisco

© 1987 Harry Waugh

Published in London by Christopher Helm Ltd.

British Library Cataloguing in Publication Data

Waugh, Harry
    Harry Waugh's wine diary.
    1982-1986
    1. Wine tasting
    I. Title
    641.2′2   TP548.5.A5

    ISBN 0-932664-53-9

    Library of Congress Number:
    First American Edition Published by

THE WINE APPRECIATION GUILD
155 Connecticut St.
San Francisco, CA 94107
(415) 864-1202

Typeset in ITC Garamond Book by Leaper & Gard Ltd, Bristol, England
Printed in the United States of America

Contents

Illustrations

All photographs are courtesy of Harry Waugh.

1

VISIT TO LOS ANGELES
January 1982

What a contrast it was with the day before of deep snow and ice in England, the worst weather for many years and the cloudless sky and a temperature of 21°C here in Los Angeles.

Our host Edward Lazarus had lent us the vast house of his late father on Roxbury Avenue North in Beverly Hills, in a block where some of the famous film stars of the 1920s used to live.

On the first day we were invited to dine at a small but good restaurant on Sunset Boulevard called La Toque, where the young American chef and owner handled his *nouvelle cuisine* with considerable skill. Our hosts, Ed Lazarus, a lawyer, and Brad Klein, a dermatologist, had brought their own wine with them. There were two 1978 chardonnays for comparison, the Zaca Mesa (barrel fermented) was good, but the Quail Ridge a sad disappointment, heavily oxidised. Two old cabernets followed, the 1968 Gemello, a good colour, lots of fruit but it tailed off somewhat. The 1968/9 Spring Mountain was much better and most attractive. Another good red wine to follow was the 1976 Ridge Zinfandel from the small Picchetti vineyard whose grapes are usually included in blends, being of such excellent quality in 1978 they were made into this highly successful wine. The meal concluded with Louis Martini's delectable Moscato Amabile.

THURSDAY, 14 JANUARY

Another lovely day. Ed Lazarus drove us along the very pretty Sunset Boulevard to Malibu where we spent a fascinating morning at the Paul Getty Museum which is a fine building in a superb setting. I am so pleased to have seen it at last. The building, full of treasures from ancient Rome and Greece, is based on the Villa dei

Papiri which stood outside Herculaneum overlooking the Bay of Naples and which was buried by volcanic mud when Vesuvius erupted in AD79.

About five years ago in Los Angeles, being dissatisfied with the usual, wineletters, a coterie of enthusiastic amateur wine lovers grouped together in order to form one of their own to accord with their own idealistic principles. As we were already aware, the 1978 vintage was unusually good for red burgundy and the research for *The Underground Wineletter* caused them to buy and taste anonymously over 400 different red burgundies of that year. Although still too young to be enjoyed properly, the meal that evening at Ed's condominium was based on a few of the more successful wines of this vintage. The other guests were Mr and Mrs John Tilson and Bipin Desai. John Tilson is the editor of the Wineletter, in association with Geoffrey Troy, Bipin Desai, Ed Lazarus and Brad Klein.

We began in fact with two chardonnays from the Hanzell Winery, in the Sonoma Valley, the 1973 and the 1974, both good vintages but of different styles. The 1974 was a bigger fuller wine, but in fact we all preferred the 1973, notable for its elegance.

There was some discussion over the first two reds, each of them also very different.

1978 Echézeaux, domaine Dujac
(a very rare wine – only twenty-five dozen,
i.e. one barrel, was made)
Dark colour, a glorious bouquet and a lovely flavour, although by no means ready yet, this had an immediate attraction

1978 Echézeaux, Henri Jayer, Vosne Romanée
Dark colour, although very closed up, the bouquet is clearly going to be very good. The wine itself more severe at present than the Dujac, very backward, but shows great promise

The second pair were both Bonnes Mares.

1978 Bonnes Mares, domaine Dujac
Dark colour, a most attractive bouquet and a delightful flavour

1978 Bonnes Mares, Groffier
Very dark colour, a superb fragrant bouquet, and a gloriously rich flavour, immense quality

But we had not finished!

1961 Bonnes Mares, Clair Dau
Good dark colour, a splendid bouquet, a lovely complete wine, at its best

1919 Bonnes Mares Delongey Vieilles Vignes
Alas, too old

It is seldom that such great red burgundies come my way. An evening such as this helps dispel the disillusion which has been growing about the Côte d'Or.

FRIDAY, 15 JANUARY

Yet another superb day, the temperature around 21°C, a heaven-sent break for us Londoners. Beverly Hills is a pretty place, not only because of its avenues of lovely houses, all of such varied styles of architecture, but also for its shops where all manner of tempting things are displayed. On the street, it was noticeable so many of the women were following the fashion of wearing knickerbockers, such a pleasant relief from the blowsy trend of the past decade.

The first session of the great 1961 tasting took place that evening in the Beverly Wilshire Hotel on Wilshire Boulevard, which has happy memories, and it was especially nice to see my old friend Hernando Courtwright, possibly one of the greatest hoteliers in the world.

The man behind this extraordinary series of tastings was Bipin Desai, a specialist in high energy nuclear physics at the University of California. Indian by birth and starting life as both a teetotaller and a vegetarian, he claims that in recent years he has been doing all he can to make up for lost time! Over the past ten years he has collected rare wines, particularly of the 1961 vintage. Then in 1978 he began to toy with the idea of a major 1961 tasting, but it is doubtful if at that time he would ever have imagined ending up with anything so important as this turned out to be.

Having assembled over 90 different 1961s in his cellar, he travelled Europe to continue his search. Eventually, with the aid of friends, including Dr Louis Skinner (who himself in 1981 had presented a tasting of some 50 1961s) and Jean-Michel Cazes of Château Lynch-Bages, he managed to reach the staggering total of no less than 131 examples of this unusually fine vintage. Admittedly nine of them were sauternes and barsacs, but that still left 122 reds!

The bulk of the wine, therefore, came from his own excellent cellar and the remainder had been gathered together more recently from the London Auction Houses as well as private cellars in Europe. In this manner, the risk of wines being spoiled by irregular storage was mitigated, a problem which, due to extremes of temperature, unfortunately has been known to occur from time to time in the USA.

In view of the magnitude of this event the tastings were spread over three days: 7.0 p.m. on 15 January (Saint Emilion and Pomerol); 11.0 a.m. on 16 January (Sauternes, Barsac, Haut-Médoc and Saint Estèphe); 7.0 p.m. on 16 January (red Graves and Margaux); and finally 11.0 a.m. on 17 January (Saint Julien and Pauillac).

An impeccable buffet (Peter Korzilius) was served during each function and, for the proper appreciation of the wine, the dishes had been most carefully selected by Edward Lazarus. (The latter and Herbert Barnard were invaluable in planning this event.) As there were 34 people present, the question of glasses raised a problem, in fact 1,200 were used at each session.

With wine already 20 years old, some bottle variation was inevitable and since two bottles from each *château* were to be used, it was decided to serve a glass from each bottle to alternate persons. Thus in a case of variance, one could always 'borrow' from one's neighbour. This, in fact, proved invaluable.

There is usually some controversy over how long a time a wine should be decanted before serving but on this occasion the timing worked admirably. The wines for the first flight of seven had been decanted by Kerry Payne immediately prior to the actual tasting and the decanting continued steadily throughout the session. Meanwhile, Dennis Foley had the task of filling each glass to the required level. Clearly these two have reduced the organisation of a great tasting to a fine art – this was to prove a masterly performance without a single hitch.

Beginning with the Saint Emilions there were five flights on the first evening. The wines were served anonymously and discussed after each flight. The names were then revealed to enable further assessment.

Stubbornly perhaps, I hold firm views about blind tastings. It is so easy to pronounce with the labels in full view, but impossible to overcome prejudice. In a blind tasting, as this event proved, wines may emerge whose merit might otherwise easily have been overlooked. Thus even if one does make the occasional mistake, an anonymous tasting is worth while in the long run. On this occasion, however, having requested an anonymous tasting when accepting the invitation, I found myself 'hoist with my own petard' for I found that, as master of ceremonies, I had to disclose my own findings first of all! To make matters worse still, with the exception of the very last flight (i.e. the Pauillacs) the finest wines were by no means reserved for the end of each phase, but somewhat unkindly distributed among the lesser fry.

As for the climatic conditions under which this vintage was born, I can do no better than to quote from the notes made late in

1961 by the present manager of Château Latour, who at that time was one of the leading brokers for the wines of the Médoc. Here roughly is the translation:

C'est le grand – le Tout Grand. In other words, the very best!

Eventually the vines gave birth to the 1961 vintage following the dreadful shock they had suffered on the morning of the 29th May. Thanks to a severe frost three quarters of the promised harvest disappeared overnight with the result that we brought in a crop almost ridiculously small, less indeed that the tiny vintages of 1956 and 1957 which were victims of the disastrous frost of February 1956, the most severe for over two hundred years.

The development of the vines in 1961 was precocious; they were in full flower at least two weeks earlier than the normal period which is around the 16th June, hence the extremity of the disaster. As though to make amends, the weather thereafter was very good until the vintage was harvested. Thus two factors, the unusual climatic conditions and the scarcity of grapes both played their part in producing a wine of extraordinary quality. The vines had been able to lavish all their bounty on the few surviving bunches.

Without pretending to explain the mysteries of nature, we can compare this vintage of 1961 with that of 1945, which was somewhat similar. In that case, the early stages were equally favourable, causing the vegetation to be three weeks in advance, but hopes were dashed by three successive days of frost on 1, 2 and 3 May.

With little rain to swell them, the hot summer of 1961 caused the grapes to form thick skins, thereby producing the tannin which has caused this vintage to take so long to mature. Happily, by this time, the art of vinification had made considerable progress, so the 1961s have not taken so long to develop as did the 1945s. Looking further back over historic vintages, that of 1928 was even harder and still more so than the great 1870s; the latter did not reach their prime for some 40 years, by which time most people had either consumed them too soon or had given up in despair.

The notes on each of the 131 wines would make this overlong, so in order to save space I can do no better, I think, than reproduce a chart which gives the rating of three of the tasters besides myself: Dr Bernard L. Rhodes, vice president of the Kaiser Institute, the man who planted what has become the now famous Martha's Vineyard in the Napa Valley; John Tilson, the energetic editor of the *Underground Wine Letter*, the Los Angeles publication which has gained a well-deserved reputation among connoisseurs; and of course Bipin Desai, the man behind this remarkable event.

For the sake of brevity, only the wines which rated 17/20 and over are included here. Every person has his own weaknesses, thus with 131 wines to be assessed I began on a more modest level of scoring than I should have and as the Saint Emilions were the first group to be tasted, I was clearly marking them too rigorously. The two main victims of this error on my part were Cheval-Blanc and Ausone and with hindsight I should have given the Ausone at least 17/20 and the Cheval-Blanc 17.5 or 18/20. Even so, of all the regions, Saint Emilion was perhaps the weakest.

By contrast the group of no less than 17 top growth pomerols was outstanding. At the time I wrote 'one runs out of superlatives, but what a blaze of glory!' Pétrus, Latour-Pomerol, Trotanoy, L'Evangile and Clos L'Eglise all first rate: the Latour-Pomerol was a proper knockout and the Pétrus a masterpiece, to say the least.

Nothing very remarkable occurred when we tackled the wines under the heading of Haut-Médoc, but among the Saint Estèphes, Les Ormes de Pez came as a most agreeable surprise, surpassing easily the de Pez from a magnum. Both the Cos and the Montrose were excellent, especially the former, but then the latter is still far from being ready.

Among the red Graves, the Haut-Brion grew and grew in the glass and subsequently I marked it up to 18.5. La Mission Haut-Brion and Latour Haut-Brion were not far behind, but for me the real surprise in this group was a wine we seldom come across, Les Carmes Haut-Brion. On inquiry later, I was told that although so little known, Les Carmes is reputed to excel in the great vintages, although it is not always so successful in other years.

In the margaux section the Château Margaux and Palmer were really in a class by themselves and since each has such a distinctive style, there was no difficulty in telling which was which. In view of its tremendous reputation, there was some concern over the Palmer, for more had been expected from it. The Margaux, preferred by most of those present, was a superb wine. As the guest of Marguerite Cruse, I have always admired her 1961 d'Issan, so it was reassuring to have my opinion confirmed in a blind tasting. As will be seen, the Boyd-Cantenac was also good.

As anticipated, the Saint Juliens came up to expectation, the general standard being high. Again as expected, the two leaders, Léoville-Lascases and Ducru-Beaucaillou were first rate with Gloria well in the running. Fine as it undoubtedly was, there was a decided difference between the two bottles of Gruaud-Larose, which could indicate the passing of the summit; from recollection, this delicious wine was better some years ago.

The Pauillacs were served in three flights and, as will be seen

Bordeaux 1961 – the Ratings of Four of the Tasters

Harry Waugh	Dr Bernard L. Rhodes	John Tilson	Bipin Desai	Points out of 20
Lafite, Margaux	Lafite, Pétrus	Latour	Lafite	19.5 (or 19 +)
Latour, Pétrus	Palmer, Trotanoy	L'Evangile, Palmer, Pétrus	Latour, Margaux, Mouton Rothschild, Trotanoy	19
Ducru Beaucaillou, Palmer, Mouton Rothschild	Latour, Margaux, Mouton Rothschild	Gruaud Larose, Léoville Lascases, Lynch Bages, Mouton Baron Philippe, Mouton Rothschild, Pichon Baron	Latour Pomerol, Palmer, Pétrus	18.5 (or 18 +)
	Ducru Beaucaillou, Latour Pomerol, Mouton Baron Philippe, Suduiraut			
Boyd Cantenac, Latour Pomerol, Cos d'Estournel, Léoville Lascases, Montrose, Mouton Baron Philippe, Pichon Baron, Trotanoy	Cheval Blanc, Cos d'Estournel, Haut Brion, Latour Blanche, Léoville Lascases, Pichon Baron	Clos L'Eglise, Gloria, Grand Puy Lacoste, Grand Puy Ducasse, Latour Pomerol, Lafleur Pétrus, Malescot, Margaux, Montrose, Pichon Lalande, Pontet Canet, Suduiraut, Trotanoy	L'Evangile, Gruaud Larose, Haut Brion, Lafleur Pétrus, Lynch Bages, Léoville Lascases, Malescot, Montrose, Pichon Baron	18
L'Evangile, Haut Brion, d'Issan, Malescot	Clos L'Eglise, Gloria, Lafleur Pétrus, Léoville Poyferré, Lynch Bages, Montrose	Boyd Cantenac, Ducru Beaucaillou, Pape-Clement, Sigalas Rabaud	Cheval Blanc, Clos L'Eglise, Ducru Beaucaillou, Mouton Baron Philippe, Rausan Segla	17.5 (or 17 +)
Clos L'Eglise, Gloria, Gruaud Larose, Haut Batailley, Latour Blanche, Lafleur Pétrus, Léoville Poyferré, Les Carmes Haut Brion, Les Ormes de Pez, Lynch Bages, Marquis de Termes, Pavie, Pichon Lalande, Pontet Canet, Sigalas Rabaud, Suduiraut	Ausone, Boyd Cantenac, Carruades de Lafite, La Conseillante, Croizet Bages, L'Evangile, Gruaud Larose, D'Issan, Les Ormes de Pez, Pontet Canet, Pichon Lalande, Vieux Château Certan	Carruades de Lafite, La Conseillante, Cos d'Estournel, La Gaffelière, Haut Brion, Lafite, La Lagune, Latour Haut Brion, Marquis de Termes, Pavie, St Pierre, Vieux Château Certan	Ausone, Belair, Cantemerle, Carruade de Lafite, La Conseillante, Cos d'Estournel, Figeac, Lascombes, Latour Blanche, Latour Figeac, Petit Village, Pichon Lalande, La Pointe, Pontet Canet, La Mission Haut Brion, Vieux Château Certan	17

from a consensus of opinion among the four tasters whose scores are mentioned, the Mouton Baron Philippe was exceptional ('a mouthful of bliss'). The Pontet-Canet also showed extremely well. The Carruades de Lafite was especially popular – it had a glorious bouquet – but the impression from my bottle was that it now may well have passed its best.

After the first two flights of Pauillacs (each of seven wines) had been tackled and the names revealed, we realised this was the only *commune* where the giants had been kept for the last and what a 'grande finale' it turned out to be!

For me the Lafite and Latour were well ahead of the others. The Lafite which I placed first was reassuring as my experience hitherto with this particular wine has been disappointing. For instance, when I tasted 25 1961s in Belgium a few years ago, it had not come within the first ten. The answer probably lies (as David Peppercorn says in his recently-published excellent *The Wines of Bordeaux*, pp. 129-39) in that the bottling of the 1961 vintage was irregular at Lafite. Anyway, on this occasion it was superb.

While I had not rated the Mouton quite so high, my note at the time read 'lovely deep bouquet (fine tobacco), a delicious sweet taste and altogether first rate': 18.5/20 points in a category such as this is something very special. As so often happens, the Latour was still very backward and will need some years yet to reach its peak.

Also grouped in the last flight were the two Pichons and Lynch-Bages, but inevitably they were overshadowed by the giants, the best so far as I was concerned was the Pichon-Baron.

In retrospect, for perfection, it might have been instructive to compare all the eight *grande seigneurs* anonymously together rather than with their districts, but there must be limits to one's demands. It is nevertheless interesting to see how they all stood out in their respective groups. Indeed, to have tasted them at all was the opportunity of a lifetime.

It was also noted how few of these 1961s, even those in the lesser categories, had scored low points. Admittedly there were instances of variation from bottle to bottle and indeed some bottles had been corked and one or two were frankly bad. Some, of course, were showing signs of age, which after 20 years is not unexpected, but generally speaking the way this vintage had held up at such a high level of quality was impressive.

Clearly there is no space for each and every wine to be noted but for readers fortunate enough still to have some of this great vintage in their cellars, these are some of the wines in which the tannin was still quite evident, therefore presumably with capacity for further improvement: Trottevieille, Pavie, La Tour Figeac, Grand Barrail, Vieux Ch. Certan, La Conseillante, Gazin, Trotanoy,

Lafon-Rochet, Calon-Ségur, Montrose, Haut-Brion, Latour Haut-Brion, La Mission, Pape-Clément, Haut-Bailly, Rauzan-Gassies, Margaux, Giscours, St Pierre, Léoville-Lascases, Lafite, Latour and Pichon-Lalande.

Some years ago at the tasting in Belgium the Saint Emilions were the weakest link and the pomerols among the first ten wines. It is fair to say that this conclusion was confirmed in Los Angeles with the pomerols competing valiantly with many of the best wines from the Graves district and the Médoc.

All too often the French press has hailed a good vintage as the year of the century, but unless one includes 1900, there really have only been four worthy of that title, 1928, 1929, 1945 and 1961, with nothing except for 1982 and perhaps the Comet year of 1985, to equal any of these since. Of these, the 1929s were the shortest lived, but how superb they were at their zenith at around 20 years old (for the writer at any rate, the most attractive of them all).

Due to their excessive tannin, both the 1928 and 1945 vintages took an 'unconscionable' time to mature, longer certainly than 1961. During the general discussion following the final session, several of those present who were fortunate enough still to possess these two older vintages in their cellars, agreed that generally speaking a number of their 1945s showed signs of the tannin having outlived the fruit. This is of course a matter for debate, but as a result of the present comprehensive exercise it would appear on the whole that the 1961 vintage has a better balance of fruit and tannin and all in all is of greater calibre than its two illustrious predecessors. It could be argued therefore that, up to date, 1961 could be regarded as truly 'the year of the century'.*

Sauternes and Barsac
It was not so easy to wax enthusiastic over the white dessert wines. Admittedly in this case the 1961 vintage was not as successful for dessert wines, but with one notable exception, the result of this tasting was not too bad. Three of them in fact were extremely good, Suduiraut, Latour Blanche and Sigalas Rabaud.

The shock was the d'Yquem. Both bottles, dark brown in colour, were heavily oxidised and there was a gasp of dismay when their identity was revealed. Some six or so years ago, while dining with Dr Rhodes in California, I made a proper fool of myself over this particular wine. Overhearing my expounding on its oxidation, etc., he produced anonymously an excellent bottle

---

*This was borne out at a major tasting of the 1945 vintage in Los Angeles in 1986.

to finish the meal and was my face red! It would appear, therefore, that there could have been some irregular bottling.

Note. For those readers who may wish for further information, here for what they are worth, are the details of the author's own scorings:

Saint Emilion
Grace Dieu 15, Troplong-Mondot 13, Beauséjour Duffau 15.5, Beauséjour Fagouet 14, Pavie 16, Clos Fourtet 13.5, Trottevieille 15.5, Belair 14, Figeac 15, Gaffelière 11, Canon 15, Soutard 14, Grand Corbin 14, Corbin Michotte 15, Corbin Despagne 13, La Tour-Figeac 15, Grand Barrail 15, La Tour-du-Pin-Figeac 13, Ausone 16, Cheval-Blanc 18.

Pomerol
Petit-Village 13, Nenin 15, Certan Giraud 14, Clinet 13, La Pointe 14, Le Gay 13, Rouget 13, Vieux Ch. Certan 16.5, La Conseillante 16.5, Gazin 15, Lafleur 14, La Fleur-Pétrus 17, Pétrus 19, Trotanoy 18.5, Clos l'Eglise 17, Latour-Pomerol 18.5.

Haut-Médoc
Citran 12, Lanessan 10, Liversan 12, Belgrave 12, Chasse-Spleen 13, Fourcas-Hosten 9, La Lagune 16, Cantemerle 15.5, Maucaillou 10.

Saint Estèphe
Cos Labory 13, Lafon-Rochet 15, Calon-Ségur 15, Phélan-Ségur 14.5, Les Ormes de Pez 16, de Pez magnum 14.5, Meyney 15, Cos d'Estournel 18, Montrose 17.5.

Graves
Carbonnieux 14.5, Latour-Haut-Brion 16, Haut Brion 19.5, La Mission 17, Domaine de Chevalier 14, Pape-Clément 14.5, Malartic-Lagravière 13.5, Smith-Haut-Lafitte 16, de Fieuzal 14, Haut-Bailly 16, Larrivet-Haut-Brion 12.5, Les Carmes Haut-Brion 17, Bouscaut 13.

Margaux
Angludet 13.5, Tour du Mons 15, Prieuré-Lichine 16, Kirwan 14, Boyd-Cantenac 17, Brane-Cantenac 15, Cantenac-Brown 13, Ferrière 14, Lascombes 16, Malescot 16.5, Rauzan-Gassies 15, Rausan-Ségla 13, Margaux 19.5, Palmer 18.5, Dauzac 13, d'Issan 17.5, Marquis de Terme 16.5, Marquis d'Alesme Becker 14, Durfort-Vivens 16.

Saint Julien
Lagrange 12, Talbot 16, Gloria 17.5, St Pierre 15, Gruaud-Larose

17, Bechevelle 16, Langoa-Barton 13.5, Léoville-Barton 14.5, Léoville-Poyferré 17, Léoville-Lascases 18, Branaire-Ducru 14, Ducru-Beaucaillou 18.5.

Pauillac

Grand-Puy-Lacoste 16, Grand-Puy-Ducasse 16, Batailley 15.5, Haut-Batailley 17, Moulin des Carruades 13, Duhart-Milon 11, Haut-Bages-Averous 14, Cuvée Commanderie du Bontemps 13.5, Pontet-Canet 17, Clerc-Milon 15, Croizet-Bages 16.5, Lynch-Moussas 13, Mouton Baron Philippe 18, Carruades de Ch. Lafite 16, Mouton-Rothschild 18.5, Lynch-Bages 17, Lafite 19.5, Pichon-Lalande 17, Pichon-Baron 18, Latour 19.

MONDAY, 18 JANUARY

Tawfiq Khoury, a noted builder, sent his chauffeur to drive us to San Diego. The journey took two and a half hours but driving along the highway was not as interesting as I had expected. Apparently the sea road is far prettier but takes very much longer.

Tawfiq and Richel Koury live in a fabulous house with a lovely garden which Hugh Johnson helped to arrange. Twenty of us sat down to a dinner that unquestionably could be described as a gastronomic event. Among our friends present were Barney Rhodes, Ben and Mayon Ichinose, Nate and Judy Chroman and Lou Skinner from Florida. So exceptional was this meal that a record of it may be of interest. The standard was equal to a two star restaurant in the *Guide Michelin*.

We began with bottles of 1961 Dom Perignon. There was naturally a little variation in bottles of this age but the wine had kept remarkably well. Canapes of pâté de saumon et avocado were served with the champagne. Then followed Éscargots Imperial Dynasty. With delicious lobster grilled with a liberal quantity of truffles we drank 1953 Corton Charlemagne Domaine Hippolyte Thevenot. Here, because of the age of the wine there was a definite difference, the bottle with the paler colour was excellent.

The tender pheasant was accompanied by an absolute master-piece from Burgundy, 1961 La Tâche in magnums. The bouquet and distinction of the first bottle had a wonderful fragrance and a glorious flavour. The second magnum took longer to develop after being poured into the glass. If the bouquet was perhaps less elegant, it was certainly a bigger, sturdier wine.

For a pause, if not a change of pace, a delectable sorbet of kiwi had been selected and we started again with rack of lamb cooked to perfection with a hint of tarragon, endives and a fine soufflé of spinach. The claret served with this course, the 1949 Cheval-

Blanc, was so good people began to wonder whether it was not better than the renowned 1947 from this *château*. Whereupon although it was not on the menu, our host went to his cellar to produce that very wine. The doubters had to admit the 1947 was the more noble of the two vintages, much richer with a fabulous bouquet. By this time we were eating an excellent cheese fondue and, as Barney mentioned, the 1947 was so rich it went better with the fondue than it would have done with the pheasant, thus we had the best of both worlds!

A beautiful 1937 Lafaurie Peyraguey accompanied strawberries and cream and we finished with a magnificent bottle of Taylor 1955 which must surely be at its superb best.

With all these good things this may sound a daunting meal, but as neither the portions or quantity of wine served were large and it took place over a long period of time, it was sheer perfection, easily one of the greatest meals of my life.

Among the guests were Mr and Mrs Richard Wing, owners of the Imperial Dynasty restaurant near Fresno in California who among other things had made a name for his restaurant with his escargots Imperial Dynasty and this particular course at the meal was his responsibility. Never have I eaten such good snails. The secret apparently is the ginger which nullifies the garlic and in turn is softened itself. Some pâté de foie gras is included in the recipe and, in order to prevent the snails becoming tough from the heat of the oven, each portion was covered with a slice of cheese and onion and with two slices of ginger root on top.

Before leaving, Tawfiq took us down to his cellar, a veritable treasure trove where apart from thousands of bottles of rare wines he has over 500 magnums, double magnums and imperials of all the greatest wines. Among the rarities are literally dozens of Cheval-Blanc 1947, Quinta do Noval 1931 and a particularly inter- esting collection of old Madeira back to the eighteenth century.

On our return to Los Angeles we stopped for lunch at a restaurant in North Beach called Bouzy Rouge where Steve McAnlis had assembled a group of enthusiasts from Les Amis du Vin and the Hi Time Liquor Store. Most of the numerous wines we tasted bore strange names to us. Steve admitted that new wineries spring up with such frequency that even the wine devotees living in California are unable to keep up with them.

It is even worse for the store proprietors. As an example a member of Hi Time told me there were so many good chardon- nays on the market, which they buy in their enthusiasm and later cannot keep trace of either in the store or in the warehouse, that many become overlooked. The financing of a liquor store in California must be more difficult than in England because here the owners have also to keep such a large and varied range of their own domestic wines. One factor of course is their cost, in some cases relatively much higher than perhaps better quality wines from Europe.

That evening we attended a session of a wine club which meets once a month to taste rare wines. Among those present were many who had been present at the 1961 tasting, Ed Lazarus, Bipin Desai, John Tilson and Geoffrey Troy, and we met at the home of Brad Klein, who also has a fascinating cellar beneath his house.

Mrs Klein, also a dermatologist, had prepared a delicious cold seafood supper with delectable sauces. The theme of the evening and one close to my heart was a vertical tasting of vintages of Taylor's Port which Brad Klein had collected. The evening began with a nice champagne new to me, called Bellecart-Salmon 1976, a wine very popular in California.

One's visits to the West Coast are instructive because new trends in the wine world appear to be more marked. I learnt, for instance, that in France, champagne from individual growers is encroaching upon the sale of the *grands marques*. And more and more growers who own fine vineyards (instead of as in the past selling their produce to the *négociants*) are now caring for the development of their red burgundy in cask, bottling it and selling it under their own label. This entails quite a new line of research in order to seek out these growers and find how to buy their wine.

The first wine, one which Brad had found at Sotheby's in London, if not in the first flush of youth had considerable academic interest, an 1899 Sillery from Champagne with the neck label Claridge, a prominent British firm in the nineteenth century but long since defunct. It had certainly disappeared from the scene long before I entered the wine trade in the 1930s. The wine had, as only to be expected, a somewhat oxidised bouquet and was only slightly effervescent, nevertheless the taste was still agreeable.

Then followed two magnums of chardonnay of the 1978 vintage from yet another winery so far unknown to me, Acacia. One called Napa Chardonnay was rather too rich and full blown for my personal taste; the other, however, from the Lakeside Vineyard in Carneros had far more style and distinction, a good wine.

Vintage Port from the House of Taylor Fladgate

First Flight

1970
Dark colour, quite a powerful full bouquet, rich but very youthful, needs at least five years   15/20

1966
Medium colour, good but not exceptional bouquet, very fruity and typical of its vintage   16/20

1963
Good dark colour, strong almost masculine bouquet, powerful with a wonderful flavour, great stuff which needs time to develop   19/20

1960
Fine colour, a mature slightly toffeeish nose, delightful flavour, probably at its best now   17/20

Second Flight
1955
Good colour, a heavenly bouquet, great fruit and concentration, a fine bottle   18/20

1948
Very dark colour, an unusually deep bouquet, also a deep enveloping flavour, a giant of port. All this in spite of the bottle being slightly corked, the underlying potential was evident 19/20

1945
Dark colour with just a hint of amber, a glorious nose with something there none of us had ever encountered before, just a hint of mint or was it cedar, anyway most attractive. The tannin at last subdued, this was a superb bottle of port   20/20

1942
Owing to the war this was the first vintage (so far as I know) which was bottled in Portugal. The colour light to medium, the nose was good but less intense, the finish sweet and gentle. This bottle hardly stood a chance following so closely on the heels of the great 1948 and 1945 vintages   16/20

Third Flight
1935 (Jubilee Vintage of King George V)
A paler colour but a well bred bouquet, not at all a big wine but there was plenty of charm   14.5/20

1927
Good dark colour, strangely not much bouquet but sound, by contrast a splendid depth of intense flavour, well knit and deep   19/20

Having always considered these famous 1927s to have been at

14

their best when about 20 years old, in spite of the lack of bouquet I was frankly surprised by the intense quality of this wine.

1924
Very good colour considering its age, a delightful bouquet, initially sweet but the brandy was beginning to become evident, quite remarkable though for its age   18/20

Fourth Flight
1912
Good colour, a distinguished bouquet, a complete wine with all its faculties, very good indeed   17/20

1904
Fairly pale colour and of course a much older nose, some spirit at the finish but lots of fruit left   16/20

1870
A pale tawny colour but anno domini had prevailed. This must have turned up its toes long ago but 'Bravo Brad Klein' for finding it for us

WEDNESDAY, 20 JANUARY

It seldom rains apparently in Los Angeles, but when it does so it is in no uncertain manner and one can get very wet. We lunched at a good Chinese restaurant with Ed Lazarus and then went shopping in an excellent area called Century Plaza.

That night, Mike McNamara drove us to his home in Palo Verdes for a delightful dinner and really spoilt us with fine wines, among them Mouton-Rothschild 1959 and 1947 Cheval-Blanc; the latter, a splendid bottle by the way. I have been told there is now some variation between bottles of this wine. The high note continued for we finished with 1959 Lafaurie Peyraguey.

THURSDAY, 21 JANUARY

A fascinating morning spent at the MGM Studios in Culver City. Robert Justman, a director is a friend of Ed Lazarus. I have met Robert during past visits to Los Angeles and he is a devotee of fine wine. He took us to the set where a TV film, *McClean's Law*, was being prepared and we saw the hero of the series, Jim Arness both rehearsing and being filmed and in fact were even introduced to him.

Our last evening reached another high level in gastronomy, a dinner party given for us by Bipin Desai at Michael's restaurant where the food was truly delectable. We had course after course but since it was *nouvelle cuisine* and beautifully prepared, no way was this tiring.

Not wishing to produce the kind of wines we are lucky enough to encounter from time to time, our thoughtful host had searched his cellar to find something different and certainly succeeded.

Among the appetisers were belon oysters and how delicious they were, every bit as good as those from France. These came from oyster beds off the Californian coast, south of San Francisco. With these we drank a wine from the Jura, Château Chalon and true to form it did have some resemblance in flavour to light sherry.

With delicious sea bass we drank a fine old semi-sweet Vouvray. A sorbet followed to clear our palates, then with lobster and copious fresh truffles we were given two splendid white burgundies:

1978 Chevalier Montrachet les Demoiselles, Jadot
Pale colour, well bred nose, not a big wine but most distinguished.

1978 Chevalier Montrachet, Leflaive
Slightly darker, a splendid bouquet with a deeper flavour. This will be wonderful in, say, two year's time.

Two red wines were then served, both of a colour to appear almost black and both the produce of that outstanding grower, Guigal in Ampuis.

1978 Hermitage
Lovely bouquet, full of flavour but still some acidity to lose. Should make a lovely bottle in five to ten years' time

1978 Côte Rotie, Côte Brune and Côte Blonde
A lovely bouquet and a huge wine packed with fruit. Will make a superb bottle. How nice to know I have a couple of cases of this in my own cellar.

With those we ate delectable grilled baby chicken.

Following on with the cheese, Bipin had chosen for us

1955 Pichon Longuéville Baron
Good nose and flavour but with too much acidity for my taste

1949 Pichon Longuéville Baron
Seemed almost dark in colour, a beautiful bouquet and wine of depth and fine quality. Much nicer than the 1955

2

VISIT TO SPAIN AND PORTUGAL
February 1983

Dick and Sally Scheer were waiting for us at Jerez Airport and wafted us off quickly to a nice lunch at a restaurant called El Bosche. Dick Scheer is the owner of what must be one of the finest retail stores in the Mid-West, The Village Corner, Ann Arbor, Michigan. With them was our friend Bob Simburger, a newspaper man from Detroit.

Rooms had been booked for us at a delightful hotel, El Corregidor in Arcos de la Frontera, some 32 kilometres from Jerez. Facing a square in which there is a fine old church as well as what looks like a Moorish castle, the hotel is situated on the top of a high cliff whence there is a fabulous view over the surrounding countryside.

The following morning, Mr Bruce Millar showed us round the Sandeman Bodegas in Jerez where an immense amount of new construction was in progress, a result no doubt of the recent change of ownership to Seagrams.

I shall always have a warm feeling towards Sandeman because it was the late Pat Sandeman who found my job for me with Harveys of Bristol immediately after the war. For generations the Bristol Milk and the Bristol Cream had been supplied solely by Sandeman and with consummate success. When I joined Harveys in 1945, it was a small but highly respected old-fashioned West Country firm specialising in port and sherry. In fact in days gone by, Harveys used to be better known for their port than sherry. It was really the successful promotion of Bristol Cream in the United States after the war by the late Jack Harvey, a former pillar of the English wine trade, which formed the basis of the tremendous expansion of business and the world-wide acceptance of

Harveys as a leader in the Sherry trade.

As sales expanded, especially in the United States, more and more supplies were needed, more indeed than Sandeman's could manage. There came a parting of the ways and Harvey's began to buy elsewhere, albeit with some problems. I suggested to my chairman George McWatters that he should approach Sandeman's to see if the two firms could join together in what might have been, at least so I thought, a perfect marriage. Unfortunately Sandeman refused the offer and subsequently each of these two fine old firms lost their independence.

Our next visit was to La Riva, a small firm now a subsidiary of Pedro Domecq, which specialises in an exceedingly good fino sold under the name of Tres Palmas. The small bodegas, a contrast to the large ones at Sandeman's are from the eighteenth century and convey an old world impression. Here, besides the excellent Tres Palmas, we tasted some remarkable wines.

Old Amontillado, average age, 90 years
Full flavoured with an unexpectedly dry finish

Old Oloroso, Solera 1806
A delightful colour, a gloriously rich old bouquet, a superb rich flavour with a fine dry finish. The taste lingered on and on in one's mouth

Palo Cortado, Solera 1800
A very rare sample of which only a very little exists. The colour was quite dark and the bouquet also revealed its age; although there was no sugar at all, the flavour was quite rich, a wonderful complete wine with a very dry finish

Before lunch we called at Pedro Domecq where the head of the firm had expressed a wish to welcome us. There we enjoyed a glass of fino in the famous cellar which contains ancient butts of sherry dedicated, among other notabilities, to Nelson and Napoleon Bonaparte. Lunching at a restaurant near the bull ring, we ate delicacies such as *anguillas*, baby eels each so small it was no larger than a matchstick. These, served in a kind of soup, are a great speciality in Spain and we were lucky to coincide with the season for them.

Hereafter our troubles were to begin. Having so far enjoyed one of the mildest winters on record in England, we had to come to Spain to find the snow. After waiting for four hours at the most uncomfortable airport imaginable, we were finally told no plane would come for us from Madrid where the runways had been snowed up. Fortunately for us, it was off-season so we were able to return to the hotel for the night.

Back to Jerez airport early the following morning our plane came hours late, but we were assured our connecting flight to Lisbon would be held for us. Of course it wasn't and we found the officials in Madrid unsympathetic to say the least. Finally, we caught a flight out at 4.0 p.m. but at Lisbon the airport was so crowded there was hardly room to sit down. Our hearts sank when we were told that, once again, there would be a delay. When at last we arrived in Oporto it was as we had feared – no luggage! This, after some twelve hours of travelling was the last straw for five very weary people, the more so since our luggage was not delivered until two days later.

The plan had been to go to the Douro where the vineyards are situated, but since all our luggage was missing, this had to be cancelled. Then we had a stroke of luck, for at the last minute, Nick Heath, the manager of Sandeman's, was able to arrange a tasting for us.

We began with the range of Sandeman wines: the Clipper, a white port which makes a good aperitif, the tawny and ruby ports which provide the main sale and the finer wines, the Partners and the Founders Ports, the latter being fuller and more robust. The 1976 late bottled had a good strong grapey flavour and contrasted with the lovely 20 year-old Imperial Tawny.

In order to demonstrate how port develops in wood, Mr Heath had put out six unblended wines all from more or less the same source:

1980
Rough, immature and almost disagreeable at this early stage

1977
Although very young, it was taking on shape as it were, lots of fruit and more pleasing to taste.

1970
A distinct difference was noticeable, the colour was lighter, more tawny in fact and the flavour far more mature

1967
A fine tawny colour, a delightful bouquet and more tawny in style

1948
A lovely bouquet, a lovely taste too, but the finish was more spirit-ous

1945
A distinguished older bouquet, an attractive taste with a faint hint of toffee! The spirit was also noticeable in this.

It was most kind of Mr Heath to arrange this instructive tasting without warning.

Until fairly recently, the bulk of the young wine produced up the Douro was transported in cask down river to Vila Nova de Gaia by picturesque river boats and at times the journey could be hazardous. Now that a dam has been built, the wine is transported more efficiently, but less romantically, in tanker trucks.

At first glance the shippers' lodges appear to be grouped together all higgledy-piggledy on the same steep hillside but now, with the increased demand for port, there is not really enough space to house all the wine. In consequence, some firms find themselves obliged to store and mature more and more wine up river, in the Douro; this has its disadvantages, because of the much warmer climate, there is more loss from evaporation.

We found a convenient place for lunch on the river side of Vila Nova de Gaia where the fish was very fresh. We regretted our good intention to walk from the restaurant to Silva & Cozens offices. They were further away than we had anticipated and by the time we had climbed the very steep hill, I for one was blowing hard!

Michael Symington showed us around his cellars which are extensive because Silva & Cozens is an important group combining such famous firms as Dow, Warre, Graham, Quarles Harris, Smith Woodhouse and Gould Campbell. All of these trade independently, but are really under the same umbrella.

At home in England where port has always reigned supreme, it is enjoyed as a post prandial beverage, whereas in France there is a strong demand for a lighter, slightly drier wine which the French drink as an aperitif. In fact, considerably more wine is shipped to France than to England.

Here also, a fascinating tasting had been prepared for us by Peter Symington who is in charge of all the blending and so on.

1981
A black impenetrable colour, fierce and extremely young and virtually impossible to appreciate

1980
A very fruity bouquet, a huge wine, still brash and uncouth, but with excellent underlying quality

1978
Not so much bouquet, lighter in style

1977
The great year, a fine nose developing, a big powerful wine, packed with fruit. Both the 1977 and the 1980 were of obviously good quality

1974
Pleasant bouquet, good fruit, but a softer wine

1964
More tawny in style both on the bouquet and the palate

Then followed a range of tawny wines:

Ten years old
Definite in style and very good

20 years old
A super bouquet and flavour

60 years old
Very fine bouquet, more delicate perhaps and aristocratic

100 years old
Very old bouquet, quite remarkable but showing its age, the spirit had taken over and there was more acidity

There had been some adverse comments in the English wine trade over the launching of the 1980 vintage so soon after the splendid 1977 vintage, but here in Oporto it was being regarded more highly even than at its launch.

There was a near disaster that evening. We had been bidden to dine with Michael and Elizabeth Symington who live at Maia, some kilometres outside the city. We lost our way in the dark while leaving the city and were in a proper mess because nobody we asked could speak anything but Portuguese. Finally we were saved by a nice shopkeeper in a village who spoke a little French and who, although he was unable to direct me, telephoned so that we could be fetched. Even so we were over an hour late.

Just before leaving the following morning, we visited the Graham Lodge higher up on the hill and there we had a final tasting:

1980 Vintage Port
Warre
The bouquet still undeveloped, but a lovely flowery, fruity flavour

Graham
A fuller nose, a wine packed with fruit and full of 'stuffing' or to use that old expression 'a grip of the gob'

Dow
A fine bouquet, which was described as 'burnt', lots of fruit and a

21

delicious flavour with a full, fairly dry finish. *Note* Dow is noted for this relatively dry finish

I think I was in a minority, but placed them in this order of preference: Graham, Dow, Warre.

A direct flight took us to Madrid where, at the airport, we picked up a nice new roomy Talbot car for the onward journey. In spite of the sunshine and bright blue sky, it was still bitterly cold and somehow in Spain one does not expect such freezing weather. After a visit to the Prado, we took a taxi to the Place Mayor with which I was just a little disappointed, having somehow expected more. However, the scene was enlivened by students in masks and so on celebrating the approach of Mardi Gras. In a nearby cafe, we enjoyed ourselves consuming innumerable glasses of fino sherry, accompanied by delicious *tapas* in the form of shrimps, clams, mussels and other appetisers. Visiting it so seldom, one tends to forget what a lovely city Madrid is, the wide avenues are particularly impressive.

On our way north we made a diversion via Segovia to see the Roman aqueduct which appears to be better preserved than the Pont du Gard in Provence. Driving was comparatively easy because at this time of the year there was very little traffic on the road.

After spending the night at the Palador de la Calzada, originally an old monastery in Santo Domingo, our first call was on the well-known establishment, the Marquis de Riscal in El Ciego. This, however, proved a disappointment. After a tour around the somewhat grubby cellars we were offered two wines to taste, a 1980 white Reserva from Rueda (Valladolid), quite fruity and very dry, and the red Marquis de Riscal 1978, a light wine which needs some years to develop.

Our reception at Paternino in Haro was very different, but it must be admitted that the new winery carries little romance – a really up-to-date factory which is kept scrupulously clean and where the talk is in millions of hectolitres. The eighteenth-century cellar, however, in the nearby village of Allauri, where this firm was founded in 1898, displays a totally different scene with its mould-covered casks and dripping walls.

There are three main wine areas for Rioja: the Alto where the finest wine comes from; the Alavesa where the terrain is more hilly and where the sandy soil is responsible for a lighter kind of wine; and the Baja which produces wine of lesser quality.

The wood fire in the reception room acted as a magnet for us all. Among the wines we tasted before lunch were 1981 Rinsol, a fresh fruity white wine and a 1973 Reserva with a deep bouquet and a fuller flavour. Finally we had a 1968 Gran Reserva with delicate bouquet and a delightful flavour.

During lunch we drank the following: 1976 Vina Vial, fruity and easy to drink, 1973 Gran Reserva, a richer more full-bodied wine with a good finish and 1967 Gran Reserva with considerable finesse on the nose, which was the best part for me.

We arrived in Bordeaux that evening in time for an excellent meal at La Chamade, but chose the wrong wine, the 1976 Marquis d'Aligre, which was very light and had little future before it.

Our host the next day was Alain Querre who was many friends both in England and the United States. Among his many activities, he runs a kind of club for some of the smaller growers of Saint Emilion to help them taste each other's wine and to improve the quality of their own. In the past, most of these growers used to sell their produce to the big *négociants* in Bordeaux, but as is happening on the Côte d'Or, they are beginning to mature the wine themselves and sell it as *château* bottled. The result has been a number of pleasant surprises.

With several of the growers present, we tasted some 30 wines of the 1981 and 1982 vintages, and it was my first experience of the latter. The local opinion appeared to be that 1981 is better than 1979 and that 1979, for Saint Emilion, is better than 1978.

Some Saint Emilions of the 1981 Vintage

Bel-Air, Saint Georges
Medium colour, a pleasant fruity bouquet, not a big wine but quite agreeable   14.5/20

Clos Domayne
Medium colour, some richness on the nose, good fruit and complete   15.5/20

Pipeau
Medium colour, a slightly sweeter bouquet, a rather special taste   14.5/20

La Croix Figeac
Good colour, scented bouquet, good fruit and flavour, perhaps lacking some finesse   14/20

Fombrauge
Good colour, with an attractive bouquet, plenty of fruit and well made   15/20

Clos Valentin
Good colour, quite a full bouquet, rounded, complete and very good   17/20

Puy Razac
Darker colour, pleasant bouquet, good fruit and flavour   14/20

Monbousquet
Good colour, attractive bouquet, rather good   17/20

Carteau
Medium colour, bouquet a little rougher, less rounded perhaps but good quality all the same   15/20

Haut-Segattes
Dark colour, attractive bouquet, a well made complete wine
15/20

Pipeau
Good colour, well bred bouquet, good fruit and body   16.5/20

Grand Corbin
Good colour, quite a good bouquet, full-bodied with a slightly rougher finish   14.5/20

Grand Mayne
Dark colour, good fruit and flavour, still some tannin but rather nice   16/20

Beauséjour Bécot
Good colour, attractive bouquet, some acidity to lose, with plenty of character nevertheless   16.5/20

Pavie
Dark colour, a full bouquet, complete and full-bodied, has plenty of depth and is rather good   18/20

Domaine de la Vieille Eglise
Pale colour, a nice bouquet, but rather light in style   14/20

La Grace Dieu, les Menuts
Good colour, attractive bouquet, full-bodied and quite a mouthful   17.5/20

The 1982 Vintage

Bel-Air Saint Georges
A big fruity bouquet, medium body but should make a nice bottle   14/20

Clos Domayne
Dark colour, a nice nose and has greater depth of body   14.5/20

Pipeau
Good colour, interesting bouquet, good flavour   14.5/20

La Croix Figeac
Good colour and quite pleasant   14/20

Fombrauge
Dark colour, nice bouquet, medium body, plenty of charm   15/20

Monbousquet
Dark colour, well bred bouquet, very good flavour   16.5/20

Carteau
Dark colour, slightly roasted bouquet, very good flavour   16/20

Haut-Sagattes
Dark colour, well bred bouquet, a nice 'solid' wine, should make a nice bottle   16/20

Ripeau
Dark colour, full bouquet, plenty of fruit, but a disappointing finish   14.5/20

Grand Corbin
Dark colour, plenty of character on the bouquet, has good fruit   15.5/20

Grand Mayne
Good colour, a fuller bouquet, good fruit and flavour with a nice finish   16/20

Beauséjour Bécot
Good colour, a pleasant full bouquet, very nice flavour, has some tannin to lose   16.5/20

Pavie
Dark colour, well bred bouquet, a fine full-bodied wine   18/20

Domaine de la Vieille Eglise
Pale colour, an attractive bouquet, but is on the light side 14.5/20

La Grace Dieu, les Menuts
Dark colour, good bouquet, a fine full-bodied wine, has considerable depth   16.5/20

Some of the 1981s were showing very well, but the 1982s were still a little too young to appreciate properly.

Our final day was spent in Bordeaux with Christopher Canan, the English broker who has teamed up with Rebecca Wasserman, who specialises in the wines of the Côte d'Or. These are some of the wines we tasted:

1980 Ramage de la Batisse, cru bourgeois supérieur
Medium colour, a pretty bouquet, rather light and should be ready early

1980 Cos d'Estournel, Saint Estèphe
A full bouquet, with a fine depth of flavour, should make a good bottle

1980 Volnay, Clos de la Pousse d'Or
A fine bouquet and a fine wine

1980 Volnay 1er Cru, Michel Lafarge
Good bouquet and quite a powerful wine

It seems strange how, in the early stages, the quality of this 1980 vintage of both burgundy and bordeaux was disparaged. Thanks to an adverse newspaper report in the United States on the 1980 vintage in Bordeaux, few Americans bought the vintage and this caused anger among the château proprietors. Although admittedly on the light side, many of the 1980s are attractive; and being inexpensive and having matured early this has proved a useful vintage.

On the Côte d'Or a well-known authority also criticised the quality of the vintage in this region, but happily, in this case, the impact was not so serious. As it transpires, many of the red burgundies of 1980 are turning out well, although some of them will benefit from another year or so in bottle. While not on the same level as 1978 or 1983 the 1980 is not by any means to be ignored.

3
AUTUMN VISIT TO BORDEAUX
1983

MONDAY, 10 OCTOBER

Having left London in pouring rain, we found the sun was shining when we arrived at La Mission Haut-Brion.

We knew the harvest had been in progress for some time, so our first question was about the quality. Our host Francis Dewavrin was quite enthusiastic and said, much to everyone's surprise, that it was far better than expected. He estimated it would turn out to be better than either 1981 or 1979, if not perhaps so good as 1978. Unsatisfactory climatic conditions until August had led to somewhat gloomy predictions as to the final quality, but the good weather in September had changed the situation more than expected. This is interesting when with hindsight we know how well this 1983 vintage has turned out.

As for the white wine, it was even better and Francis was expecting his Laville Haut-Brion to be as fine as in that good year 1970.

The wines we had for lunch were:

1974 Latour Haut-Brion
Very dark colour, full-bodied, robust and most enjoyable from a half bottle

1964 La Mission Haut-Brion
Good colour, delightful to drink now, this must be about at its best

At dinner we began with the 1970 Laville Haut-Brion, already beginning to take on colour, but really good

1970 Latour Haut-Brion
Very dark colour, a big wine which is still rather backward

1967 La Mission Haut-Brion
Dark colour, not so big as the 1970, but well matured. This must be among the few successful wines of this somewhat awkward vintage

TUESDAY, 11 OCTOBER

We arrived at Château Pichon-Longueville in time for lunch. The de Lencquesaing's had made further progress with their terrace which overlooks the vineyard of Latour. A part of the old *chai* was being converted to make a reception area with its doors opening directly on to the terrace.

The first wine at lunch was:

1970 Pichon-Comtesse
Very dark in colour with heaps of fruit. It is still firm though and it looks as though it will need three or four more years in order to release the hidden charm

1964 Pichon-Comtesse
This was just right; a lovely bottle

Monsieur Godin, the *régisseur*, drove us out to see how the picking was progressing. It is amazing how all the vineyards are muddled up together, Beychevelle, Ducru-Beaucaillou and Gloria on the Saint Julien side of a track with the vines of the two Pichons on the other.

Further purchasers of this 1983 vintage may have to be selective. On our way from Bordeaux we had noticed areas where the vines were looking sick and dispirited, their leaves sparse and much too brown. This had been caused by the bad weather during August which had brought on *pourriture* as well as a strong attack of red spider. The vineyards which had suffered were those where no spraying had been done during that critical period of bad weather. One of the reasons why spraying had not been done in August was because on some estates the proprietors and their staff had been away on their annual holiday. This was partly thanks to the President, Monsieur Mitterand, who introduced such severe labour laws, i.e. a thirty-nine hour week and five weeks' holiday.

With foresight Madame Eliane de Lencquesaing had left two tractor drivers at Pichon-Comtesse and between them they had managed to keep up with the spraying, but other vineyards had not fared so well. It was possible to see the distinct difference between the vines of one proprietor where the leaves were green and healthy looking and those of a neighbour where the leaves were brown and sparse.

Before dinner I paid a visit to the *chai* where all the vats were full, but apparently it is not such an easy vintage to handle as was the 1982. The 1982 of Pichon-Comtesse has a fine dark colour, a deep flavour and heaps of fruit. This should turn out very well.

The property is run by Eliane de Lencquesaing, but her son Hugh who is studying art in Paris will take over in due course; he has already taken his degree in oenology and is helping to make the wine. He was working in the *chai* until 11.0 p.m. and so was unable to join us for dinner.

After the *soupe de vendange*, and very good too, Eliane had prepared a magnificent *magret de canard* and rarely have I eaten better. I was unaware that the area in the south-west of France is reputed to be the best for *magret de canard*; it seems that here the ducks are larger and have very plump breasts.

We began with the 1971 Pichon-Comtesse. I know this fairly well because we have had a case at home, but never have I had a better bottle. Even so short a time as a few months before must have been too soon to drink it. It is extraordinary how a wine changes. People say the 1971 médocs need drinking, but this particular one is only now approaching its best.

WEDNESDAY, 12 OCTOBER

One of the purposes of our visit to Bordeaux was to taste the famous 1982 vintage, a long-delayed visit because of my car accident while in Burgundy in April. Some of my charming Bordelais friends told me it had served me right for going to Burgundy!

An Anonymous Tasting of the 1982 Vintage

The dark colour of all the wines was remarkable and due to its special quality, the vintage was easier to taste than usual. There was very little excess acidity and the tannin was not over pronounced.

Croizet-Bages, Pauillac
Fruity bouquet, medium body, easy to taste, not much depth or tannin and appears forward

Gloria, Saint Julien
Very good bouquet, has more tannin and depth but some stridency

Rauzan-Gassies, Margaux
Scented bouquet, good fruit and body, well balanced

Desmirail, Margaux
Lovely nose, plenty of fruit, good quality, still backward

Durfort-Vivens, Margaux
A full bouquet, good fruit, but tannic with some acidity

Haut-Batailley, Pauillac
Very nice bouquet, rounded, charming and easy to taste, very good

Saint-Pierre, Saint Julien
A deep bouquet, rounded and full-bodied, has both charm and harmony

Haut-Bages Liberal, Pauillac
Fruity bouquet, good structure, but with less immediate charm, good depth of flavour though

Brane-Cantenac, Margaux
An attractive bouquet, lighter in body with some acidity

Calon-Ségur, Saint Estèphe
A deep scented bouquet, lovely fruit with both depth and balance, will make a good bottle

Beychevelle, Saint Julien
Attractive bouquet, good fruit and body but there is some greenness – or is it stridency?

Grand-Puy-Lacoste, Pauillac
A rich bouquet, full-bodied, plenty of tannin, but very good

Pichon-Comtesse, Pauillac
Lovely bouquet, lots of fruit and body with a nice finish, fine quality

Pichon-Baron, Pauillac
An attractive bouquet, a good full-bodied well made wine, good quality

Lynch-Bages, Pauillac
Rich bouquet, packed with fruit and flavour, first rate

Ducru-Beaucaillou, Saint Julien
Very good nose, good fruit and a lovely rich flavour, has considerable depth

Léoville-Lascases
Fine bouquet, a big well made wine with a lot of depth, fine quality

Margaux
Lovely deep bouquet, packed with fruit, a fine wine of considerable depth. Has plenty of tannin

Mouton-Rothschild
A splendid bouquet (gorgeous smell!) rich, rounded and great depth of flavour. A lot of tannin to lose, but altogether delightful, the best of all

Latour
Excellent bouquet, a big, full-bodied wine, rounded with masses of fruit. This also should make a great bottle

Lafite
A lovely bouquet, not quite so big a wine as those preceding but has lots of fruit and is of fine quality

The order in which I placed the last four wines was Mouton, Latour, Margaux and Lafite. It was useful to have to taste these anonymously otherwise prejudices might well have intervened!

THURSDAY, 13 OCTOBER

The fine weather continued, a final chance for those vineyard which had not yet gathered in their last loads of grapes.

This was a day devoted to the wines of Pomerol and Saint Emilion and it was a rare treat to taste more of the 1982 vintage which was so successful in these two districts, especially the former. All the wines had a wonderful dark colour.

Before the tasting began in earnest, Christian Moueix showed us the 1982 vintage from his own *château* in the Fronsadais, Château Canon, Canon-Fronsac, a good vinous bouquet, not a big wine, but nicely rounded. This should make a good bottle for everyday drinking.

Saint Emilion, the 1982 Vintage
Fonroque
A big fruity bouquet, medium body but good fruit, with a trace of acidity

Magdelaine
A full bouquet, again not a very big wine, but is rounded with a lovely balance. A fine well bred wine

Belair
Very nice nose, very good fruit and flavour, with a pleasant finish, will make a good bottle

Figeac
Very fruity bouquet, medium body, fine quality

Pomerol, the 1982 Vintage
La Grave Trigant de Boisset
A delightful bouquet, medium body with a rich and altogether delightful taste. The best vintage I have tasted since Christian took over this vineyard

Latour-Pomerol
A very full bouquet, more like heavy cavalry here! This has more depth than La Grave Trigant and will make an excellent bottle

La Fleur-Pétrus
Another big one! Full bouquet, a big full-bodied wine, without the depth of the Latour-Pomerol, but with more breeding perhaps, this will make a lovely bottle

L'Evangile
A delightful bouquet, a lighter wine than the two predecessors, but good flavour and well bred, excellent

La Conseillante
Pleasant bouquet, medium body and very good fruit, has a beautiful balance

Trotanoy
Beautiful bouquet, a fine depth of flavour, lovely fruit and very well bred. Still plenty of tannin, superb quality

Les Trois Grands Seigneurs
Ausone
A fine full bouquet, a big, rich, rounded wine, packed with quality and distinction

Cheval-Blanc

Excellent bouquet, rich and round, a great mouthful of delight with a splendid finish. Very great quality

Pétrus

A huge bouquet, another lovely mouthful of fruit and flavour, still some tannin, but wonderful quality

Christian drove us to La Fleur-Pétrus to lunch with about 20 of the regular staff who were busy handling the young wine. The picking had finished a few days earlier, but there was plenty to do. It seemed that whereas the 1982 vintage had been faultless, causing no trouble at all, this year, 1983, there were all sorts of problems arising during the making of the wine. Among the guests were those well-known authorities from London, David and Serena Peppercorn, and Robin Daniels, Christian's new partner in the vineyard at Yountville in the Napa Valley. When Inglenook was sold to Heublein's in the 1960s the Daniels' family had kept back the best portion of its vineyard for themselves. It is this small vineyard which is now to be developed and managed by Christian Moueix and Robin Daniels.

FRIDAY, 14 OCTOBER

There was some sadness attached to this visit to Bordeaux for it was to be our last to La Mission Haut-Brion. Thanks to the kindness of that genius among wine makers, the late Henri Woltner, La Mission had become our second home as it were, in Bordeaux. This had continued after his death during the all too brief management of his brother Fernand and the five happy years with Francis and Françoise Dewavrin, the late Fernand's daughter. However, on 30 October, La Mission Haut-Brion was to pass into the hands of Haut-Brion across the road. This would end a great rivalry which began when around 1929, Henri Woltner began to produce such exceptional quality at La Mission. Yet at the same time it would reunite a property which was divided as long ago as 1642, and happily the vineyard was to be under the management of that splendid man, Jean Delmas.

The *régisseur* at La Mission, Henri Lagardère, had worked with Henri Woltner since 1965, but it had been his son Michel who had actually made the wine since Henri Woltner's death. If anything under the aegis of the Dewavrins, the reputation of La Mission Haut-Brion had become even greater than before. Now, because of family differences and in part the difficulties under the socialist regime of Monsieur Mitterand, it was all to go.

The Dewavrins had departed for Paris and their place had been taken for the weekend by Henri's ex-son-in-law Mario Zurer and his new wife and two of their friends. Some of the wines that Mario brought up from the cellar were so exceptional that they have to be recorded. On the Friday, we began with Latour Haut-Brion 1961. This may be the second wine here, but the quality is excellent and this 1961 would stand up well against many of the successes of this great vintage from the Médoc.

It was followed by something even greater, a magnum of 1947 La Mission Haut-Brion with a bouquet and a depth of flavour it is impossible to describe with justice. For those who have not had the good fortune to taste this particular wine, a brief diversion may not come amiss.

The summer of 1947 was very warm and similar conditions did not really recur until the summer of 1982. As we all know, the 1982 vintage has been a great success, but had it not been for the temperature-controlled stainless steel vats recently installed in a number of *châteaux*, the story might have been different. Towards the end of September the weather had become so torrid that had it not been for the temperature control, volatile acidity could have been widespread, as indeed happened in 1947. Some of the proprietors with wooden fermentation vats still had some problems, but of course were aided by the vast improvement in the art of vinification which has taken place over the past 30 years.

I can remember those 1947s very well – thanks to the hot summer, the young wine in cask tasted far more attractive than usual and we had great expectations for the future. It was not to be though, because in many cases the volatile acidity became apparent after the course of a few years and some of the 1947s from the Médoc were never the success which had been envisaged. All the same it was a superb vintage for the wines of Pomerol and Saint Emilion. In fact, it is considered that until 1982 came along, there had never since been such a good year for Pomerol.

The huge success of 1947 was of course the Cheval-Blanc. It is a fabulous wine and in my notes on its progress over the first ten years there is frequent mention of its resemblance to vintage port! Almost of similar stature were some of the pomerols I bought for Harveys, wines such as Lafleur, L'Enclos, La Croix de Gay and L'Evangile. The 1947 of La Mission Haut-Brion, however, has always been outstanding and I have been fortunate to share many a good bottle here at the *château*. I had never, however, been so fortunate as to have it from a magnum, so this was an unforgettable experience.

The last wine that evening, and one which somehow managed to hold its own after the 1947, was a bottle of 1934 La Mission. Here again there was a touch of the late Henri Woltner's genius, because although 1934 was only a reasonably good vintage, indeed the only one in that dreary decade of the 1930s, there were not many successes. This La Mission was certainly one of them and here it was showing well after nearly 50 years!

On the Saturday evening Mario Zurer tried a different tack for we began with two rather poor years, 1977 and 1968, and here again the produce of La Mission stood up well. So many of the 1968s were more or less undrinkable, yet after 15 years the La Mission although not great of course was still in command of all its faculties. The final bottle, in fact a magnum, was La Mission 1952, a marvellous dark coloured wine which at 30 years old must have been near its best.

There was another fabulous array on the Sunday evening. To begin with there was the 1981 vintage which although not ready showed a lot of promise. Michel Lagardère, who made the wine, considered it is better even than his 1982. Then there appeared a magnificent bottle of La Mission 1961, dark of colour and full of sweetness, vigour and charm. I wondered what could follow that 1961, or rather stand up to it, but the 1949 did and nobly. Most of us will agree that the 1949 Mouton is the best of that vintage, with Latour a little way behind; in my opinion the latter is marred sometimes by a trace of acidity but much less than with many other 1949s. This 1949 La Mission had no apparent acidity and was a wonderful bottle.

MONDAY, 17 OCTOBER

It had begun to rain the previous day, the first time in a whole month. It is unusual, however, for the vintage to have been gathered in without any rain at all.

We drove to Château Cissac where Danielle Vialard had prepared a tasting of the leading *crus bourgeois* of the 1982 vintage.

Some Crus Bourgeois *of 1982*

Potensac, Médoc
Very dark colour, a good fruity bouquet, good fruit and well made. A nice 'solid' wine

Abiet, Haut-Médoc
Dark colour, a pleasant sweet bouquet, medium body with a nice finish

Tour de Mirail, Haut-Médoc
Very dark colour, a nice nose, with a good depth of flavour. This may take a little while to develop

Cissac, Cissac

Very dark colour, a full bouquet, a big wine packed with fruit. One of the best of this tasting

Lanessan, Cussac

A nice full bouquet, lots of fruit, powerful and full-bodied

Belgrave (St Laurent)

Very dark colour, nice scented bouquet, has some fruit but altogether a thinner wine

Maucaillou, Moulis

Good colour, nice fruity nose, full-bodied with a good flavour. Rather good

Chasse-Spleen, Moulis

Dark colour, fine bouquet, heaps of body and good flavour, should make a very good bottle

Les Ormes de Pez, Saint Estèphe

Very dark colour, very fruity bouquet, a complete very 'solid' wine. Another winner

Phélan-Ségur, Saint Estèphe

Dark colour, fruity bouquet, a big wine, but perhaps a little coarser, a nice mouthful nevertheless

Tronquoy-Lalande, Saint Estèphe

Scented bouquet, a lighter but thinner wine than Les Ormes de Pez

Gloria, Saint Julien

A charming bouquet, not a big wine but well bred with lots of style. Very good

Plantey, Pauillac

A slightly more severe bouquet, good fruit and body, but lacks the style of the Gloria

Labégorce, Margaux

An attractive scented bouquet, medium body, good fruit and rather good

This was a remarkable tasting, all the wines were on a much higher level of quality than anything I can remember for years. One expects quality from the *crus classés*, but not like this from the *crus bourgeois*.

TUESDAY, 18 OCTOBER

We were welcomed at Château d'Issan by Marguerite Cruse and her daughter Nicole Tesseron. There we tasted the 1982 vintage, which is every bit as good as its reputation, alongside the 1981 vintage. The latter may perhaps lack some of the depth of the 1982 vintage, nevertheless it is beautifully balanced and very good.

By the end of the war both this vineyard and its *château* had been allowed to fall into disrepair. It was purchased by the late Emanuel Cruse in 1945 and since 1950, his gallant widow has been pulling it together again. Her care and attention have been well rewarded and although it has taken years to be recognised, the wine from this vineyard is now in the first flight.

4

THE CÔTE D'OR AND THE RHÔNE
February 1984

This was to be our fourth visit to the vineyards with our friends from Michigan, Dick and Sally Scheer and Bob Simburger. We met at Heathrow and flew to Lyon where we picked up a car to drive to the Hostellerie du Vieux Moulin at Bouilland near Savigny-les-Beaune, a pleasant place set in delightful rural surroundings with excellent food and a good wine list. Most of those wines had been supplied through the good offices of Becky Wasserman who lives in the village.

I had first met the remarkable Becky some four years before and funnily enough, while visiting the Scheers at Ann Arbor in Michigan. She had been married to a painter, who had settled in this neighbourhood because of the good light. In order to help make ends meet, Becky had begun by selling wine barrels made by a local *tonnelier*. From barrels to wine is not a far step and in no time Becky had got to know some of the local growers and to acquire an enthusiasm for their produce.

In the past, with a few exceptions, the distribution of burgundy was handled almost entirely by the *négociants*, some of whom were and still are first rate, but others were not so good. Thanks to the good *autoroutes*, many wine lovers have become more mobile and like to seek out their burgundy themselves and this is but one of the reasons for the tendency towards *domaine* bottling. In consequence, during recent years more and more of the important growers, many of whom formerly sold their produce to swell the blends of the *négociants*, are now selling their wine under their own labels. This 'renaissance' as it were, of burgundy appears to have been brought about largely by the younger generation and has meant the installation of up-to-date equipment in the cellars and the acquisition of the skill of handling young wine. The successful repercussions on the large American market have been thanks largely to the enthusiasm and untiring efforts of Mrs Wasserman.

Our first call was on Alain Gras, a young grower whose vines are in Saint-Romain, an outlying district beyond Auxey-Duresses on the Côte de Beaune. Both red and white wine are produced in this area but until recently, thanks to the influence of a powerful distributor, the emphasis was on white, but now that the distributor has retired one or two growers have begun to plant more *pinot noir* vines. The resultant red wine is not intended to compete with the *grands vins* of the Côte d'Or, but on a lesser level perhaps similar to a *cru bourgeois* or a *petit château* of Bordeaux.

Alain Gras is a typical example of the new generation here in Burgundy. His father and indeed all his forebears had always sold their wine in cask soon after it had been made to the *négociants*, but after finishing his vinous education in Beaune, Alain persuaded his father to change their policy and sell their products in bottle and under their own label. He explained that he could not bear to see all the wine they had made with such loving care being blended and sold anonymously to the public. As expected, his father had had mixed feelings and when he saw the large stack of new bottles arriving on the premises he had told his son that he must be crazy.

1983 Saint-Romain, white
The bouquet full of fruit, a pleasing well balanced wine, quite strong in alcohol, 14°

1982 Saint-Romain, white
An attractive and more developed bouquet, fairly full-bodied with a dryish finish

1982 Auxey-Duresses, white
Pleasant bouquet, a wine with more depth and flavour, more serious, but with a trace of acidity at the finish

1979 Saint-Romain, white, the first vintage made by Alain Gras
A nice concentrated bouquet, good fruit and well balanced

1982 Saint-Romain, red, made from 20-25-year-old vines
A rather pale colour, a fruity bouquet reminiscent of cassis, very nice taste.

1982 Auxey-Duresses, red, made from 50-year-old vines

Medium colour, pleasing bouquet, has greater depth and concentration, unexpectedly good

The next grower was Monsieur A. Mussy who lives in Pommard. Sadly, only two years before, this poor man lost his only son while driving his tractor among the vines.

1983 Beaune Epenottes
Good nose, plenty of fruit and substance

1983 Pommard les Epenots 1er Cru
Medium colour, pleasant bouquet, a good 'solid' wine with plenty of depth, but some acidity to lose

1982 Beaune Epenottes
Good ruby colour, attractive bouquet, good fruit and body, but there was something odd about the aftertaste

1982 Pommard les Epenots
Medium colour, an attractive bouquet, good fruit with body, but the finish a little disappointing

1976 Pommard les Epenots, made from 60-year-old vines
Good colour, well developed bouquet, plenty of body with a delicious flavour

Monsieur Pierre Boillot lives in the village of Meursault.

1980 Meursault
A fruity wine but very sharp

1981 Meursault
A somewhat smokey bouquet with more fruit and body. Well balanced and rather good

1981 Meursault Goutte d'Or
An attractive slightly sweet bouquet, a fuller more rounded wine, rather good

1982 Meursault
Fresh fruity bouquet, similar flavour, but with some acidity

1982 Meursault Charmes
Very nice nose, a lovely full flavoured wine which should make a good bottle

1982 Volnay Santenots
Pale colour, full fruity flavour, well made

1983 Volnay Santenots
Good dark colour, quite a big wine with some tannin. Good as the 1982 was, the 1983 was definitely better

WEDNESDAY, 8 FEBRUARY

Still pouring with rain and there were floods everywhere. The winter here had been fairly mild, but so far had been much too wet.

A reception by Madame Lalu Bise Leroy is a red letter day for any visitor to Burgundy. Her firm surely has the largest stock of fine burgundy on the Côte d'Or. As will be seen from the details of that day's tasting, her library of wines must be unmatched. Who else for instance could produce 13 good examples from Volnay Santenots going all the way back to 1949? To begin with, however, we were to taste six vintages of Meursault les Perrières.

Meursault les Perrières

1974
A distinguished bouquet, clean, fruity, dry, just a little severe perhaps, but certainly well bred. Mme Bise Leroy considers this will be about at its best by 1994!

1973
A supple more developed nose, plenty of fruit. Has less character perhaps, but is attractive and easier to drink and is ready now

1972
Quite a rich bouquet reminiscent of sweet corn! Lighter in body and just a little sharp, but better than expected

1971
A rich bouquet, a deep concentrated rather masculine wine with a fine finish, excellent quality

1970
A marvellous vanilla bouquet, a wine of lovely balance and now approaching its best

1969
Golden colour, a rounded mature bouquet, again with a hint of vanilla. A fabulously rich concentrated wine of quite exceptional quality

Volnay Santenots

1978

An unusually dark colour, a heavenly velvety bouquet, full-bodied, rounded and concentrated. Nothing like ready and will last for years. Remarkable quality

1976

Medium colour, a good individual bouquet, a big fruity wine, with masses of tannin. This stood up surprisingly well after the outstanding 1978

1972

There were two examples of this vintage, presumably from two growers:

First wine Rather pale colour, lots of bouquet though, medium body and the acidity of this vintage was not apparent

Second wine Medium colour, a more elegant nose and a bigger more 'solid' wine with a fine finish

1971

Medium colour, good bouquet and body, tender, easy to drink and ready now, rather good

1970

Very dark colour, quite a full bouquet, rich, full and delicious, long in the mouth and unexpectedly good for this vintage

1969

Very good colour, the bouquet full of fruit and character. Has fine structure and balance and what a marvellous flavour

1964

Good colour, fine bouquet, lovely fruit and flavour, still firm, even so ready now, superb quality

1962

Medium colour, a classic bouquet, rounded with lots of fruit, a little drier than the others, but gentle nevertheless. Similar in style perhaps to the first 1972, but nicer. Very good.

1959

Fine bouquet, fuller and deeper than the 1982, a great powerful wine. Still some tannin and will continue to improve. Twenty-five years old and remarkable

1955
Medium colour, a pleasant nose, lighter than the 1959, but is well balanced with plenty of fruit, distinguished with heaps of quality

1953
Medium colour, a bouquet reminiscent of roasted coffee beans! An elegant wine packed with charm, not unlike the 1962 for style

1952
A marvellous dark colour, a kind of nutty bouquet, a massive 'solid' wine, seemed more masculine than the 1953, with a slight taste of cedar

1949
Very good colour, a lovely gentle bouquet. Another lovely 'solid' wine of superb structure and balance. A masterpiece with a heavenly finish

Later on at the farm of Monsieur and Madame Bise Leroy, our aperitif was no less than a 1976 Montrachet and this we continued to enjoy with a splendid dish of *lotte à la nage* (called monkfish in England). Then with roast beef we had the following four wines, all of the successful 1964 vintage.

Nuits-Saint-Georges les Boudots
A fine dark colour, a fine wine with heaps of fruit and flavour

Grands Echezeaux Domaine de la Romanée Conti
A slightly lighter colour, a lighter body too, but packed with elegance and charm. This fairly blossomed with the cheese

Chambolle-Musigny Charmes
A fine dark colour, an excellent bouquet, masses of fruit and flavour and so worthy of its name 'Charmes'. For most of us, this was the best wine of the four

Chapelle Chambertin
Good colour and bouquet, a little harder and firmer than the others, it probably needs more time to develop

This had been a fabulous experience and where else could it be equalled? There has been some disillusionment about red burgundy, but here was a perfect example of a family which has never let the standard drop.

THURSDAY, 9 FEBRUARY

The premises of the two brothers Henri and Jean Boillot are situated fairly high up on the hillside of Volnay and are much larger than most in this region. It was interesting to see their new Vinimatic Fermenting Machines which have been in use here for several years. In order to break up the *chapeau*, or thick crust of skins which forms on the surface, these machines turn over the fermenting must twice a day. The Boillots claim this method produces wine with a darker colour and is *plus gras*.

The cellars are kept very clean and around 240 new barrels are bought every year. At the time a new barrel was costing 1,000 francs. There was a very large stock of wine in bottle and as individual growers go, this is quite a big operation. Since all the wine comes from their own vines, unblended that is, this was to prove an interesting comparison in both red and white for the three vintages of 1982, 1981 and 1980.

Puligny-Montrachet Clos de la Mouchère
1980
Well bred bouquet, very nice flavour which filled the mouth

1981
The bouquet fiercer, a similar flavour, but has more acidity and will take some time to mature

1982
A pretty bouquet, a full, very nice flavour, fruity and well balanced. The best wine of the three

Volnay (not Vinimatic)
1982
Pale colour, very fruity bouquet, fairly full-bodied with some tannin. There was, however, a suspicion of bitterness at the end of the taste. Some of the stalks are left in the fermenting must and that may account for it

1981
A better colour, hint of raspberry on the nose, less tannin, but good fruit, still a little bitterness. Monsieur Boillot mentioned that astringency is one of the characteristics of the 1981 vintage

1980
Good colour and a very *pinot noir* nose. Delightful flavour with a pleasant finish. The best of the three

Some of the growers were then saying the 1980 vintage is proving better for red wine than 1979, the latter beginning to dry up a little. It is certainly finer than either 1981 or 1982.

Volnay Chevrets (Vinimatic)

1982
Medium colour, pleasant scented bouquet, good fruit and body, more depth in fact and a better finish

1981
Good colour, not much bouquet, lighter and thinner with less charm. Monsieur Boillot claimed this has a good future, but it did not appeal to me

1980
Good colour, attractive bouquet, lots of fruit and nicely rounded. Still backward, but has a good future

1969
Dark colour, delightful scented bouquet, heaps of fruit, some acidity to lose

From this tasting of red wine, from the quality point of view, the vintages would appear to be in the order of 1980, 1982 and 1981.

Michel Lafarge in Volnay

A fine looking man who is also the mayor of Volnay. Parts of his cellar date back to the thirteenth century.

Bourgogne Aligoté 1982
Nice nose and a most attractive wine, of unusual quality for an aligoté

Volnay 1982
Good colour, lovely nose, nice depth of flavour

Volnay 1er Cru 1982
Distinguished bouquet, good fruit and flavour, a fine example of Volnay. This should make a very good bottle

Beaune Grèves 1982
Good colour and bouquet, not a big wine but is complete

Volnay Clos des Chènes 1982
Dark colour, lovely bouquet, delicious flavour, definitely a wine to buy

Volnay 1981
Medium colour, medium body and a little drier, prefer the 1982 of this wine.

Clearly 1981 is not a good vintage, there was a lot of rain earlier in the year and it continued to rain during the harvest

Volnay 1981 1er Cru
Medium colour, nose closed in, a bigger and better wine with more depth

Volnay Clos des Chènes 1981, grapes picked before the rain
Dark colour, a bouquet of character, full fruity and well made. Good for the vintage

Volnay 1980
Good colour and bouquet, plenty of body and a nice taste. Some acidity though

Volnay 1er Cru 1980
Dark colour, a delightful bouquet, has a good depth of flavour and balance, fine quality

Volnay Clos des Chènes 1980
Masses of bouquet, a lovely flavour, full of charm, will make a very good bottle

These wines of Monsieur Michel Lafarge were impressive.

Domaine Daniel Rion et Fils, Premeaux
Formerly the cellars were scattered all over the village, but recently the family business has been concentrated in a fairly large modern building which is full of the latest equipment. Patrice, the eldest son who now runs the business, was in the United States on a visit, something that rarely happened in the past, but now appears to be normal practice. The young growers are going there to see what is going on and also to meet some of their customers. I asked one well-known grower if he had learned a lot and he replied that it had been interesting rather than instructive. This sounds like chauvinism, but that man does produce first-rate wine. Under the circumstances the tasting was conducted by Monsieur Rion *père*, a somewhat shy and very modest man.

1981 Nuits-Saint-Georges
Very dark colour, a pleasant bouquet, not a big wine, but well made with plenty of fruit. Quite easy to taste and rather nice for a 1981

1980 Côtes de Nuits
Good colour, pleasant bouquet, light to medium body, agreeable and almost ready to drink

1980 Nuits-Saint-Georges
Very dark colour, very full bouquet, lovely fruit with a lot of character, a good mouthful. Complete and excellent

1981 Vosne-Romanée
Good colour, attractive bouquet, nice flavour but a disappointing finish

1980 Vosne-Romanée
Lovely colour, the bouquet still closed up. Good fruit though with plenty of depth. Rather good

1981 Vosne-Romanée les Beaux-Monts
A dark colour, fine fragrant bouquet, delicious taste, a wine packed with charm. Remarkable for a 1981!

1980 Vosne-Romanée les Beaux-Monts
Dark colour, a distinguished bouquet, a powerful 'solid' wine with masses of fruit with considerable depth. Will make a fine bottle

1983 Vosne-Romanée les Chaumes
Dark colour, fragrant bouquet, not a big wine but has charm and a nice finish

1983 Nuits-Saint-Georges 1er Cru, Les Vignes Rondes
An oaky nose, nicely rounded with a lot of tannin

1983 Nuits-Saint-Georges les Pruliers
Good colour, lovely fruit, full of charm with considerable depth. A wine of enormous potential

1983 Clos Vougeot
Dark colour, intense bouquet, a mouthful of concentrated flavour, almost 'solid', a lot of tannin. Should make a splendid bottle

A wonderful dinner at the fabled Lameloise at Chagny, a restaurant fully worthy of its three rosettes in the *Guide Michelin*. When some 30 years ago, I used to visit the Lameloise, it was smaller, the interior decoration more modest; although the cooking was every bit as good in those days, Monsieur Lameloise had yet to gain his first rosette. The wines were good, the 1979 Puligny-

Montrachet of Etienne Sauzet and an excellent Auxey-Duresses les Duresses of Dicoinne.

FRIDAY, 10 FEBRUARY

The morning was spent tasting in the cellar of Madame Pitoiset-Urena in Meursault, a large lady who owns three hectares (about seven and a half acres) of well situated vines.

1983 Meursault les Pellands
Pleasant bouquet, good fruit and flavour

1983 Meursault les Poruzots
Full-bodied and quite powerful

1983 Meursault Genevrières
A fine rounded wine with masses of body

1983 Puligny-Montrachet les Chalumeaux
A lovely nose, very good fruit and a delightful flavour

All of the above were of course still in barrel, but somehow the wines in bottle which followed were not so attractive, at least to me, they had a kind of strike about them. These are some of the better ones:

1982 Meursault les Poruzots made from 70-year-old vines
Definitely nicer with a rich flavour

1982 Meursault les Genevrières
A fine long wine, well bred and needs time to develop

1982 Puligny-Montrachet les Chalumeaux
Still closed up, but clearly fine quality

1979 Puligny-Montrachet les Chalumeaux
Well developed bouquet, a fine wine

Comte Lafon in Meursault

This was like old times, I used to buy a lot of wine from this man from the early 1950s until 1966 while I was a director of Harveys of Bristol. One of the finest of all the growers, the Comte believes in meddling as little as possible with his wine and leaves it longer in barrel than most people. A heating engineer by profession, he can afford not to sell his wine too soon. His theory is that particular care should be taken immediately after the grapes are crushed and once the initial period is over the wine is left on its lees and is never racked. He claims the secret is to have the courage to do nothing. This policy clearly works because the quality of the wine he produces is excellent.

1983 Meursault Clos de la Barre still undergoing malalactic fermentation

Quite sweet. Comte Lafon said this wine resembles his 1963 vintage which he had to keep in cask for five years and he was the only man to be successful in that disastrous vintage. During the course of a single afternoon masses of *pourriture* (rot) had developed among the vines and that was followed by a jump of 2° in the sugar content. In a way, 1983 had been similar with an unusually high degree of sugar in the white wine, but this time the change took place over three to four days.

1982 Meursault Desirée

A scented bouquet, silky and easy to taste, good fruit with a nice balance

1982 Meursault Goutte d'Or

Fragrant bouquet, heaps of fruit and character

1982 Meursault Charmes

Scented bouquet, a distinguished wine with an attractive flavour, fine quality

1982 Meursault Genevrières

Fine bouquet, full of elegance, but going through a phase with a little bitterness at the end of the taste, plenty of promise though

1982 Meursault les Perrières

A splendid rich bouquet, reminiscent of peaches. Well bred with a lovely flavour. Should make a really good bottle

1982 Montrachet

A heavenly bouquet but still a slumbering giant

In 1983 Comte Lafon made more Montrachet than he has ever done before, four casks, two of which he intended to bottle in 1985 and the rest in 1986. In poor years he has made as little as half a cask or one cask.

White Wine in bottle

1980 Meursault Charmes

A powerful bouquet, a leaner wine though with some acidity. Our host told us it had been a difficult year for white wine

Red Wine in Bottle

1980 Volnay Santenots

Dark colour, an attractive well bred bouquet, plenty of fruit and of good quality

1979 Volnay Champans

Dark colour, masses of fruit, rounded and charming. *Note* In accordance with some other growers, Comte Lafon is beginning to prefer his red 1980 vintage to the 1979

1963 Montrachet

Pale golden colour, a bouquet like a German Auslese, a lovely rich wine and almost unbelievable for this poor vintage. This was the wine Lafon had kept in cask for five years. As it was so full of sugar, at vintage time every year he had added a little of the new fermenting wine to reactivate it and help to complete the fermentation

Hubert de Montille in Volnay

A lawyer from Dijon who, like Comte Lafon, is independent and can afford to make wine that takes time to mature. In fact we were to find these particular wines unusually slow to develop. As a result they seemed less attractive than others, but later on as we tasted the older vintages we could appreciate the reasoning behind his methods.

1982 Volnay Champans

Medium colour, a bouquet reminiscent of plums, medium body, good fruit, but very firm

1982 Pommard 1er Cru Les Pezerolles

Darker colour, a concentrated bouquet, plenty of fruit with more depth, but somewhat acid and severe, in fact very backward

1982 Pommard les Rugiens

Good colour and bouquet, a lot of body with good depth, also severe and backward

1983 Pommard les Rugiens

Dark colour, a lovely flavour and full of charm

This grower hardly chaptalises at all and of course not at all with the 1983s. His cellar is very cold and his wines taste much younger than those of other growers.

1981 Pommard les Rugiens, in bottle
A berry like bouquet, some body but on the lean side. Quite good
for this unforthcoming year

1980 Pommard les Rugiens
Dark colour, a fruity bouquet, with greater depth and of good
structure

1978 Pommard les Rugiens
Good colour, scented bouquet, good fruit with nice depth of
flavour, but still very closed up

SUNDAY, 12 FEBRUARY

At last the sun had begun to shine in a cloudless sky. A few
kilometres away up in the hills are the ruins of the eleventh-
century Abbaye Ste Marguerite and this provided an excuse for a
much needed walk. Then we settled down to a tasting of sundry
wines which Becky had collected from other regions for Dick
Scheer to taste. Among them were two of the best wines I have
ever come across from the Côtes de Provence, the 1982 St Andre
de Figuière, surprisingly easy to drink and worthy of its silver
medal and another from the same grower but with a gold medal
which was more serious and really rather good. Unfortunately
they were quite expensive. The best wine of the lot for me
though was the 1981 Château Fonbadet, Pauillac, a dark colour
and packed with good flavour.

MONDAY, 13 FEBRUARY

This was a day devoted to *négociants* rather than individual
growers. Our first stop was with Faiveley, a much respected firm
in Nuits-Saint-Georges where Monsieur Guy Charles Nicolle
provided a tasting for us, a nice young man who through selling
his wine to all the great restaurants in France was well versed
in gastronomy. There were some attractive wines from their
own vineyards, 1982 Rully, 1981 Mercurey, white, 1981 Nuits-
Saint-Georges Clos de la Marechal and 1964 Latricières Cham-
bertin.

After an excellent lunch at the Hotel Côte d'Or in Nuits-Saint-
Georges we drove to Gevrey-Chambertin to call on the small but
very good family firm of Pierre Bourée. This visit also evoked old
memories, because in the distant past, I used to buy quite a lot of
wine for Harvey's but that was in the 1950s and 1960s in the days
of the late Paul Bourée. His nephew and young assistant at the

time was Marcel Valet who is now head of the firm with two grown up sons. This firm always produced wine of excellent quality and from the notes which follow, it will be seen that Monsieur Valet has kept up the family tradition. The latter told us he had thought little of the quality of the red wines of 1981 so had bought the minimum quantity. His 1980s were clearly carefully selected.

As we tasted no less than 28 wines here, there are too many to relate so I will concentrate on those which impressed us most and in fact were some of the best of this vintage we had come across.

White Wine

1982 Meursault
A nice gentle bouquet, delightful flavour with a good finish

1982 Corton Charlemagne
Very good nose, a lovely flavour, classic

Red Wine, All of the 1982 Vintage and All From Cask

Volnay
Good colour and bouquet, lots of fruit and body, rather good

Chambolle-Musigny
An attractive scented nose, a wine full of charm

Gevrey-Chambertin Clos de la Justice
Good colour and bouquet, an attractive complex wine, long on taste

Gevrey-Chambertin Cuvée Reserve, i.e. a blend of *premier crus*
Good colour and bouquet, a fine big wine with attractive sweetness, should make a very good bottle

Vosne-Romanée Les Suchots
Medium colour, fruity bouquet, a lovely flavour, a wine with style and considerable quality

Charmes-Chambertin
Dark colour, fine bouquet, full-bodied, a beauty

Mazis-Chambertin
Dark colour, fine bouquet, full-bodied, rounded with a lot of charm, excellent

Morey-Saint-Denis Clos de la Roche
Dark colour, distinguished bouquet, a most attractive taste, really delightful

Bonnes Mares
Dark colour, beautiful bouquet, a lovely mouthful almost of essence, a great treat

TUESDAY, 14 FEBRUARY

A cloudless sky but still very cold. At ten o'clock we arrived at the offices of Lupé-Cholet in Beaune where Giles de Courcey received us and took us to an attractive fourteenth-century cellar for a tasting mainly of the 1982 vintage, a good commercial year rather than a great one. Even if the 1980s are not destined for a long life, they should develop reasonably early.

I must have known the de Lupé family ever since the war. Until he was killed tragically in a motor accident, the late Jacques de Lupé used to come to England where his firm was highly regarded among the leading circles of the wine trade. Since his death many years ago the business was carried on chiefly by Inez de Lupé. This is an old family and their *château* in Nuits-Saint-Georges is packed with lovely furniture. The family has owned the *premier cru* vineyard of Château Gris for many years and it was around 1907 that they joined the Comte de Cholet to become *négociants*.

Meursault 1982
An attractive bouquet, full, rounded with a good depth of flavour

Puligny-Montrachet 1er Cru les Champs 1982
Nice bouquet and flavour, good quality

Savigny-les-Beaune 1er Cru les Lavières 1982
Good colour and nose, rich and charming

Beaune 1er Cru Clos du Roi 1982
Nice spicy bouquet, good 'solid' stuff with some tannin

Nuits-Saint-Georges, Château Gris 1982
Very special bouquet, complete with a delightful flavour

Vosne-Romanée les Malconsorts 1980
Darker colour, rich bouquet, deep, full-bodied, but much more backward. The better quality of this vintage was noticeable

Later with Inez we went to the Hotel Côte d'Or for lunch. The restaurants with one rosette in the *Guide Michelin* can vary in quality but there can be little doubt that the proprietor here fully deserves his. The white wine was 1982 Petit Chablis from Lupé-Cholet which is always so good. Inez told us her family have bought this for many decades from the same grower. The red was a magnum of 1978 Château Gris. Although not ready to drink, this is going to be a lovely wine.

That afternoon we drove south through Lyon to the Hotel Beau Rivage at Condrieu on the right bank of the Rhône and just south of Vienne, a delightful hotel and well known to those of us who are interested in the wines of nearby Côte Rotie.

Condrieu is noted for its white wine made from the *viognier* grape, of which the leading light is of course the tiny but well-known vineyard of Château Grillet. These wines of Condrieu have a special bouquet and flavour all of their own and as they are hard to find elsewhere, one seizes the opportunity to enjoy them on their native heath.

Note It is sad that the much loved Inez de Lupé has died since these notes were written.

WEDNESDAY, 15 FEBRUARY

As our appointment with Monsieur Chave at Mauves had fallen through as well as that with Paul Jaboulet in Tain l'Hermitage, we spent the morning sightseeing. First of all we had to look at the vineyard of Château Grillet and then drove south to Tain l'Hermitage where we explored the country behind the steep hillside on which the vineyards of Hermitage are situated. This was the country of Crozes-Hermitage and there are glorious views of the Rhône valley to be had from the hilltop.

Further south we called on two growers in Cornas and I must admit that it is strange, in spite of the many visits I have paid to the Rhône valley, I had never been there before. The wines are very full-bodied and very tannic with a very dark colour; because of this heavy tannin, it takes the better vintages a good ten years before they reach their best. One wonders what the future of this area will be, the slopes on which the wines grow are so steep, the difficulty of production is immense and not very rewarding. In consequence, the younger generation has been reluctant to follow in their fathers' footsteps. We were told there are no men under 35 now in the business and this was borne out by the two growers we were to meet, both of whom had an only son and neither son wanted to work in the family vineyard. Admittedly, the holdings are very small.

It seems that 1983 is a very good vintage for this region with 1982 somewhat disappointing. Unlike the Côte d'Or, 1981 was a good year with 1980 better still.

Monsieur Guy de Barjac, who owns about six acres

1983 Cornas, from 80-year-old vines
Almost black in colour, a huge wine packed with fruit with masses of tannin. This will be used for blending

1982 Cornas, a blend of young and old vines
Very dark colour, a deep bouquet, much easier to taste with heaps of flavour

As elsewhere, due to the excessive heat at vintage time, there had been problems at the time of the harvest and the subsequent vinification in 1982. The ideal temperature is around 25°C but in 1982 the temperature rose up to 30°C. Consequently, the 1982 has less colour than usual.

Our next visit was to Monsieur Auguste Clape whose premises are on the Route Nationale and, with some six hectares, he is the biggest grower in the district; in his office there are numerous diplomas for the gold medals won by his wines.

The excessive tannin in the wine means, according to Monsieur Clape, that it is fatal to use new oak casks; he always buys old ones from *négociants* on the Côte d'Or where the tannin in the oak has diminished.

1983 Cornas, made from 30-to-40-year-old vines
Good colour and nose, a well balanced, well bred wine

1983 Cornas, from another slope
Dark colour, very good bouquet, with more depth and body

1982 Cornas
Not so dark as the others but a lovely nose, not a big wine but good for its year

1981 Cornas
Good bouquet and lots of fruit

1978 Cornas
A marvellous bouquet, a lovely deep full flavoured wine

1973
Less colour, a pleasant bouquet, but less powerful. Ready now

1972
Wonderful colour and a fabulous nose, a big velvety wine of unusual quality. No wonder this man has such a fine reputation

THURSDAY, 16 FEBRUARY

Colder still, but a glorious day. The frost is just what the vines needed after the excessive rain of the past week.

Condrieu is an unusually small district, even so the production is considerably less than in the past. In fact, there are only about ten growers in all and the production of one or two of them is no more than one barrel. The grape used for this wine is 100 per cent *viognier* and half of the area is owned by one man. It is a wine which should be drunk while it is young because as it ages it tends to lose its fruit.

Our first call was on Monsieur Jean Pinchon who produces about six barrels in an average year. Unexpectedly, he lives in a modern villa with his cellar beneath. This is how he rated some of the recent vintages:

1983: Good well balanced wines which should keep well

1982: Powerful, up to 14.7°, ripe wines but with insufficient acidity

1981: A successful vintage, good fruit acidity, will keep well, 13.5°

1980: Reasonably good, the grapes were less ripe

1979: Similar to 1982, good very ripe grapes, but insufficient acidity

We had the impression that Monsieur Pinchon expected us to drink up all the wine in our glasses, but as it was only ten o'clock in the morning, this might have had disastrous results.

1982 Condrieu

A dry fruity bouquet, a pleasant flavour with a good long after-taste

1983 Condrieu

The malalactic fermentation still in evidence, but this appeared to have plenty of depth and quality

In order to find the next grower we had to drive right up into the hills to the Château de Rosay. The owner Monsieur M. Multier told us his family came from Lyon and had made their living by making braid and so on for military uniforms. His vineyards are some way away, near those of Château Grillet, and his pink-painted *château* with its three towers is quite imposing. The original building was smaller until around 1830 when the property was bought by an industrialist who had made his fortune by buying up the debris from the battlefields of Napoleon. He has three hectares of vines, but only one with the *appellation* of Condrieu.

1983 Condrieu

An attractive fresh bouquet with an intensity of fruit and a lot of character

1981 Condrieu, in bottle

A fine fragrant bouquet and a delicious taste

The visit to the vineyards ended on a high note for we spent the rest of the day with the well-known firm of Etienne Guigal in Ampuis, a firm which produces wines of excellent quality. Because of strong demand and limited production, the wines of Guigal are hard to find.

The firm is run by Marcel Guigal, but was founded by his father who began to earn his living when he was only eight years old. At 14 he left his native valley of the Loire to obtain work with the firm of Vidal-Fleurie which at that time was very small. Through the years he worked his way up from cellarman to head cellarman and in his time planted the firm's most important vineyards. Having worked for Vidal-Fleurie for 20 years, he left in 1946 to start his own business of which he has made an astonishing success. Now in his eighties he says with modesty how fortunate he is to have such an able son as Marcel to carry on the good work. At the time, there was the ironic situation that the important firm of Vidal-Fleurie, which had never prospered since the departure of Etienne Guigal, was for sale. If they were successful over the purchase, the Guigals would be the owners of some of the finest vineyards of Côte Rotie. They are already owners of two of the finest, La Mouline on the Côte Blonde and La Landonne on the Côte Brune.

1982 Condrieu

An attractive racy taste with a full flavour

In spite of the heavy cost, the red wine is mostly matured in new oak for three or four years depending upon the vintage. It seems that 1982 was not a very good year for Côte Rotie.

1982 Hermitage, blanc

Quite a powerful bouquet, plenty of fruit and body. This has been matured in new oak for six months

From the cask:

1983 Côte Rotie, La Mouline, Côte Blonde
to be kept in cask for three years with no filtering or fining
A very dark colour with a powerful bouquet, a rich, rounded wine which is full of tannin. Should make an excellent bottle in time

1983 La Landonne, Côte Brune
Extremely dark colour, heaps of fruit and flavour. Not so massive as La Mouline, but perhaps more elegant. Will keep for many years

1982 Hermitage
Good colour, not so full-bodied as La Mouline, a lovely flavour though and very well bred. Excellent quality.
The predominant feature of the bouquet of red Hermitage is cassis and that of Côte Rotie raspberry or blackberry and violets. Of the two, the Hermitage style is the more definite, but because of the various elements, Côte Rotie is more difficult to pick out

1982 Côte Rotie
Good colour, a fragrant bouquet, not so rich as some of the others, good nevertheless

1980 Côte Brune et Blonde
Dark colour, a most attractive bouquet of raspberry, a lovely 'solid' well made wine. Needs a long time to develop

1979 Chateauneuf du Pape, Guigal label and from vines
specially reserved
Very dark colour, a cedary bouquet, a fine big well balanced wine with a nice finish

1980 La Mouline
Very dark colour, the bouquet still closed up, rich rounded and altogether marvellous, a huge mouthful of flavour

1980 La Landonne
Dark colour, a deeper bouquet than La Mouline, lovely flavour, great quality

1976 La Mouline
Very dark colour, a lovely mouthful of flavour, rounded with a fine finish, splendid quality

1978 La Mouline
Deepest colour of all, a huge powerful bouquet, the flavour quite lovely, a wine packed with promise

Marcel Guigal took us to a restaurant on the right bank of the Rhône to the north of Vienne called Camerano, where the young chef specialises in fish; certainly our turbot was admirable. With this we drank the 1982 Condrieu of Guigal which had been good at the tasting but was even better with food. As one can find with a good Condrieu, this had an exciting taste with the faintest hint of sweetness in spite of the fact this is a dry wine. With our cheese Marcel produced his 1978 Brune et Blonde, still firm but possible to drink, but how good it will be when fully matured. I have some of this at home and will keep it for a few more years. Incidentally, at home I am drinking an excellent 1980 Côtes du Rhône from Guigal as the daily fare. Marcel told me he buys the grapes from the same grower every year.

Finally this visit provided a splendid opportunity to get to know the wines of Condrieu better, because there are five or six growers' wines on the list at the hotel. Except perhaps at La Pyramide at Vienne there can be few other places in the world where such a wide selection is available. We should, I suppose, have tasted the Château Grillet which has the great name, but it was almost double the price of the others.

On our first evening we tried the 1982 Vernay* which was pleasant, but not exceptional.

The second night the 1982 Côteau de Vernon, the best wine from the same source and it has a fine individual taste. On the last evening, the non vintage of Mons. Guilleron, but it was dry and rather flat, much better in fact was the 1982 from Mons. Perret which was fresh and exciting.

These wines of Condrieu have an individuality, a delightful special appealing flavour which is different from anything else and they alone helped to make our three day visit even more enjoyable.

---

*I have the same wine, but of 1983, at home and it is delicious.

5
VISIT TO BORDEAUX
1984

We arrived in the midst of a rainstorm, not a good augury for the vintage which was to commence in ten days' time. At Château Latour, we learned the weather had been dry and cool during the preceding week but that an unsettled spell had begun and indeed was to continue.

This day, 21 September, was to be one of the highlights of my life, a dinner given by the President of Latour to celebrate my eightieth birthday. It was also the first time the *salle de reception* was going to be used since its reconstruction by Colefax & Fowler, the well-known London decorators. Formerly rather gloomy (one of the legacies of the previous owners) it has now become a beautiful room. There were about 50 of us altogether, all the leading *châteaux* proprietors were present as well as some of my oldest friends from Bordeaux. Many had been friends for well over 30 years and some even longer, like Ronald Barton whom I first met before the war.

The food cooked by a *traiteur* from Bordeaux was delicious, better even, I thought, than that of the great dinner held at Château Margaux about two months before to celebrate 50 years association between Bordeaux and the United States. That dinner had been held in honour of Sam Aaron, who in 1934 founded his famous business of Sherry Lehman in New York.

1967 Domaine de Chevalier, white, accompanied the *filets de poissons en terrine* and the sturdy 1961 Latour provided an excellent match for the pigeon. This is a fabulous wine, but to be truthful, it was not really ready; it had a heavenly flavour of course, but it was still firm and rather resistant, masking no doubt, all kinds of delights. Words fail to describe the 1928 Latour, a superb wine with years still to go, but surely now at its summit. The delightful sweetness which had been hidden under a cloak of tannin for half a century had at last broken through. I overheard Daniel Lawton saying it was the finest claret he had ever drunk and that, coming from him, must be something!

Perhaps by the turn of the century the 1961 will be showing equally well. By then it will only be 40 years old, which is nothing for a good vintage of Latour, let alone a great one.

Both Alan Hare, our President, and my old friend Guy Schyler said a few words and I had to reply with my English accent, but at least I was understood! Surrounded as I was by old friends, it was an evening I shall never forget. Even so, there were two friends, both of them unwell, whose presence I missed, Jean-Paul Gardère and Edouard Cruse.

SATURDAY, 22 SEPTEMBER-SUNDAY, 23 SEPTEMBER

It was a weekend for raincoats and umbrellas; the weather was thoroughly unsettled. At the time there was no *pourriture* on the grapes, perhaps because the weather had not been warm enough, perhaps owing to the beneficial effect of the new sprays. The *merlot* grapes were few and far between, but the *cabernet sauvignons* looked very healthy. Together with Alan and Jill Hare, we lunched at Pontet-Canet with Guy and Nicole Tesseron and among the other guests were Hugues and Micheline Lawton. The Lawton family have been prominent in the wine world of Bordeaux since the eighteenth century.

The 1982 and 1983 vintages were tasted from the barrel and both of them were attractive, especially the 1982, a fine big wine. Guy told us he intends to start a second wine at Pontet-Canet, probably with the 1985 vintage. From my memory of those two exceptional vintages, the 1945 and 1929 of Pontet-Canet, the possibility of producing great wine here is feasible. In London some 12 years ago I remember serving the 1945 Pontet-Canet anonymously alongside the 1945 Mouton-Rothschild and all those present preferred the Pontet-Canet.

At dinner that evening Alan Hare produced the 1909 Latour, a wine I cannot remember tasting before. Expecting it to be thin or at least over the hill, it was a pleasant surprise to find how good it was. One might have guessed it was 40 or 50 years old, but certainly not 75!

MONDAY, 24 SEPTEMBER

Intermittent rain continued all day. At Château Cissac, Pascal

Vialard had set out a range of the *crus bourgeois* of 1983 as well as a few of the classified growths. Cissac is one of the more attractive *châteaux*, a fine example of Médocain building of the eighteenth century. Even the office block across the small intervening road has a delightful village charm.

Some Wines of the 1983 Vintage – First Group

Potensac, Médoc
Dark colour, a nice fruity bouquet, a 'solid' well made wine which should make a good bottle 18/20

Abiet, Cissac
Good colour and bouquet, some tannin, but a nice depth of flavour, rather good 15/20

Lamothe, Cissac
Medium to pale colour, good nose, light but attractive 15/20

La Tour du Mirail, Cissac
Good colour and bouquet, good fruit and flavour 15/20

Coufran, St Seurin de Cadourne
Good colour, a slightly rougher nose but good flavour and well made. Just a trace of acidity 15/20

Verdignan, St Seurin de Cadourne
Good colour, a little more strident, but good fruit 15/20

Lanessan, Cissac
Dark colour, a full scented nose, medium body, good flavour and nicely balanced 18/20

Malescasse, Lamarque
Dark colour, full bouquet, medium body, plenty of fruit and some tannin 15/20

Cissac, Cissac
Dark colour, good bouquet, a lot of fruit and very good 18/20

Beaumont, Haut-Médoc
Very dark colour, fruity bouquet, medium to full-bodied, rather good 17/20

Maucaillou, Moulis
Good colour, scented bouquet, medium body 15/20

Gloria, Saint Julien
Medium colour, nice perfumed bouquet, good flavour, but expected more from this 16/20

Les Ormes de Pez, Saint Estèphe
Dark colour, nice scented nose, good fruit and flavour, excellent quality 19/20

Tronquoy-Lalande, Saint Estèphe
Good colour, attractive bouquet, medium body, well made 16/20

Haut-Bages Averous, Pauillac
Good colour, scented bouquet, medium body, an attractive wine 17/20

Labégorce, Margaux
Dark colour, nice nose, light to medium body, rather good 16/20

Second Group, with separate marking
Chasse-Spleen, Moulis
Good colour, a good fruity, rounded wine with a lot of charm, also a lot of tannin 16/20

Léoville-Lascases, Saint Julien
Dark colour, a fine bouquet, a fine wine, with style and breeding 19/20

Ducru-Beaucaillou, Saint Julien
Good colour, beautiful bouquet, full-bodied, full-flavoured with considerable depth, excellent quality 19.5/20

Pedesclaux, Pauillac
Dark colour, scented bouquet, medium body, well made and well bred 15.5/20

Lynch-Bages, Pauillac
Dark colour, fruity bouquet, full-bodied with a lot of flavour, very good 18.5/20

Haut-Batailley, Pauillac
Dark colour, pleasant bouquet, light to medium body, well bred 16/20

Grand-Puy-Lacoste, Pauillac
Good colour, a fine concentrated bouquet, attractive flavour which fills the mouth 18.5/20

La Tour Martillac, Graves
Good colour, a rather closed bouquet, good fruit with some
charm   15.5/20

Although not big, spectacular wines like the 1982s, these 1983s
are really very good. They have plenty of charm and are typical of
a good vintage. Particularly noticeable from this tasting was the
great increase in quality of the *crus bourgeois* during the last
20 years.

We had moved to Château d'Issan in Cantenac to stay with
Marguerite Cruse. This beautiful moated *château* was completed
between 1602 and 1604 on the site of a fortress built by the
English and destroyed by them after their defeat at the battle of
Castillon in 1453. Before that the Greeks had settled here. In the
old *chai*, which is of the same period as the present house, there
is a fine rafted roof and it is there that Mme Cruse holds her
concerts which are a feature of the summer season in Bordeaux.
In the *cuvier* on the far side of the moat, a fine range of stainless
steel fermentation tanks were installed in time for the 1984
vintage and her son Lionel maintains it has made all the difference
at harvest time.*

1983 d'Issan
Dark colour, an attractive bouquet, fruity, rounded and first rate

1982 d'Issan
Fine dark colour, delightful bouquet, full flavoured with a lovely
taste, a fine big wine

TUESDAY, 25 SEPTEMBER

Considerable reconstruction was under way at Château Lynch-
Bages, both around the house and especially in the *chais*. The
latter were being modernised and extended. The new labelling
machine from Germany has a feature I had not seen before, the
labels are on an already prepared adhesive roll. Jean-Michel Cazes
claims it is highly efficient. The other guests were Xavier Borie
and his wife, the proprietors of Grand-Puy Lacoste.

Les Ormes de Pez
1983
Good dark colour, a nice vinous bouquet, full-flavoured with a
delightful taste

---

*d'Issan is one of those *châteaux* where the quality is improving all the time.

1982

Dark colour, a fine full bouquet, a huge wine with the flavour and body filling the mouth. This should make an excellent bottle and I am glad I have bought quite a lot of this for my own cellar

1981

Good colour, an elegant bouquet, lighter in body than the other vintages, but good all the same, well balanced with a pleasant finish

Haut-Bages Averous, the second wine of Lynch-Bages

1983

Good colour, fresh bouquet, a delightful fruity flavour

1982

Dark colour, an attractive bouquet with a touch of cassis, full-bodied, rounded with a hint of sweetness. A very good wine with heaps of charm

1981

Good colour, a more developed bouquet, good fruit and well made, a nice wine

Lynch-Bages

1980

Quite a good colour, a fruity bouquet, not a big wine but pleasant and easy to taste. Not great of course, but useful for present consumption

1983

Dark colour, the bouquet still closed up, but full and fruity, heaps of fruit, a complete wine with considerable promise

1982

Very dark colour, a fine deep bouquet, a big wine with masses of fruit and some tannin. Almost massive in style and should make an excellent bottle

1981

Dark colour, fruity bouquet, it seemed thinner after the huge 1982, but is nicely rounded nevertheless

1979

Dark colour, a pleasant mature bouquet, plenty of fruit, but a trace of acidity. A little disappointing after all the others

1975

Good colour, a concentrated bouquet, quite a big wine with plenty of fruit, rather dry though on account of all the tannin. At the time of tasting this could have had more charm, but it is typical of the 1975 vintage

During lunch we drank the 1977 Lynch-Bages, nothing special naturally, but agreeable and easy to drink. Then came the 1952 vintage, a big wine and still somewhat firm, this should continue to improve and must surely be ready before too long.

The general date for the commencement of the vintage was 1 October, but this was by no means obligatory. Since the weather had been so unsettled this year, some growers had considered starting as much as a week later. While discussing this subject with Jean-Michel Cazes, I mentioned a start was to be made at Latour on the 1st and he said he intended to begin three days later giving a reason I had not heard before. It seems that because of its favoured situation close to the river, the grapes at Latour usually ripen about three days before some of the other local vineyards and the same applies to the flowering of the vines around the end of May, which also begins earlier. Thanks to its location, the vineyard of Latour has thus two advantages, less liability to frost and grapes which ripen a day or so earlier.

WEDNESDAY, 27 SEPTEMBER

After some early mist, the weather improved and it was a better day altogether. Our first appointment was with Monsieur Michel Delon of Léoville-Lascases, a man who is noted for making good wine. The *cuvier* where the grape juice is fermented is over 200 years old and the roof is supported by splendid oak beams. In these days it comes almost as a surprise to see the fermentation vats are the old kind, that is made of oak, but handsome is as handsome does; the quality of the wine produced regularly at Léoville-Lascases is hard to beat.

The wine in cases is stored across the main road and in common with other properties, the area has been enlarged and even further extension was in progress.

The revolution in the sale and distribution of the great médocs has had a profound effect on the *château* proprietors. Until 20 or so years ago, the produce of each vintage was purchased by the powerful *négociants* in Bordeaux while the wine was still very young. It was then transported to their cellars beside the river where it was 'nursed' through its infancy, and then, when about two years old, was either sold in cask to other merchants or put into bottle on the spot. Now that the *négociants* have become fewer in number and no longer have the capital to buy on a large scale, much of the sale of the wine is carried out on a brokerage basis with merchants abroad and even with their retail customers buying their claret *en primeur.* A good example of this is what has happened to both the 1982 and 1983 vintages.

Even so, if much of the wine is sold in this manner and much of it *en primeur,* it still has to be kept somewhere. Thus, instead of disposing of the bulk of their stock soon after the vintage, the *châteaux* proprietors have had to find extra space for storage and this in turn must have caused a problem of finance. Happily, thanks partly to the independence stemming from almost universal *château* bottling, the proprietors have possibly more money than ever before and so are in a better position to pay for the enlargement of their premises for holding wine stock.

There are three wines at Léoville-Lascases: the *grand vin,* Clos du Marquis, and Potensac which ranks among the best of the *crus bourgeois.*

Potensac

1983
Very dark colour, a full, fruity bouquet, a big wine with a nice concentration of flavour. This confirmed our opinion when we had tasted the same wine at Château Cissac two days earlier

1982
Dark colour, good bouquet, a powerful wine, *charnu* i.e fleshy and well made, but still rather firm. This will make a good bottle

Clos du Marquis

1983
Dark colour, an attractive full bouquet, has a lovely taste, a wine to buy

1982
Dark colour, an attractive bouquet, a fuller, richer wine, but a query perhaps concerning its finish

Léoville-Lascases

1983
Lovely colour, lovely bouquet and flavour, which fills the mouth. Elegant and full of promise

1982
Very dark colour, delightful bouquet, a deeper wine than the 1983, well bred with a lovely finish, a beauty

1981

Medium colour, distinguished bouquet, lighter in body of course, but classic and well balanced, this will certainly make a good bottle

1978

Dark colour, powerful bouquet, a concentrated taste with a fine finish, better even than expected

When we arrived at Château Malescot for lunch there were three generations of the Zuger family to meet us, Roger Zuger, the proprietor whom I have known since he was a boy, his 20-year-old son and his mother, with whose husband I used to work closely in my Harvey days, some 30 years ago.

For lunch Roger had decanted a bottle of 1945 Malescot, still just a little severe but typical of its great vintage and the 1907 which was his mother's year of birth. Considering its age and the fact that 1907 was never a great year, it was surprisingly good.

Château Malescot, 3rd growth, Margaux

1983

Good dark colour, a delightful bouquet (Malescot is noted for its bouquet), plenty of fruit and a good flavour

1982

Dark colour, fine bouquet and flavour with a nice finish.

These wines were typical of their *commune*, light perhaps but full of elegance and charm.

THURSDAY, 28 SEPTEMBER

Early mist was followed by the first fine day since our arrival a week before. At this time of the year Patrick Danglade and Jean-François Moueix, who together direct Duclot, the leading *négociant* of Bordeaux, arrange a tasting for the wine brokers and a few extra guests such as ourselves. This time it was the turn of the 1981 vintage, a good one of course, but which has been overshadowed by the more spectacular vintages of 1982 and 1983. The wines, were grouped into their areas, Graves, Saint Emilion, Pomerol, Pauillac, etc., and presented anonymously without even an indication as to the *commune*. The marking was from zero to five.

1981 Vintage, an anonymous tasting in the order of placing

La Conseillante, Pomerol
Very good bouquet, lovely fruit and flavour
Total 82 points, my score 5

Pavie, Saint Emilion
Pleasant bouquet, not a big wine and for me a slightly sharp finish
Total 81.5 points, my score 2

Pichon-Lalande, Pauillac
Fine bouquet, lots of fruit, still a little hard, but has lovely depth, fine quality
Total 80 points, my score 5

Lynch-Bages, Pauillac
Quite a good bouquet, not a big wine, with less charm
Total 79 points, my score 3

Léoville-Lascases, Saint Julien
Fine bouquet, plenty of fruit and a good full flavour, well balanced
Total 77.5 points, my score 5

The next two wines both scored the same total points.

Vieux Ch. Certan, Pomerol
Good fruity bouquet, good fruit and body and is well made
Total 76 points, my score 3.5

Canon, Saint Emilion
Pleasant bouquet, medium body, finishes nicely
Total 76 points, my score 5

Pape Clément, Graves
Nice nose, good fruit, well made with a nice finish
Total 73 points, my score 3.5

Domaine de Chevalier, Graves
Fruity bouquet, quite good fruit and flavour, spoilt by a sharpish finish
Total 71.5 points, my score 2

Figeac, Saint Emilion
Query bouquet, not a big wine, also with a slightly sharpish finish
Total 70.5 points, my score 3

Ducru-Beaucaillou, Saint Julien
Pleasant bouquet, good fruit, also a trace of acidity
Total 70 points, my score 3

L'Evangile, Pomerol
Attractive bouquet, good fruit with plenty of body
Total 69.5 points, my score 5

Beychevelle, Saint Julien
Disappointing bouquet, plenty of fruit and quite full-bodied
Total 67 points, my score 4.5

Carbonnieux, Graves
Pleasant bouquet, good fruit but lacks charm
Total 66.5 points, my score 3.5

Pontet-Canet, Pauillac
No special bouquet, some acidity and lacks charm
Total 65.5 points, my score 2

For what they are worth the notes on these wines are my own. There was some variation of course as to our assessments, but on the whole the quality was good.

After Patrick took us to the famous Saint James restaurant on the hill on the far side of the river. It was a delicious meal, worthy of the two rosette status. The wines we enjoyed were the 1980 Lynch-Bages, on the light side, but very drinkable, and a more serious 1976 from Ducru-Beaucaillou.

Although with somewhat jaded palates, we dined most agreeably that evening with Donald and Anne Biddle at Le Chalut, a restaurant which specialises in seafood. Amongst other activities Donald has been a most successful chairman of the Wine Committee of the Carlton Club in London. The grilled turbot with sauce bearnaise was excellent.

FRIDAY, 28 SEPTEMBER

The fine weather continued, in fact it was a glorious day. These are the details of another anonymous tasting of the 1983 vintage.

1983 Red Bordeaux

Les Ormes de Pez, Saint Estèphe
Dark colour, medium body with an attractive flavour, this should make a good bottle: *Note* First rate for a *cru bourgeois*   11/20

Gloria, Saint Julien
Dark colour, plenty of bouquet, a nice wine of medium body which has some charm   13/20

Desmirail, Margaux
Dark colour, nice nose, good flavour and quite full-bodied   12/20

Durfort-Vivens, Margaux
Medium colour, plenty of bouquet, with good fruit and depth but how disappointing considering this is a second growth   12/20

Haut-Batailley, Pauillac
Medium colour, good fruit, medium body, rather too much acidity   11/20

Calon-Ségur, Saint Estèphe
Medium colour, pleasant bouquet, good fruit and flavour, some tannin, rather good   14.5/20

Montrose, Saint Estèphe
Dark colour, pleasant bouquet, not a big wine, but the flavour is good   14.5/20

Grand-Puy-Lacoste, Pauillac
Medium colour, attractive bouquet, good fruit and body with some tannin, good quality   15.5/20

St Pierre, Saint Julien
Dark colour, very nice nose, good fruit and flavour, fairly full-bodied   15.5/20

Pape-Clément, Graves
A paler colour, rather nice nose, good fruit with a pleasant finish   16/20

Beychevelle, Saint Julien
Dark colour, nice nose, medium body, some tannin but too much acidity   14/20

Brane-Cantenac, Margaux
Dark colour, well made with a lot of fruit and tannin, rather good   16/20

Lynch-Bages, Pauillac
Dark colour, very good bouquet, not a big wine but it has a nice flavour coupled with a good finish   17/20

Pichon-Lalande, Pauillac

Very dark colour, fine bouquet, heaps of fruit, soft and rounded   18/20

Pichon-Baron, Pauillac

Medium colour, lots of fruit and flavour, some tannin, a little coarser perhaps than the Pichon-Lalande   16.5/20

Ducru-Beaucaillou, Saint Julien

Good colour, lovely bouquet, a big 'solid' wine, still hard, but it has a lot of charm   18/20

Léoville-Lascases, Saint Julien

Medium colour, a fine bouquet, medium body, with a lot of charm. Fine quality   18/20

Cos d'Estournel, Saint Estèphe

Medium colour, fairly full-blooded with an attractive flavour, some tannin   18/20

Mouton-Rothschild, Pauillac

Dark colour, a lovely bouquet, full-bodied with lots of fruit, fine quality   19/20

Lafite, Pauillac

Dark colour, fine bouquet, full-bodied, but still rather closed up. With its tannin, difficult to assess   19/20

Margaux, Margaux

Dark colour, lovely bouquet, lighter in style, but beautifully balanced with a lovely flavour. Very fine   19.5/20

Latour, Pauillac

Dark colour, a big wine here with masses of fruit and body. Fine quality   19/20

It is evident that these 1983s have considerable quality as well as charm and we will hear much more of them as they develop.

MONDAY, 1 OCTOBER

The weekend had been spent at an unpretentious hotel with a rosette called La Guitoune on the Bassin d'Arcachon; the decoration may not be very exceptional but the food is good. The rainy weather continued and we moved to another small but pleasant hotel in Libourne called, of all strange names, The Backgammon.

It is on the *quai* facing the river Dordogne and the proprietor is a fisherman who owns oyster beds at Arcachon.

The day was spent with Alain Querre, the owner of Château Monbousquet in Saint Emilion and who is also a *négociant* in Libourne. These are some of the wines we tasted with him:

Puy Razac 1982, Saint Emilion
Good colour with an attractive bouquet and plenty of fruit and flavour, but a trace of acidity to lose

1982 Monbousquet, Saint Emilion
Good colour, a fuller bouquet, fruity, rounder and richer, rather nice

1982 Saint Louis, Saint Estèphe
Dark colour, a full bouquet, lots of fruit, a distinctive flavour with a long finish. Needs two or three years to develop. An interesting vineyard which is not even listed in *Bordeaux et ses Vins*

1982 Bodet la Justice, Canon Fronsac
Dark colour, a delightful bouquet, good fruit and a wine to buy

1983 Monbousquet, Saint Emilion
Dark colour, attractive bouquet, good flavour with plenty of charm. At the moment it seemed more attractive than the 1982 vintage

What an extraordinary vintage this 1982 vintage is; even some of the *petits châteaux* already taste nice and some can even be enjoyed now.

We lunched at La Plaisance in Saint Emilion where they now have a very good chef who is also the proprietor. As the bedrooms were being redecorated, this will be a nice place in which to stay, provided of course one can get a room. From experience this is not often the case.

After lunch we called on Monsieur Hebraud, whose 1983 Château Cheval-Blanc looks as though it is going to be really fine.

TUESDAY, 2 OCTOBER

Bright and sunny to begin with, but it began to rain again and never stopped all day. The situation had become so serious that some of the *châteaux* had had to begin their harvest.

All the same, a visit to the Moueix family is always a sunny day. We found Christian philosophical over the rather grim situation. The prospect of a poor vintage over the past months had seemed so inevitable that this final disaster of rain during the harvest did not seem so serious as it might have done there been even a chance of a reasonably good vintage. This bad news had already caused the price of ordinary Saint Emilion to rise some 20 per cent since the summer and with the continued bad weather it was likely to increase still further.

Better news was that the firm of Jean-Pierre Moueix had just bought two of the finest vineyards in the Fronsadais, namely La Dauphine and Canon-de-Brem. As will be gathered from my diaries, I have followed these two properties closely for the past 20 years. Christian paid me the compliment of saying I was the only person who has ever done any good for the wines of Fronsac, but in view of the results, any success I may have had has been limited. None of it seems to have done much good, because this district is still undervalued and unappreciated. This is strange when many wines of Fronsac are superior in quality to some of the Saint Emilions. Such is the magic of a name!

The 1983 Vintage

La Dauphine, Côtes de Fronsac
Dark colour, a fruity bouquet, not a big wine, but it has an attractive flavour and finishes well

Canon de Brem, Canon Fronsac
Dark colour, a nice full bouquet, a more powerful wine with masses of flavour, remarkable quality

Lafleur, Saint Emilion
Dark colour, pleasant bouquet, medium body and easy to taste

Fonroque, Saint Emilion
Good colour, fairly full body, similar taste, deeper and more full-bodied than Lafleur

Magdelaine, Saint Emilion
Dark colour, distinguished bouquet, elegant and well bred with a lot of charm, lots of quality

La Grave Trigant de Boisset, Pomerol
Very dark colour, delightful bouquet, medium body, but charming and easy to taste

La Fleur-Pétrus, Pomerol
Very dark colour, the bouquet still closed up. A fuller wine with more depth, still backward, but this will make a fine bottle

Trotanoy, Pomerol

Very dark colour, a copious bouquet, well structured with a good flavour, harder though than the La Fleur-Pétrus. Not showing so well now, but may be better in the long run

Since, in spite of the weather, the harvest was in full swing, we drove in the heavy rain to Château La Fleur-Pétrus to join the pickers for lunch. There must have been about 60 of them, clad in every kind of waterproof. The food was excellent: the lovely traditional *soupe de vendange* and then some very good roast duck. Although it bore no label, the wine was notable. Jean-Claude Beyrouet who makes the wine for Jean-Pierre Moueix explained it was a blend of classified growths of Saint Emilion in recent vintages, all of which have been good.

Fellow guests were two visitors from California, Mr and Mrs Barrett, the owners of Château Montelena in the Napa Valley. Accustomed as he is to the warmth and fine weather at harvest time in California, it must have been quite a revelation for Jim Barrett to see the problems facing the poor wine makers of Bordeaux when the weather was as bad as this – all the latter could do was to laugh!

WEDNESDAY, 3 OCTOBER

Back in Bordeaux, we stopped for a tasting with Philippe Casteja and Charles Boisset at Borie-Manoux in the Cours Balguerie-Stuttenberg. Although this firm owns the Domaine de L'Eglise in Pomerol and Trottevieille in Saint Emilion, they were not too despondent; the greater part of their properties lie in the Médoc where there is a preponderance of *cabernet sauvignon* whose grape skins are tougher and more resistant to bad weather. Here, we were to taste more of the attractive 1983 vintage. We began in fact with a pleasant white graves, the 1983 Château Baret.

The 1983 Vintage

Baret, red graves

Good colour, pleasant bouquet and flavour

Beausite, Saint Estèphe

Good colour, medium body, plenty of fruit but I preferred the Baret to this

Haut-Bages Monpelou, Pauillac

Good colour, also attractive with a nice flavour

Lynch-Moussas, Pauillac

Good colour and bouquet, plenty of fruit, but a harder more severe wine

Batailley, Pauillac

Dark colour, a nice bouquet, fruity and quite robust with a good finish

Bergat, Saint Emilion

Good colour, the bouquet still immature, rounded and nicely full-bodied. Needs time to develop

Trottevieille, Saint Emilion

Dark colour, medium body, good nose with fruit and flavour

Domaine de l'Eglise, Pomerol

Dark colour, very good bouquet, a nice rich wine which I preferred to the Trottevieille

Looking back, this visit to Bordeaux afforded a good insight into the quality of the 1983 vintage and I could not help being impressed. On the whole, the 1983s may lack the massive almost luscious charm of the 1982s which is a vintage so very easy to appreciate. All the same, overshadowed as they may be for the time being, the 1983s are more typical of a fine vintage from Bordeaux and, whatever happens, they can only turn out well in the long run.

6
THE CÔTE D'OR
April 1985

Thanks to the excellent railway system in France, there is now a better way to reach Burgundy than in the past and that is to take the plane from London to Paris and then travel by train from the Gare de Lyon to Dijon. As this comfortable train travels at some 250 kilometres an hour, the railway journey only takes an hour and a half!

We had come primarily to find out for ourselves just how good the 1983 vintage is for red wine. I had heard that the quality was highly irregular and this is understandable when one considers the difficult climatic conditions which prevailed. There was the hailstorm during the summer which badly damaged the vines on the Côte de Nuits, especially those of Chambolle-Musigny and Vosne-Romanée. Then came the heavy rain in September which caused so much rot in the same area. Happily the Côte de Beaune was not so badly affected.

Until the time of our visit the weather in 1985 had been unfavourable. After the intense cold in January, it remained unsatisfactory and it was still distinctly cool when we arrived. I found the vines definitely more backward than those I had seen in Saint Emilion just two weeks before. They appeared to be about three weeks behind in their development and the growers were praying for some sunshine to hurry them along.

MONDAY, 13 APRIL 1985

It was an early start for we had to be in the attractive village of Chambolle-Musigny by 9 a.m. The Roumier house is situated in a delightful corner on the hillside. This is a father and son operation. Christophe, the son, a fine looking young man, explained we would have to see mainly the 1984 vintage, because most of their 1983s had just been bottled, an operation which tires the wine and makes it difficult to taste for a few months. He said the weather had been so bad in the previous weeks that there had been little else to do other than work in the cellar.

Apart from some *coulure* (non-pollination of the tiny buds) he told us that the weather in 1984 had been most promising until the heavy rain in September caused rot among the grapes. The final result therefore is somewhat disappointing; although not too bad, these wines lacked both flesh and charm and have some acidity. After trying some of the 1984s M. Roumier père joined us to taste some of their wines already in bottle.

1982 Chambolle-Musigny
Good colour and altogether a rounder wine with more richness.

Note: In general the 1982 vintage may have been lacking in depth, but was pleasant on the whole and has the asset of being ready to drink reasonably early

1983 Chambolle-Musigny, bottled in February 1984
A fine dark colour, an attractive flavour with plenty of depth, should make a good bottle

1983 Bonnes Mares, bottled the previous week
A splendid colour, tremendous fruit with great concentration, such richness and a lovely mouthful of wine. Should make a great bottle

1978 Chambolle-Musigny, half bottle
Good colour, good fruit and body and, of course, a much more mature flavour

Our next call was to Domaine Mongeard-Mugneret in the nearby village of Vosne-Romanée where Monsieur Jean Mongeard can trace his ancestry back to 1639. His early forebears were all either wine makers or coopers. Here we were more fortunate because his 1983s were still in cask and so could be tasted.

1983 Bourgogne Rouge
Although this was only in the form of a mouthwash, it was rather good

1983 Vosne-Romanée
Good colour, fruit and flavour, a very nice well balanced wine

1983 Echézeaux
Dark colour, a fine 'solid' wine, good quality

1983 Vosne-Romanée les Suchots
Good colour, lots of fruit and a lovely flavour with a good finish in spite of the tannin

1983 Grands-Echezeaux
An unusually dark colour, a concentrated bouquet, a truly 'solid' wine and my word what concentration, rich and wonderful. This should make a great bottle

1983 Clos de Vougeot
Very dark colour, a lovely bouquet, well bred with a heavenly taste and such finesse. Another masterpiece

As a *bonne bouche* our host opened a bottle of

1972 Echézeaux
Fine dark colour, packed with lovely taste and none of the prevalent 1972 acidity. Elegant, well balanced and still youthful – what a wine

We left feeling impressed.

The rain had started again by the time we had driven up the steep hill that lies behind Chagny to the Domaine de la Folie, the home of Xavier Noel-Bouton, who owns nine hectares of some of the finest vines of Rully, most of which are quite old. The wines of Rully still remain relatively unknown, but now that those of Pouilly-Fuissé have become so expensive as well as hard to find, they are proving their usefulness. I have always had a sentimental feeling for the wines of Rully, because my first purchase ever was a cask of Rully in 1939 which was shipped just in time before the war broke out. Happily it turned out very well, or so I was told, because by that time I was away in the army.

1984 Aligoté, just racked
Not a big wine, but pleasing to taste with a nice finish

1984 Rully Clos Saint-Jacques
An attractive rounded flavour with a fragrant bouquet

1983 Rully Close Saint-Jacques
A lovely rich flavour with a nice fresh finish (This is excellent and I hope we can buy some for our own cellar)

Note: From our tasting so far, it would appear that 1984 is a better vintage for white wine than it is for red. In general, the red wines are all right, but they lack flesh and generosity. The white wines are better, it seems, than in 1980, but less good perhaps than in 1981, 1982 and 1983.

The vineyard of the late Monsieur Guy Roulot is now managed by his son and his nephew and the cellar is spotlessly clean.

1984 Meursault les Vireuils
Good fruit, has some depth

1984 Meursault les Luchets
Fine fruit, well balanced and rather good

1984 Meursault les Perrières
Good fruit and flavour, has greater depth and fills the mouth nicely

1983 Meursault les Luchets
Much richer and sweeter than the 1984 vintage, heavier as well, perhaps a little too rich and heavy. This was a good example of some of the richer wines of this vintage which lack the necessary degree of acidity

1983 Meursault les Tessons
Another big wine, but a little less clumsy

1979 Meursault les Tessons, in bottle
Well developed bouquet, good fruit and well balanced, still youthful and elegant

1975 Meursault Charmes
Golden colour, has fruit but is leaner and lacks depth. 1975 was not a good year for white burgundy and this was a typical example.

Comte Lafon
Still in the village of Meursault, it was Bruno Lafon, a younger son, who showed us his family wine.

1984 Meursault Clos de la Barre
Not a big wine, but it has a very nice flavour

1984 Meursault Charmes
More body and a good flavour, fine quality

1983 Meursault Clos de la Barre
Lots of fruit and a delightful flavour, definitely would be a wine to buy, that is if there were any available!

1983 Meursault Desirée
A bigger wine with more depth, well bred, but it appeared to lack acidity

1983 Meursault Goutte d'Or
Medium body, better balanced than the Desirée and rather nice

1983 Meursault Perrières
Fine bouquet, a lovely flavour with lots of style. Fine quality

1983 Meursault Genevrières
A delightful flavour, masses of breeding, but it seems to have less acidity than the Perrières, very good all the same.

Note: It seems that some of these 1983s are almost too rich and overwhelming

1982 Meursault Clos de la Barre, in bottle
Medium body, plenty of fruit and a very nice taste

1982 Meursault Genevrières
Full-bodied, medium rich and full of breeding, fine quality

In Volnay, at the Domaine de la Pousse d'Or, we were welcomed by Gerard Potel and his wife. The *domaine* was purchased by its present owner in 1964 and Gerard Potel has been responsible for making the wine ever since. He is among the *avant garde* of the wine makers and his produce enjoys a well deserved reputation.

There is a splendid view from his house up on the hillside above the village, looking across the broad plain towards Switzerland. I had never before realised how much rape was grown in this part of France; it was in full flower and splashes of brilliant yellow enlivened the landscape like a chessboard. Monsieur Potel was gloomy about the weather and told us that unless it improved quickly, the growers might be faced with disaster.

He talked about the revolution that is taking place in Burgundy. When he arrived in Volnay in 1964, 95 per cent of all the wine was handled by the *négociants* and at present it is only some 60 per cent. This has led to some ill-feeling on the part of the merchants, who now have new, very strong competition and, in addition, many of the growers who are aware of the high potential of their vines, have turned to *domaine* bottling, thus depriving the merchants of much of the high quality wine necessary for their blends.

Be that as it may, while for a number of years now the reputation of red burgundy has been under a cloud, there has been a splendid 'renaissance' in quality, which looks as though it will continue to expand. These remarks are by no means intended to denigrate the *négociants*, firms such as Leroy, Drouhin and Bourée, to mention just a few who produce excellent quality.

Here also the 1984 vintage had been spoilt at the last minute by heavy rain in September and during the harvest. Monsieur

Potel had managed to limit the damage by putting the grapes on racks to drain off excess water before fermentation. He also ran off more juice once the grapes were in the vat – an operation called a *saignée*, literally 'bleeding' the vat – to concentrate the must and achieve a better solid-liquid balance in the *cuve*. All of his wines have a fine dark colour.

1984 Volnay Clos d'Audignac
Medium body, fruity and rather dry

1984 Volnay Caillerets
A good flavour with a little more depth, but in common with many 1984s, there is a lack of substance

1984 Volnay Caillerets, Clos des Ouvrées, from old vines
A dark colour, good fruit and body, fine quality

Domaine de la Pousse d'Or
1984 Volnay Clos de la Pousse d'Or
Very dark, firm fine flavour and more substance

1984 Pommard Jarollières
Plenty of fruit, full-bodied and very good. The difference from the Volnays was striking; this was a bigger wine altogether, if perhaps a little less elegant

1983 Volnay Caillerets
Noticeably rounder after the 1984s, complete and well made. Plenty of 'gras', i.e. fatness of flavour, but still rather backward

1983 Volnay Clos de la Pousse d'Or
Another rounder, more generous wine, well balanced with a fine flavour. Will make a fine bottle

1983 Pommard Jarollières
A fine big 'meaty' wine, lots of fruit and lots of tannin. May take ten or more years to develop

In Bottle
1980 Santenay les Gravières
Good fruit and very nice

1976 Volnay Caillerets Clos des 60 Ouvrées
Very dark colour, a lovely rounded, full-bodied wine with a fine finish, still backward

1964 Volnay Clos de la Pousse d'Or
Very dark colour, a splendid wine with fine aromas variously

described by my companions as truffle, white mushroom and 'sous bois' (a French term meaning leafy undergrowth), generous and complete with a firm tannic grip. A remarkable bottle, still not at its best

Domaine Michel Gaunoux, Pommard

Michel Gaunoux died a few years ago and his widow is carrying on until her eleven-year-old son will be able to take over. The winery is beautifully clean which is something that could not be said in the past for all burgundian cellars. All the same, things have improved immensely since I first began to visit the region some 40 years ago. This remains one of the few properties where men still actually tread the grapes at vintage time.

1982 Beaune
Medium body, good fruit and flavour, with a pleasant finish

1982 Pommard Grands-Epenots
A fine dark colour, clean bouquet, medium body, complete with a hint of richness. Good all through

1979 Pommard Grands-Epenots
A fine dark colour, still somewhat reserved, but a delightful flavour, great quality

1962 Corton-Renardes
A nice smell of old leather, a heavenly taste, delicate and charming, great finesse, a lovely bottle

Note: In so far as the vineyards of Corton are concerned, the Bressandes, Clos du Roi and Renardes are perhaps the finest.

Domaine Simon Bize, Savigny-les-Beaune
Another father and son operation.

1983 Savigny-les-Beaune, bottled only a week before
A rather pale colour, medium to light body, pleasant flavour

1982 Savigny-les-Beaune, in bottle
Good colour with plenty of depth and finesse, an attractive wine

1982 Savigny-les Marconnets
Good colour, full of flavour and has a fine structure, first rate quality

It was still very cold, so we were glad to sit by a huge log fire to eat our lunch and with this we tasted the following:

1982 Savigny Aux Guettes

Dark colour, a lovely rich flavour, excellent quality and if available a wine to buy

1980 Savigny-les-Beaune

Good fruit with an attractive taste

1952 Savigny les Vergelesses

A sweet smelling bouquet, a big 'solid' rich wine, which has kept remarkably well

Domaine Blain-Gagnard, Chassagne-Montrachet

This family has so many names that they are confusing. Young Monsieur Blain is the grandson-in-law of the Monsieur Delagrange from whom I used to buy such splendid wine in the 1950s and 1960s for John Harvey & Sons. He had no son, his daughter married a Monsieur Gagnard, who in turn had two daughters, one of whom married Monsieur Blain and he now looks after the grandfather's vineyards and the making of the wine.

1984 Chassagne-Montrachet Morgeot

Has good depth and substance and should make a good bottle

1984 Chassagne-Montrachet les Caillerets

Well bred with a very nice flavour

1984 Criots-Batard-Montrachet

Rich and fairly full-bodied

1983 Chassagne-Montrachet les Caillerets,
bottled in February

Clean with a hint of sweetness, delightful to taste. Has much elegance and is extremely good

1983 Bâtard-Montrachet, bottled in February

Still a little undeveloped, but has such depth and such splendour it is almost majestic. It was possible almost to feel the weight of this wine in one's mouth*

Our last stop on this day was in Mercurey on the Côte Chalonaise to meet a delightful character called Michel Juillot. A dynamic man resembling in a way that other powerful personality of the wine world, Bob Mondavi of the Napa Valley. Like him, Monsieur

---

*At home I still have one bottle left from a cask of Monsieur Delagrange's 1971 Bâtard-Montrachet that I bought for Jackson's of Piccadilly, a glorious wine.

Juillot has carried out experiments with oak casks to investigate the most suitable species of oak to use. Here was another perfectionist who puts almost all his young wine into new oak casks. How these Burgundian cellars have changed since I first came to buy wine, which must have been in 1947. In those days they were primitive, dirty and bitterly cold in winter. Now by contrast most of them are kept scrupulously clean and have up-to-date equipment such as stainless steel fermentation vats.

1984 Mercurey Clos l'Evèque
Rather a pale colour, but a nice perfumed bouquet, a fresh fruity taste, sweet and attractive

1984 Mercurey Clos des Barraults
Good colour, a delightful taste with charm and greater depth

1983 Mercurey
Medium colour, most pleasantly rounded with good balance and a nice long finish. First rate

1983 Mercurey Clos l'Eveque
Medium colour, good fruit and body, a lot of quality

1983 Mercurey Clos des Barraults
Good colour, firmer on account of its tannin, very good underlying quality

1983 Aloxe-Corton
A charming wine with masses of fruit

1983 Corton Perrières
A lovely bouquet with a fine depth of flavour, quite a sturdy wine. This should turn out well

The Juillots joined us for dinner in a local restaurant called L'Hostellerie du Val d'Or which has a rosette in the *Guide Michelin.* It was an evening of laughter egged on no doubt by the delicious wines that Michel Juillot had brought with him: his delectable white Mercurey of 1983 of which, alas, already there is no more available to buy and an equally agreeable magnum of his red 1978 Mercurey Clos des Barraults.

WEDNESDAY, 15 APRIL 1985

At last the weather had changed, it was both sunny and warm and how badly this was needed.

In Nuits-Saint-Georges we called on a young, bearded very serious wine maker called Alain Michelot, who succeeded his father some ten years ago. He is producing wine of excellent quality.

1983 Morey-Saint-Denis
Rather a pale colour, but a nice taste

1983 Nuits-Saint-Georges
Also rather pale, has good depth though and an attractive flavour

1983 Nuits-Saint-Georges les Cailles
Medium colour, good structure with a pleasant finish

1983 Nuits-Saint-Georges Vaucrains
Medium colour, a bigger, sturdier wine with both fruit and power in evidence. May take time to develop

1983 Nuits-Saint-Georges les Porets
A paler colour, but a fine bouquet, well constituted with lots of fruit as well as some tannin

1983 Nuits-Saint-Georges les Chaignots
A pretty colour, a fine fruity bouquet, good body with plenty of charm. Enjoyable now, but will be much better say by 1990

In Bottle
1972 Nuits-Saint-Georges les Porets
Good colour, a delightful taste, masses of fruit, will continue to improve

Note: Alain Michelot considers his 1982s will develop in much the same manner as his 1979s, both are similar in style

1976 Nuits-Saint-Georges Vaucrains
A beautiful colour and a fine bouquet. A lovely rich wine, indeed a proper mouthful. Tannic

1972 Nuits-Saint Georges-les Chaignots
An intense colour, rich, rounded and magnificent, a masterpiece here. Easier to taste than the tannic 1976, a truly splendid wine

Domaine de la Romanée-Conti
I hate to think how long it is since I came here, perhaps 30 years. Since then, one has heard such conflicting reports on the *Domaine,* that confidence has been lost and of course the cost of the wine has always been beyond the purse of most people.

This was a particularly interesting visit and all the more so as there have been some changes recently at the *Domaine* after the retirement of their long-serving winemaker, Monsieur Noblet, and the appointment of a young, very impressive oenologist, Monsieur Le Ferrer. We were all greatly struck by the quality of the wines, even by that of the 1984s, which, after all, come from a modest vintage. The *cuverie* was spotlessly clean and it was interesting to see a whole range of new stainless steel fermentation tanks.

We were shown around by Monsieur Le Ferrer. As is to be expected, all the young wine here goes into new oak casks.

1984 Echézeaux
Medium colour, a clean sweet bouquet, good fruit with an attractive, slightly sweet flavour

1984 Grands-Echézeaux
Medium colour, very nice nose and flavour, quite rich as well, with a hint of sweetness and a little more tannin

1984 Romanée-Saint-Vivant
Medium colour, a bigger, more robust wine with a very nice taste

1984 Richebourg
A deeper colour with much more stuffing to begin with and then it tailed off a little

1984 La Tâche
Good colour, plenty of fruit and body, well balanced with some tannin

1984 Romanée-Conti
Dark colour, masses of fruit, a fine concentrated wine with plenty of tannin. I, for one, was surprised by these wines which were so much better than the reputation of the vintage had led me to expect

1983 Echézeaux
Good colour, very good fruit and body, rounder than the 1984 vintage

1983 Grands-Echézeaux
A pretty colour with greater depth and density of flavour than the Echézeaux, an extraordinary density in fact and a very fine wine

1983 Romanée-Saint-Vivant
Good colour, a lovely big, 'meaty' wine with a lot of tannin. This is very fine

1983 Richebourg
Good colour, a lovely nose, fruit and flavour, an immense concentration of richness and what a bottle this will make!

1983 La Tâche
A lovely colour, superb bouquet, tremendous style, tremendous quality. Less robust perhaps than the Richebourg, even more severe, or should one say serious: anyway, it is terribly good

1983 Romanée-Conti
Dark colour, a heavenly bouquet, superb fruit and flavour, an essence almost, rather than a beverage. A huge wine, so big one could almost eat it. What more can one say?

There have been many things both good and bad written about the wines of the Domaine de la Romanée-Conti, but here surely we had been tasting one of the great vintages and how privileged we were! The 1983 demonstrates that this famous *Domaine* is right back on form.

Down in another cellar – more like an Aladdin's cave – where all the bottled stock is stored in large bins, Monsieur Le Ferrer opened for us a bottle of La Tâche 1979. This had a lovely dark colour, a distinguished bouquet and a heavenly taste, rich, sweet, velvety and concentrated. A delectable bottle which, because of the tannin, will continue to improve.

Domaine Coche-Dury
Our final effort was to call upon Monsieur Jean-Francois Coche of Domaine Coche-Dury, who lives in a modern house on the outskirts of Meursault, but it was bad luck on any grower to be visited hard on the heels of the Domaine de la Romanée-Conti. Monsieur Coche is a tall dark young man who likes to play the saxophone. He enjoys a well deserved reputation and his wine stood up to the test nobly.

1984 Meursault Casse-Tête
Pleasant bouquet, good fruit and flavour with a dryish finish

1984 Meursault Rougeots
Good nose, fruit and flavour, with a little more depth

1984 Meursault Perrières
A bigger, richer wine altogether, this should make a good bottle

1984 Monthelie, Red
Pleasant bouquet, on the light side with an agreeable sweet flavour

1983 Volnay
Dark colour, good fruit, a nice 'solid' wine

In Bottle
1982 Bourgogne Blanc
Robust and fruity, needs time to mature

1983 Meursault Narvaux
Good nose, fruit and body, a serious wine

1983 Meursault Perrières
Lovely nose, full-bodied, rich, excellent

1982 Meursault Rougeots
Fine bouquet, fresh exciting taste, complete and well balanced. This is reputed to be one of the most successful wines from Meursault of the 1982 vintage

1981 Meursault Perrières
Pale golden colour, fresh bouquet, good fruit, rather dry with some acidity at the finish

What does one say in conclusion? Of white wine we had tasted mainly the 1982 and 1983 vintages, both of which are good, but in some cases I found one or two of the white 1983s almost too rich and almost overblown.

We did not taste many of the 1981 red wines, but the 1982s were better than I had expected. 1982 appears to be a useful vintage, for while it is not by any means great, with more time in bottle the wine should improve. In addition, many of the 1982s can be enjoyed from now.

With a few exceptions of course, it was not possible to enthuse over the red wines of 1984, for in general they appear to be somewhat lean and lacking in generosity.

However, it was undoubtedly a good moment to come to Burgundy, if only to see some of those red 1983s, because really fine vintages for red burgundy are comparatively rare. Although some of the 1980s are very good, 1983 is clearly the best year since 1978. From all accounts, however, this 1983 vintage is tremendously variable, but thanks to the skill of Simon Taylor Gill, who had planned the visit, we only went to see growers who had been successful and their produce was impressive to say the least. The culmination at the Domaine de la Romanée-Conti was more than I, at any rate, had dared to hope.

7

A VISIT TO THE UNITED STATES
April 1985

The excitement over this visit had been building up for weeks, because this time our eleven-year-old twins were to accompany us and even the heavy rain which greeted us on arrival in Miami did little to dampen their spirits.

Our hotel had been recommended by Pan Am in London so we had expected the usual airport place, but the Sheraton River-house was anything but that. The view over the river and golf course beyond was unexpectedly attractive and the swimming pool a great magnet for the children.

The following morning we made our way to nearby Fort Lauderdale to spend a couple of days with Joe and Betty Schagrin. Joe must be one of America's leading retail wine merchants, but he also specialises in food and says his three stores were modelled along the lines of Fortnum & Mason in London. He put me to work at once at a meeting of his local Chapter of Les Amis du Vin. The subject was the recently arrived 1982 vintage from Bordeaux, a vintage which has already captured American imagination in a manner which has not been equalled since the American public first began to take an interest in Bordeaux some 25 years ago. It is also the first vintage in which the American wine lover has ever considered investing in wine.

Investment in wine, which used to be as heavily frowned upon by the English trade, first began seriously in the late 1960s, but ground to a disastrous halt as a result of the economic crisis which began around 1973 when a lot of people burnt their fingers. However, circumstances were now different. The glamour of the 1982 vintage had proved irresistible and that, coupled with the immensely strong dollar, had captured the imagination of a new section of the American public. How fortunate that it was a prolific vintage because an enormous amount of it was bought as soon as it appeared on the market. All the same, the result was inevitable, within a year the value of the first growths had more than doubled and some of the lesser classified growths such as La Lagune had trebled. The rare Château Pétrus had gone almost out of sight!

Apart from everything else, 1982 was a magnificent vintage for the wines of Pomerol and unless one grabbed up some of the successes from that district immediately, the chance of acquiring them in the future is remote except perhaps at an astronomical price. Another attractive attribute of this vintage is the excellence of the lesser wines such as the *crus bourgeois* and the *petits châteaux*. Some of the latter were agreeable to drink almost as soon as they had been put into bottle. This may have been caused by the unusually ripe grapes whose tannin was less aggressive than usual.

This particular evening was of interest for me as it was to be the first time I had had an opportunity to taste this vintage after it had been bottled.

1982 Red Bordeaux

Fourcaud, Médoc
Medium colour, pleasant bouquet, a light wine and easy to drink   Group average 13.2/20

Grand Monteil, Entre Deux Mers
Good colour, with greater depth of flavour and a nice finish (I rated it as 15)   Group average 14/20

Pierredon, Bordeaux Superior
Good colour, of average quality with too much acidity (I rated it lower!)   Group average 14.8/20

La Tour-du-Pas-Saint-Georges, Saint Emilion
A darker colour, nice bouquet, rounder with plenty of flavour and rather good   Group average 16.5/20

d'Angludet, Cantenac
Dark colour, very nice bouquet, has both fruit and body with a nice rich flavour (I gave it over 18)   Group average 17.7/20

Palmer, Margaux
Dark colour, fine bouquet with fruit and flavour but it seemed to lack concentration   Group average 18.2/20

I had a feeling the assembled company had been influenced by the Palmer label! Joe told me he had received a flood of orders for it the following day and not nearly as many for the Angludet. I wish I had some of that Angludet in my own cellar.

MONDAY, 15 APRIL

We flew to Tampa where for the first time the children had a glimpse of the Caribbean Sea. Our host was Bern Laxer whose Steakhouse is known all over the United States. He is also noted for having the longest wine list in the world for it contains some 3,000 items!

His restaurant must be popular because he serves no less than 500 covers every evening. A large room has recently been opened for the consumption of after dinner wines with a selection of 120 different varieties, including of course vintage port which is becoming increasingly popular in the USA. All of these are served by the glass and by a method which prevents all risk of oxidation.

WEDNESDAY, 17 APRIL

Our plane for Los Angeles left Tampa airport at 8.30 a.m. Incidentally, this airport is far the most attractive I have seen. It proved a long day, however, as we were to gain three hours but there was time for a rest before dinner.

That meal at the Bel Air Hotel in Beverly Hills proved to be memorable, for our hosts John Brincko, the President of the Los Angeles Chapter of The Society of Bacchus, and Ed Lazarus had brought with them wine such as no normal restaurant could provide. To begin, two meursaults, both from that much respected *négociant* Leroy, a 1969 which was still fresh and delightful and the 1945 vintage, full of body and magnificent – how well this had kept. To be really good after 40 years in bottle is an unusual feat for any white burgundy.

There was then a comparison of two red wines and both of the good 1971 vintage, the Bonnes Mares, Comte Georges de Vogué, a delightful full-bodied wine and the La Tâche. Of the two we all preferred the Bonnes Mares.

The following evening we were the guests at the annual dinner of The Society of Bacchus and this took place at that very good restaurant, Michael's. We were happy to find a number of old friends among those present.

This event is always based on the great growths of the previous vintage from Bordeaux and how lucky we were that the vintage in question happened to be 1982! Unfortunately, it had not been possible to find bottles of either Ausone or Pétrus, so in their place we tasted Canon from Saint Emilion and L'Evangile from Pomerol, but both of these were so good, we did not suffer from the substitution. The dark colour of all the wines was remarkable.

Great Wines of the 1982 Vintage

Canon, Saint Emilion
Very good fruit and flavour and it finished well. This is every bit as good as it is reputed to be

L'Evangile, Pomerol
Masses of fruit, masses of flavour, rich and delightful. It made me wish I had bought some!

Haut-Brion, Graves
A fine bouquet and a special taste, smooth and excellent, so well balanced and so distinguished. In truth, *un grand seigneur*

Margaux, Margaux
A well bred wine, but thinner after the Haut-Brion with a slight hint of acidity at the finish, but this could easily have been a bad example

Lafite, Pauillac
Lovely fruit and a lovely flavour with a whole gamut of tastes, but I still preferred the Haut-Brion

Mouton-Rothschild, Pauillac
The recognised success of the vintage in so far as the Médoc is concerned and the one I had put first in a 'blind' tasting in 1983. Still fierce with youth, but a heavenly flavour and still a lot of tannin. More open than the Latour and perhaps easier to appreciate now

Latour, Pauillac
Still very closed up, there is enormous depth of flavour underneath the thich cloak of tannin. Although still very immature, the breeding is evident and I was surprised that this time I preferred this to the Mouton, but then I am prejudiced

Cheval-Blanc, Saint Emilion
Fine bouquet, again an enormous depth of flavour, a rich wine of simply superb quality

This was the first time I had had an opportunity to taste the great wines after they had been bottled and the quality was certainly impressive. What was remarkable though was that we were able actually to enjoy drinking them as the meal began to be served, and that is something I have never experienced before with such young wine.

The meal was so good that the menu may be of interest:

Le gravlax, le foie gras sauté, les pommes de terre au caviar, sashimi au gingembre
Le pigeon au cassis, sauce Gazin
Selle d'agneau aux truffes noires, sauce Duhart-Milon, pommes gallettes
Salade Camembert
Les sorbets, les fruits frais avec crème anglaise
Les truffes aux framboises

With these delights the 1955 Château Latour was served, still youthful, but with a fine depth of flavour. A full, rich 1976 Rieussec accompanied the dessert. What an evening.

FRIDAY, 19 APRIL

While my wife and the children were taken to enjoy the pleasures of Disneyland, I had a very good lunch at The Regency Club with Randal Sultan, Joe Masterson and Steve Weiner. Randal had brought with him three wines which certainly deserve mention.

1966 Léoville-Lascases
Dark colour, fine bouquet, well balanced with a lovely flavour

1964 Léoville-Lascases
Another good wine, but not of the calibre of the 1966

1961 Léoville-Lascases
The colour beginning to turn brown, a good bottle but we all felt it was a little past its best

SATURDAY, 20 APRIL

The day of the great tasting at the Century Plaza Hotel, a popular event because over 50 people were present. It is on such occasions when one meets old friends and renews acquaintances. This tasting, in honour of Jean-Michel Cazes, had been planned by Bipin Desai, already noted for the brilliant events he has arranged over the past five years. He had invited me to act as a kind of Master of Ceremonies or something similar.

Jean-Michel had taken the opportunity to bring with him some bottles of his 1984 vintage, drawn of course from the cask. For most of us, this was our first glimpse of this so far somewhat disparaged vintage.

Thirty-eight Vintages of Chateau Lynch-Bages

1984, made primarily from *cabernet sauvignon* grapes
A nice dark colour, plenty of fruit and a good 'solid' construction with a pleasing finish – an agreeable surprise

1983, from the cask
Dark colour, good fruit and flavour, well balanced and attractive. In time this should make a good bottle

1982
Very dark colour, full-bodied, rich and rounded with plenty of depth. A fine example of this excellent vintage which will make a lovely bottle in the not too distant future

1981
Dark colour, with the first hint of maturity. Well made and well balanced with a most attractive flavour. Not quite so luscious as the 1982 but a first rate wine from a good but less fashionable vintage. In due course no doubt, the 1981s will be more appreciated

1980
Quite a good colour, good fruit but lighter of course than the preceding wines and almost ready to drink. While never a great vintage, some of the 1980s are proving very useful

1979
Good colour and fruit with an attractive flavour, but there was some acidity which was disappointing

1978
A splendid colour, good depth with plenty of concentration, fine quality and much better than the 1979. This will take some time to mature

1977
Medium colour, lighter and thinner with a trace of acidity. Typical of its vintage but quite agreeable

1976
Good colour, much fuller than the 1977 with more fruit and flavour. This is attractive, what is more, it is ready to drink

1975

Dark colour, far more massive and full-bodied, still has a lot of tannin. A fine wine, but one which may take years to develop

1973

Good colour, medium body, of average quality but it has a pleasant flavour. This needs drinking up

1972

Medium colour, although this has some fruit, it is thin and definitely rather sharp. To quote an old saying 'you can't make a silk purse out of a sow's ear'!

1971

Medium colour, much nicer than either the 1972 or the 1973, but there is some acidity, quite a pleasant wine, but by no means a great one

1970

Very dark colour, delightful fruit and a flavour which fills the mouth, first rate. A wine which has lived up to its early promise

1969

Quite a good colour, plenty of fruit, but again some acidity. Typical of its indifferent vintage

1967

Medium colour, good fruit and a much more attractive flavour, rather good for this somewhat disappointing vintage

1966

A fine dark colour, a delightful wine which fills the mouth with a lovely taste. A success in this fine vintage

1964

Average colour, good fruit but altogether thinner, not a success

1962

Good colour, good fruit with such an attractive flavour, a lovely wine of a charming vintage and is still showing well

1961

Very dark colour, very good flavour, but not one of the really great 1961s, nevertheless a good example of its year. Finished well in spite of the tannin

1961, from a magnum
Darker still, stronger and more powerful, even fiercer perhaps, but fierce in the correct sense. Tremendous fruit and from a magnum will take some years to develop fully

1960, also from a magnum
Medium colour, altogether smoother after the 'tough' magnum of 1961. A fine wine and in a magnum must be at its very best now. Thank you, Jean-Michel

1959
Very dark colour, a powerful almost massive concentration of flavour. Still quite youthful and another really fine wine

1957
Very good colour, much harder, but still has plenty of fruit. Definitely firm. Lynch-Bages was one of the few successes of this awkward vintage

1955
Medium colour, good fruit and easy to drink

1955, from a magnum
Fairly dark colour, altogether bigger and better than the bottle, a lovely wine

1954
Medium colour, an off-vintage, so one cannot expect much, nevertheless good for its year

1953, from a magnum
A delightful taste and such a nice finish. A delightful wine which has kept well, retaining all the charm of this attractive vintage, exceptional

1952
Good colour, much firmer as was to be expected, but with more depth. Still needs time to develop fully and then should be a lovely bottle

1950
Good colour, typical 1950, much lighter body and seems to have lost much of its fruit with a little acidity at the finish

1949
Good dark colour, lots of fruit, but as with too many wines of this much respected vintage, there is too much acidity

1948

Dark colour, some fruit but the flavour was overwhelmed by the acidity. This vintage was never popular, sandwiched as it was between 1947 and 1949 and rightly perhaps because when young some of the 1948s were harsh and unattractive. Léoville-Barton, Pétrus and Cheval-Blanc were among the few successes of this year

1947

Dark colour, an initial sweetness, very good flavour with masses of fruit. A great success for this vintage in which as they matured so many of the médocs developed some volatile acidity

1945

Very dark colour, plenty of flavour, but it has dried out. A little disappointing in fact. Jean-Michel explained that unlike most of his neighbours, at Lynch-Bages the 1947 was more successful than the 1945

1937

Good colour, good fruit and flavour, but lacking generosity and kindness. There was some acidity as well, but as 1937s go, it was not bad. This was a very tannic vintage in which the tannin in most cases has outlasted the fruit

1936

Medium colour, some acidity and a lack of charm, this was such a poor vintage, one must not expect much

1934

The only reasonable vintage of its decade. Good colour and a strong flavour, but could have more charm, better of course than either the 1936 or the 1937

1929, from a magnum

Very good colour and so much more attractive than the preceding vintage. A rather faded beauty all the same and showing signs of her age

1928

Very good colour with far more depth and solidity, but with just a trace of sharpness at the finish. Now ageing, but had it been from a magnum, how much better it might have been than the 1929

What a treat to have had all those magnums!

    This was a specially interesting tasting for me because it covered all the vintages with which I have been associated since I joined the wine trade in 1934. The span of vintages had been made by three generations of one family and it was bad luck on the grandfather who, with old fashioned methods and equipment, had had to handle the early vintages, many of which had been from indifferent to bad! Jean-Michel has had better luck with the weather, even so the quality of the vintages since he took over from his father in 1973 has been impressive. Much of this of course can be attributed to technical progress, but the human element also deserves recognition. If further proof were needed, one has only to consider the quality this skilful winemaker is producing with his two other wines, Haut-Bages Averous and Les Ormes de Pez.

8

VISIT TO BORDEAUX
Autumn 1985

SATURDAY, 21 SEPTEMBER

On the few occasions we take our car to Bordeaux we usually go via Newhaven-Dieppe, but this time we caught the mid-day ferry to Calais and drove down the autoroute to Elincourt Ste Marguerite, near Compiègne, where a large _château_ has been converted into a hotel. The welcome was warm and the food good.

By the time, some 24 hours later, we had reached Blaye on the river Gironde, the weather had become definitely hot. The hotel, La Citadelle, lies within the walls of the sixteenth-century fortress designed by that master of martial art, Vauban. The setting was perfect for our apéritif, especially when the brilliant red sun began to descend across the ultra-broad estuary. The restaurant has a rosette in the _Guide Michelin_ and specialises in fish. From here one crosses the river by the ferry to Lamarque, conveniently set in the heart of the Médoc, thus avoiding the long drive into and from Bordeaux.

MONDAY, 23 SEPTEMBER

Our tasting at Château Ducru-Beaucaillou was arranged by Xavier Borie, the elder son of Eugène Borie and himself the owner of Château Grand-Puy-Lacoste. The produce of the latter has always been good, but now under Xavier's management it is becoming even better. The direction of a _château_, as this one demonstrates, is of supreme importance. Hard as it may be to believe now, the wine of Ducru-Beaucaillou was by no means in the first flight during my early days in the wine trade. As far as I can remember, the improvement really began with the 1955 vintage. Since then,

Ducru has gone from strength to strength and is now well among the leaders, including the first growths.

The 1984 Vintage

Lacoste-Borie, the second wine of Grand-Puy-Lacoste
and made mainly from young vines
Quite a good colour, light but attractive, this may develop early

Lalande-Borie
Good colour, has greater depth and concentration than the Lacoste-Borie and rather good

Haut-Batailley
Good colour, has depth and a good flavour, but there was a trace of bitterness at the finish

Grand-Puy-Lacoste
A darker colour, delightful taste with a fine finish, should make a good bottle

Ducru-Beaucaillou
Dark colour, the first impression was the fine breeding, then the lovely flavour, this is a fine wine

Later on, during lunch, we drank the following:

1978 Grand-Puy-Lacoste
Good colour, still very young, but has a good future

1970 Haut-Batailley
Dark colour, plenty of body, but disappointing for this fine vintage

1966 Ducru-Beaucaillou
Dark colour, a splendid wine which must be among the finest of its vintage and near its best now

Shortly after arriving at Château Latour, I walked all around the vineyard and it was a pleasure to see everything looking so healthy. Clearly the flowering of the vines must have been successful for there was only a minimum of green grapes among all the bunches. By contrast with 1984, the *merlot* grapes appeared to be particularly good this year. Thanks to the fine weather, the ripening had been earlier than anticipated, so in some vineyards, the harvest was to begin at the time of our visit.

On the reverse side, some of the younger vines seemed to be

suffering from the drought and a few shrivelled grapes were to be seen. This was not really surprising, because there had been no rain at all for six weeks. Some of the older generation were saying the situation seemed similar to that prior to the vintages of 1945 and 1949.

With their usual thoughtfulness, Alan and Jill Hare had invited some of my old friends for dinner, Guy and Nicole Tesseron of Pontet-Canet and Lafon-Rochet, Peter and Diana Sichel of Angludet and Palmer, General Hervé de Lencquesaing and Mai Eliane, the owners of Pichon-Lalande. It was a delightful evening, during which we drank the 1976 Les Forts de Latour, quite sweet and easy to taste and possibly at its best now. This was followed by a wine which astonished us all, the 1916 Latour. We were all amazed by its depth and fine quality, for although quite good, 1916 was by no means an exceptional vintage. With an unusually dark colour for its age, it is remarkable how well this almost seventy-year-old wine has kept.

TUESDAY, 24 SEPTEMBER

Another glorious day, the temperature must have been in the mid-20°C. Nothing much of note occurred except for a visit to Pichon-Lalande for tea when I took the opportunity to taste the 1984 vintage. While not so fine as the 1983, this is attractive and will certainly make a good bottle.

Professor Pascal Ribereau Gayon, the oenologist, and his wife came for dinner and again Alan Hare spoiled us by producing two exceptional wines. The first, and not so bad for a starter, was Latour 1961! According to this bottle, after 25 years, the 1961 has finally turned the corner and is now simply magnificent. For the first time, for me at any rate, all the hitherto hidden delicious sweetness was bursting through. It was undoubtedly the best bottle of this particular wine I have ever tasted.

To match such perfection was impossible, but the Latour 1924 did its best. Well I remember this wine some 30 years ago, then in its prime; it is now *un grand seigneur*, just a little frail perhaps, but it has stood the test of time with both dignity and charm.

WEDNESDAY, 25 SEPTEMBER

The first signs of autumn, a misty morning but by eleven o'clock the sun had broken through.

We spent the day with Christian Moueix in Libourne. On the way, while driving through the Médoc, we could see the harvest had already begun at several properties, another proof of how, thanks to the fine weather, the vines had managed to catch up.

As a result of some successful planning, our visit coincided with that of Eddie and Meg Penning-Rowsell, so an agreeable day was doubly assured. It had not yet been decided whether there is to be any Château Pétrus of 1984 and since that vintage has been a disappointment for the wines of Saint Emilion and Pomerol, Christian had arranged to show us some of his 1982s from the Fronsadais district.

Henceforth I imagine the firm of Jean-Pierre Moueix will be taking more and more interest in this hitherto overlooked region, particularly since it has recently purchased the two excellent vineyards of La Dauphine and Canon de Brem. Christian himself has owned the nearby Château Canon, Canon-Fronsac, for the past ten years or so, but unfortunately the production is only around 2,000 cases.

The quality of the wines of the Fronsadais has been overlooked, as indeed has been the case with the wines of Pomerol. Regarding the latter, my voice has been one crying in the wilderness ever since I was made aware of its potential by that splendid man, Edouard Cruse. Thanks to him, I bought heavily of the very good vintage of 1945 and of the even greater 1947. I have sung the praises of Pomerol ever since, but it is only now, thanks to the quality of the 1982 vintage, that the wine has begun to be recognised as it indeed deserves.

My acquaintance with the Fronsadais is of a more recent date, a mere 20 years. My introduction to them was through Patrick Danglade who, with Jean-Francois Moueix, directs Duclot, the leading *négociant* in Bordeaux. Patrick's family has owned Château Rouet, Côtes de Fronsac, for some 200 years and his family house was built by the architect Louis, one of whose major achievements is 'Le grand Théâtre de Bordeaux'. It was Patrick who introduced me particularly to the wines of La Dauphine and Canon de Brem, whose quality is so impressive.

One of the problems with these wines has been their slow maturity, for example the 1970 vintage of each *château* is only now becoming ready to drink. Happily, I still have a few bottles of the excellent 1966 Canon de Brem which is marvellous now. Patience is still needed in so far as my 1970 is concerned. For a long time now I have also been a follower of Christian's own Château Canon (the duplication of names is confusing and if any proof were needed, the 1966 Château Canon on the wine list of the Ritz Hotel must surely represent the best value of any restaurant in London). The only reason why this was not drunk up ages ago can only be because most enthusiastic wine lovers lack acquaintance with the wines of the Fronsadais.

Heaven knows, I have done my best to educate, for in 1967 or thereabouts I persuaded Michael Broadbent to join me in a comprehensive tasting of the wines of Fronsac and subsequently he conducted an auction at Christie's devoted entirely to them. At the same time I wrote an article for *Decanter* magazine under the title of 'The Cinderellas of Bordeaux'.

After all that preamble, these are the wines of the fine 1982 vintage we tasted in the company of Christian and Jean-Jacques Moueix and Eddie Penning-Rowsell:

1982 Côtes de Fronsac and Canon-Fronsac

Plain Point Fronsac
Good colour, a pleasant fruity bouquet, medium body with heaps of fruit, virtually ready to drink and very nice

Moulin-Haut-Laroque, Fronsac
Medium colour, pleasing bouquet, less forward than the Plain Point, with less charm perhaps but to compensate a good depth of flavour

Richelieu, Fronsac
Good colour, though there was a query regarding the bouquet. A little more aggressive than the others, but again a good depth of flavour

La Dauphine, Fronsac
A darker colour, a fine vinous bouquet, good flavour and well balanced with a lot of quality. Outstanding and a wine to buy

Mausse, Canon-Fronsac
Scented bouquet, good fruit, medium body, has some charm

Canon de Brem, Canon-Fronsac
Good dark colour, deep bouquet, lots of fruit and heaps of flavour, with even more depth than the La Dauphine. Also outstanding, this needs time to develop

Canon, Canon-Fronsac (Christian's own wine)
Good colour, lovely bouquet, rounded, rich and full-bodied, excellent quality. If not quite so big a wine, this has even more charm than the Canon de Brem

Tasting again the La Dauphin and the Canon de Brem makes me thankful I bought quite a lot of these two wines *en primeur* in 1983!

The lunch which followed was a pastoral perfection with the table set under the tall trees in the garden and with the river Dordogne but a few metres away. Christian's own pomerol, La Grave Trigant de Boisset 1976, with a touch of sweetness, was charming; so much so, good as it was, the Pétrus 1950 had a job to follow it.

Edouard Cruse introduced me to La Grave Trigant immediately after the war with the 1929 vintage, which was a dream. I promptly bought the 1945 and 1947 vintages and continued to follow this *château* until I retired from Harvey's in 1966. Subsequently, through poor management, the vineyard suffered a decline, but now, after some ten years of Christian's ownership, it has began once again to show its potential.

THURSDAY, 26 SEPTEMBER

The fine weather continued and it appeared that the harvest for the younger vines and the *merlot* grapes had now begun in earnest. Whatever was to happen, even if there were to be any rain during the picking, the long spell of fine weather, especially during the month of September, had established the quality.

When we arrived at Château Batailley we asked Emile Casteja to take us to Lynch-Moussas, his other *château* in Pauillac where he has added a new wing and renovated the rest of the house. In the *chai* of Batailley we tasted the three last vintages of the Borie-Manoux properties in the Médoc.

Beau-Site, Cru Bourgeois, Saint Estéphe

1984
Good colour, a pleasing bouquet, medium body, nice flavour, but there is some acidity

1983
Good colour, altogether a bigger wine than the 1984, with more depth and quality

1982
Dark colour, a more concentrated bouquet, lots of fruit, a nice wine which should be ready fairly soon

Lynch-Moussas, Fifth Growth, Pauillac
1984
Quite a good colour, a lighter wine than the Batailley, but nicely rounded with a pleasant finish

1983
A lovely dark colour, fuller than the 1984 with a good finish

1982

Good colour, lots of fruit, a distinctive flavour and rather good

Batailley, Fifth Growth, Pauillac

1984

Dark colour, an attractive bouquet, good fruit and flavour, good for a 1984

1983

Dark colour, quite a deep bouquet, good concentration with a very nice flavour, this may take some time to mature

1982

Dark colour, an attractive bouquet, rich, rounded with plenty of depth and substance. Will make a fine bottle in the not too distant future

Fellow guests at lunch were three members of Aer Lingus and the wines we drank were the 1971 Batailley, which we know well because we have some at home, and the 1959 vintage, a lovely rich wine. How well some of these 1959s are drinking nowadays; I wish I had more in my cellar!

The approach to Château d'Angludet is charming; one passes a small but pretty lake on which swans and ornamental ducks cavort. Also dining with Peter and Diana Sichel were old friends Hugues and Micheline Lawton and a Mr and Mrs Alan Johnson-Hill who have a vineyard called Meaume whose produce is mostly sold in England. Two vintages of Château Palmer were served with the meal, the 1966, which must be one of the very best of that vintage, and the 1962, fading but still sweet and charming.

FRIDAY, 27 SEPTEMBER

We went next to Bordeaux where the heat was stifling. In the offices of Duclot in the rue de Macau, Patrick Danglade and Yves Pardes had prepared the following anonymous tasting:

The 1983 Vintage

La Tour Saint Bonnet, Saint Christoly de Médoc

Quite a good colour, a pleasant bouquet, not a big wine, but it has a nice taste   14/20

Patache d'Aux, Begadan

Good colour, an attractive bouquet and a good depth of flavour   15/20

Chasse-Spleen, Moulis

Darker colour, with a distinguished bouquet, a deeper flavour than the Patache d'Aux and rather good   16.5/20

Terrey-Gros Caillou, Saint Julien

Dark colour, a fruity bouquet, medium body, but somewhat coarser   15/20

Gloria, Saint Julien

Dark colour, pleasant bouquet, medium body with an attractive taste, rather good   16.5/20

La Lagune, Ludon

Dark colour, average bouquet, rather strident with little charm, disappointing. Of course this may have been a bad sample   15/20

Prieuré-Lichine, Cantenac

Dark colour, an attractive bouquet, medium body, a nice well bred wine   16.5/20

Montrose, Saint Estèphe

Good colour, a more austere nose, pleasant flavour though and rather good   17/20

Pichon-Comtesse, Pauillac

Dark colour, distinguished bouquet, a lovely 'solid' wine, the best of all   19/20

Bel Air, Lussac St Emilion

Dark colour, fruity bouquet, like wild strawberries! Not a big wine, but it has some charm   16/20
(Inexpensive and good value)

L'Angelus, Saint Emilion

Dark colour, a nice fruity bouquet, pleasantly rounded   17/20

La Dominique, Saint Emilion

Dark colour, scented bouquet, a big full-bodied wine, very tannic but excellent   19/20

Certan Giraud, Pomerol

Dark colour, pleasant bouquet, medium body, soft and nicely rounded   17/20

Here we had a cross section of this attractive vintage which showed how it is improving in bottle. Nobody took much interest when I was lecturing in the United States during the autumn of

1984, but now some authorities in Bordeaux consider 1983 as equally serious as the more spectacular 1982. It is certainly more typical of fine bordeaux.

For those who like to eat fish, it is worth trying Chez Philippe in the small but lovely Place du Parliament, in the old part of the city where on a fine evening one can eat out of doors. The weakness is the wine list, there is only one white burgundy and Carbonnieux is the only white bordeaux of note. I must admit though that we enjoyed the 1982 Château Piron, one of the lesser white graves.

SATURDAY, 28 SEPTEMBER

We had a rendezvous with Nicole Tesseron at Château Malescasse, a *cru bourgeois* in Lamarque which her husband Guy purchased some three years ago. When I first met Guy, soon after the war, he told me it was his ambition to own a *château* in the Médoc and now he has not one, but three! All these properties are managed by his youngest son Alfred. Another son, Gerard, married my god-daughter who in turn is godmother to my daughter so I have ties with this family.

Malescasse Sixty per cent *cabernet sauvignon*; 25 per cent *merlot*; 10 per cent *cabernet franc*

1984
Good colour, pleasant bouquet, not a big wine but rather nice, should be ready fairly soon

1983, bottled June 1985
A darker colour, fruity bouquet, has greater depth than the 1984, but a little acidity

Lafon-Rochet, Saint Estèphe

When Guy bought this property in 1959 it was in a run down state with far too many *merlot* vines. Many of these were promptly pulled up and replaced by *cabernet sauvignon* vines which have now reached maturity.

1984
Good colour, nice nose, medium body with plenty of fruit and a sufficient depth of flavour. Should make a nice bottle

1983, bottled June 1985
Dark colour, quite a rich bouquet, good fruit and body and more generous than the 1984, which helped to emphasise the difference between these two vintages

1982

Dark colour, a fine deep bouquet, with lots to come out with maturity, full-bodied and very good. With this *château* I found the 1983 deeper and in time it may perhaps make a better bottle

Pontet-Canet, Pauillac

The 1983 vinntage had just been bottled and so was unavailable. In accordance with the present fashion, Guy Tesseron has recently produced a second wine, a policy which can only do good, because inevitably it must improve the quality of the *grand vin.* In fact it is surprising that he has not done so before. At Latour, for instance, although we were by no means the first in Bordeaux, we were certainly among the pioneers of the present trend in the Médoc. We produced our first Les Forts de Latour with the 1966 vintage and this policy has proved successful.

Les Hauts Pontet-Canet

1984

Good colour, pleasant bouquet and flavour, easy to taste

1982

Nice nose, good fruit but a trace of astringency at the finish

Pontet-Canet

1984

Dark colour, nice nose, medium body with a nice 'solid' middle, well knit with a pleasing finish

1982

Good dark colour, nice bouquet, quite a big wine, well balanced with plenty of fruit, leading to a pleasant finish. This may take some time to mature

Staying here at Pontet-Canet evokes happy memories of the past, of delightful meals in the company of the previous owners, the late Christian and Emanuel Cruse and particularly of Edouard, Christian's son. On many an occasion I have been to the cellar with Edouard to pull out and decant a bottle of the fabulous 1929 Pontet-Canet, one of the finest examples of that heavenly vintage.

For dinner that evening, our host produced:

1966 Pontet-Canet

Lovely bouquet, medium body, but well balanced. An attractive wine and easy to drink. Better than many of this highly acclaimed vintage which is now turning out to be somewhat irregular

1964 Lafon-Rochet

Good colour and bouquet, good fruit and flavour. A successful wine when many of the médocs did not fare so well

SUNDAY, 29 SEPTEMBER

What a time it was to be in Bordeaux. Although at Pontet-Canet the picking was not to commence officially until the next day, the unusually warm weather could not fail to ripen the *cabernet sauvignon* grapes. Since the weather had been so exceptional, Alfred Tesseron had decided to begin his harvest a day earlier, a decision which would not have been so easy to make in the past when the picking was all done by hand. There is no problem now though, with the harvesting machines. There are still vineyards where the picking is done by hand, but in the Médoc more and more are gathered by machine. During the past ten years there has been a great improvement in the efficiency of these machines; they are now more selective of the bunches that are picked and of course over all, the saving of manpower is considerable.

The initial cost is high, but it is reckoned that the reduction of labour pays for the purchase within three years. In addition, all responsibility for finding, housing and feeding the *vendangeurs* is avoided. Here at Pontet-Canet the harvest can be handled by a dozen men instead of the 200 formerly employed. A further advantage is that, if necessary, the machines can be used during the night, that is until the dew begins to fall. This is a great asset during uncertain weather when the grapes have to be gathered in quickly. Two mechanical harvesters are employed at Pontet-Canet, one at Lafon-Rochet and one at Malescasse. Since the harvest in Charente begins after that of Bordeaux, Guy Tesseron is able to transfer his harvesting machines to Cognac to gather the grapes in his vineyards there.

The type used here is Braud 1112 and it appears to be very efficient. On careful inspection of the grapes gathered, there were no signs of damage and the amount of leaves collected was very small. A harvester is particularly useful in a vintage such as this when, thanks to the successful flowering of the vines, all the grapes have ripened more or less at the same time. When I asked what happened in an irregular vintage. I was informed the machines can be regulated accordingly and somehow the unripe bunches are left on the vines.

Later, our host drove us through part of the neighbouring vineyards of Grand-Puy-Lacoste, Croizet-Bages and Lynch-Bages and everywhere the grapes, although smaller perhaps than usual, looked very healthy. Mechanical harvesters were to be seen on all sides, even in a part of the Mouton-Rothschild vineyard. Guy Tesseron assured me that the wine produced by means of the new harvesters was of exactly the same quality as that previously picked by hand.

Up to date there had never been any restaurant of importance in the Médoc. In the past, the few visitors that there were, were entertained by the proprietors or *négociants* in their own *châteaux*. Now, with the greatly increased interest in the wines of Bordeaux, there are many more visitors, so a good restaurant called the Relais de Margaux has been opened, not far in fact from the famous *château*. An old *château* has been renovated and enlarged and there is a pleasant atmosphere; but one cannot help wondering what will happen during the winter months when the visitors dwindle to a trickle.

MONDAY, 30 SEPTEMBER

The last morning of this remarkable visit. I can seldom remember a period when there were so few worries about the nascent wine coupled with such settled weather. How different from the situation 12 months before following the disaster of the *merlot* grapes, especially in the districts of Pomerol and Saint Emilion. Consequently the 1984 vintage emerged on the market somewhat under a cloud but happily the situation was not nearly so serious for the *cabernet sauvignons* which preponderate in the Médoc. Indeed just prior to the harvest of 1984 I walked all around the vineyard at Latour and noticed how healthy all the vines were looking. Since there are only about ten per cent of *melot* vines at Latour, the ultimate result (except for a greater preponderance of *cabernet sauvignon* than usual) was not at all unsatisfactory. Thus, although 1984 is by no means one of the great years, it is not at all bad for the wines from the Médoc, indeed better perhaps than 1980. This was borne out by the following tasting which Louis Vialard had arranged for me at Château Cissac.

Some wines of the 1984 Vintage, Tasted Anonymously

La Croix Landon, Bégadan
Medium colour, pleasant bouquet, good fruit with a suspicion of acidity   13/20

Potensac, Ordonnac
Good colour, a somewhat earthy bouquet, well made though with a good follow-through   15.5/20

Soudars, Haut-Médoc
Good colour, average nose, nothing special   14/20

Malescasse, Lamarque
Good colour, nice nose, good fruit and is well made   15.5/20

Verdignan, St Seurin de Cadourne
Darker colour, bouquet quite good, plenty of fruit, but preferred
the Malescasse   14/20

Coufran, Haut-Médoc
Good colour, the bouquet a little fierce, good if a trifle severe
                                                        14/20

La Tour de Mirail, Cissac
Good colour, an attractive bouquet, a nice wine and it finished
well   15.5/20

La Fleur Becade, Haut-Médoc
Darker colour, perfumed bouquet, fruity and attractive   15.5/20

Sociando-Mallet, St Seurin de Cadourne
Darker colour, nice nose, but could have more charm   14/20

Cissac, Cissac
Good colour, fruity bouquet, a good 'solid' wine   16.5/20

Lanessan, Cissac
Medium colour, a pretty bouquet, good fruit, medium body 16/20

Belgrave, St Laurent
Medium colour, a fruity bouquet, medium body, some acidity,
lacking charm   13/20

Tronquoy-Lalande, Saint Estèphe
Medium body, pleasant bouquet, a good complete wine with a
nice finish, plenty of tannin   16/20

La Commanderie, Haut-Médoc
Darker colour, well made, but not exciting   15/20

Les Ormes de Pez, Saint Estèphe
Dark colour, very attractive bouquet, plenty of fruit and body,
very good   17/20

Lafon-Rochet, Saint Estèphe
Good colour, a fruity bouquet, lots of fruit with a very nice
finish   17.5/20

Capbern Gasqueton, Saint Estèphe
Good colour, a fruity bouquet, plenty of fruit, medium body, somewhat overwhelmed by its predecessors   15/20

Chasse-Spleen, Moulis
Medium colour, a full fruity nose, medium body with a nice finish   16.5/20

Maucaillou, Moulis
Good colour, lovely fruity bouquet, good body, very good   18/20

Brillette, Moulis
Medium colour, a fruity bouquet, attractive with plenty of charm   17.5/20

Clos du Marquis, Saint Julien
Dark colour, a delightful bouquet, plenty of fruit and body, first rate   18/20

Gloria, Saint Julien
Dark colour, nice nose, elegant, good quality   17/20

Pedesclaux, Pauillac
Medium colour, quite a good bouquet, but has an odd flavour, disappointing for a classified growth   15/20

Haut-Bages Averous, Pauillac
Dark colour, full-bodied, rich and rounded, some tannin   17.5/20

Lynch-Bages, Pauillac
Very dark colour, a nice blackcurrant bouquet, richer and rounder than all the others with a fine depth of flavour   19/20

Labegorce, Margaux
Good colour, a nice fruity nose, attractive and well balanced 17/20

How indebted I am to Louis Vialard and his son Pascal for arranging such an instructive tasting. I also received some interesting information. The Co-operative which in the past has made the bulk of the wine for the *commune* of Cissac, has, through poor management, fallen on hard times. The whole affair has been taken over by Louis Vialard, who must be one of the most able and dynamic men in the Médoc. He intends to make changes and because of his high standards it will be interesting to watch how this Cave Co-operative will develop.

In order to enlarge on the result of the above tasting, here are the notes from another anonymous tasting I attended.

1984 Red Bordeaux

Belgrave, St Laurent
Medium colour, pleasant bouquet, medium body, quite nice 11/20

Camensac, Saint Laurent
Good colour, nice nose, plenty of fruit with more depth than the Belgrave   13/20

Dauzac, Labarde
Good colour, softish bouquet, a lighter wine, not bad   12/20

Gloria, Saint Julien
Darker colour, a somewhat edgy bouquet, good fruit though
13/20

Prieuré Lichine, Cantenac
Good colour, attractive bouquet, good fruit and flavour, some tannin, rather nice   14.5/20

Rauzan-Gassies, Margaux
Medium colour, good fruit and flavour, has more depth as well as more tannin   16.5/20

Haut-Bages-Liberal, Pauillac
Good colour, fragrant bouquet, medium body, but plenty of fruit and flavour   15.5/20

Pontet-Canet, Pauillac
Darker colour, nicely rounded, good fruit with plenty of depth   15.5/20

Duhart-Milon, Pauillac
Good colour, very nice nose, quite a good flavour, but hard and tannic   14.5/20

Clerc-Milon, Pauillac
Good colour, fruity bouquet, pleasant flavour and well balanced   15.5/20

Léoville-Poyferré, Saint Julien
Medium colour, interesting bouquet, medium body and has some charm   16/20

Lagrange, Saint Julien
Good colour, attractive bouquet, well balanced, has some depth and plenty of flavour   16/20

Durfort-Vivens, Margaux

Medium colour, fruity bouquet, good fruit, but a rather aggressive finish   16/20

Branaire-Ducru, Saint Julien

Medium colour, fruity bouquet, has more depth and is rather good   17/20

Léoville-Barton, Saint Julien

Good colour and bouquet, plenty of fruit and is easy to taste 16.5/20

Brane-Cantenac, Margaux

Good colour and bouquet, a fine wine with plenty of depth
17.5/20

Beychevelle, Saint Julien

Good colour, an attractive bouquet, easy to taste, an attractive well made wine   17.5/20

Calon-Ségur, Saint Estèphe

Medium colour, pleasant bouquet, good fruit and flavour with a very nice finish   17.5/20

Lafite, Pauillac

Good colour, fine bouquet, good fruit, fine quality   18.5/20

Montrose, Saint Estèphe

Medium colour, nice nose, rounded and full of fruit   17.5/20

Latour, Pauillac

Medium colour, fine bouquet, an excellent full-bodied wine, fine quality   19/20

Ducru-Beaucaillou, Saint Julien

Good colour, an attractive bouquet, quite a big wine, packed with fruit, beauty   19/20

Mouton-Rothschild, Pauillac

The darkest of all, very good bouquet, a fine wine, full of fruit and flavour   19/20

Margaux, Margaux

Very good colour, deep bouquet, quite a big wine which is packed with fruit and flavour. For me the best of all   19.5/20

It was a pity the Léoville-Lascases and the Cos d'Estournel were not included in this tasting, but there were some surprises when the names were revealed. The Rauzan-Gassies was better than expected, also the Lagrange, a wine which in earlier vintages has usually been somewhat unattractive. In this last case, the change of ownership may already be having a beneficial effect. Among the others, the Branaire-Ducru, Brane-Cantenac and Calon-Ségur all came out well. The Ducru-Beaucaillou was extremely good and stood up well with the first growths. If not quite so charming as the preceding vintages, there is no doubt that the médocs of 1984 are quite good and they will fill a useful role in the years to come.

Commencing our journey home, we took the ferry from Le Verdon at the northern tip of the Médoc, across the broad mouth of the river Gironde to Royan and thence to Chatellerault where an unexpected surprise awaited us. Good as most of them are, the restaurants with a single rosette in the *Guide Michelin* can vary one from the other. Yet happily we found the food, service and general ambience at the Hotel Moderne unusually good and not too expensive. This ensured a finish on a high note for an enjoyable ten day visit.

9

SOME NOTES ON THE 1983 VINTAGE ON THE MOSELLE AND IN ALSACE

Originally planned for earlier in the year our visit had had to be postponed until October 1983. This in fact was just as well as it gave this excellent vintage a little more time in which to develop in bottle.

Besides my wife there were two friends from Detroit, Bob Simburger and Dr Norman Simpson and our first stop was at a nice new hotel in Traben Trabach on the Moselle, called Moselschlosschen. The building itself is not new, its former role was as a winery and indeed it continues to devote itself to the cause of wine. Under the direction of a graduate of Geisenheim, the equivalent perhaps of an English Master of Wine, there are courses to attend as well as wine tastings. The situation is superb, facing directly on to the river with a fine view across to the vine-covered slopes on the far bank and a steep hill which is surmounted by the ruins of an ancient castle.

We were the guests of the progressive firm of Rudolf Muller in Reil which owns many vineyards along the Moselle, but which recently has become known throughout the world for its brand of moselle called 'The Bishop'. It is a sad fact that very few firms in the wine business have succeeded merely by selling wine of high quality. The ideal solution is a bread and butter brand such as Havery's Bristol Cream for mass sale to the general public so as to produce the capital for indulgence in wine of finer quality.

This old established business is directed by two brothers, Richard and Walter Muller who, on their mother's side of the family, can claim forebears in and around Reil for 800 years. During dinner that evening we drank two R. Muller wines, the

1982 Scharzhofberger Riesling Spatlese and the 1983 Ockfener Bockstein Riesling Auslese. Both were attractive, but demonstrated the difference between the two vintages, the 1983 being fuller and having more depth.

WEDNESDAY, 9 OCTOBER

As in England it had been a wet summer on the Moselle. In consequence the harvest was delayed, which was perhaps as well because there was still plenty of rain about. A good sign, at least, was that the vegetation of the vines was much greener than usual for the time of year.

Walter Muller has no children but Richard's daughter Barbara, together with her husband Eric, help run the business. I can safely predict that before too long this attractive girl will be one of the leading personalities of the wine world. Formerly the Rudolf Muller firm was based in the riverside village of Reil, but the business has now moved to vast new premises about a kilometre away with the most up-to-date equipment and a storage capacity of some 12 million bottles.

These are the wines we tasted:

1984 The Bishop of Riesling Q.b.a.
A pleasant bouquet, fresh with an attractive fruity flavour

1982 Kanzemer Sonnenberg Riesling Q.b.a.
A nice bouquet, a little sweeter perhaps with more fruit acidity, rather good

1984 Saarburger Antoniusbrunnen Riesling Q.b.a.
A fragrant bouquet, a fuller but blander wine

1982 Wiltinger Scharzberg Riesling Kabinett
A fruity bouquet, good flavour and plenty of character, very nice

1983 Deidesheimer Hofstuck Kabinett
Pleasant bouquet, a slightly sweeter and fuller wine, a little dull perhaps

1983 Niersteiner Spiegelberg Kabinett
A spicy bouquet, an attractive wine with nice fruit acidity, more exciting

1983 Johannisberger Erntebringer Riesling Kabinett
An attractive bouquet, still a little closed up, but fresh with plenty of fruit

1983 Piesporter Tröpfchen Riesling Kabinett
A spicy bouquet, fresh, light and attractive

1982 Ockfener Bockstein Riesling Kabinett
A fruity bouquet, on the light side, but attractive nevertheless

1984 Bernkasteler Badstube Riesling Kabinett
Pleasant bouquet, lots of fruit and flavour, but just a little too much acidity for my liking.

In fact this was the Bernkasteler Doktor which had been declassified because of its poor vintage

1983 Deidesheimer Herrgottzacker Riesling Kabinett
Pleasant nose, good fruit with a nice depth of flavour, good quality

1983 Hattenheimer Mannberg Riesling Spatlese Langwerth von Simmern
An attractive bouquet, a delightful flavour, excellent quality

1983 Erbacher Steinmorgen Riesling Spatlese, Wagner-Weritz
A fine bouquet, more full-bodied with plenty of flavour as well as a little sweeter, has a good aftertaste

1982 Scharzhofberger Riesling Spatlese, R. Muller
A fruity nose, a nice fresh flavour, pleasant but not outstanding

1982 Saarburger Antoniusbrunnen Riesling Spatlese, R. Muller
A flowery bouquet, lots of character, exciting and very good

1983 Ockfener Bockstein Riesling Spatlese, R. Muller
A fruity bouquet, good quality

1983 Ockfener Geisberg Riesling Spatlese, R. Muller
Attractive bouquet, good fruit with more depth than the Bockstein, more 'alive', very good

1983 Ockfener Geisberg Riesling Auslese, R. Muller
A fuller richer wine with more depth and a very nice finish, fine quality

1983 Ockfener Bockstein Riesling Auslese, R. Muller
Fine bouquet, good fruit with even more depth, good fruit acidity

1983 Herzheimer Honisack Riesling Auslese, R. Muller
Heaps of fruit and richer still, a very fine wine

From such a tasting, one could not help but receive a favourable impression of the 1983 vintage, which is clearly as good as it has been portrayed.

The cellars of the Bernkasteler Doktor of Dr Thanisch in Bernkastel lie directly beneath the famous vineyard and one enters through a decorative copper gate. The production is small and the entire stock of the 1983 vintage had already been sold. The cellars were swathed in a kind of ethereal mist because the ancient casks were being cleaned in preparation for the new vintage.

THURSDAY, 10 OCTOBER

The day started well, but was to prove a very long one. It began with a visit to the impressive Staatsweingut cellars in Trier where the cellarmaster invited us to taste several of his wines.

1983 Ockfener Bockstein Kabinett
On the light side with a certain amount of acidity, which no doubt will disappear in due course

1982 Avelsbacher Hammerstein Riesling Spatlese
Attractive and probably at its best now

1976 Ockfener Bockstein Riesling Auslese
This was lovely with a full and very pronounced flavour. The cellarmaster said he thought his 1983 would develop along the same lines

1983 Serriger Vogelsang Riesling Eiswein
Glorious fruit acidity with a superb finish. A splendid wine which will need another five years to develop and then, as the cellarmaster said, it will last for decades

There is a current fashion is Germany for extremely dry wines (trocken) but by no means are all the leading growers in favour. We were to experience some of these trocken wines during our lunch at an excellent restaurant in Trier called Pfeiffer Muhle. We tried three wines each from well-known vineyards and they were all disappointing.

Our confidence was soon to be restored by a memorable tasting prepared by Herr Egon Muller of Scharzhofberg, one of the great men on the German wine scene.

1983 Wiltinger Scharzberg Qualitatswein
A fresh fairly dry wine

1983 Scharzhofberger Kabinett
Clean and fresh, fairly dry and slightly fuller than the others

1983 Wiltinger Braune Kupp Spatlese
An attractive flavour, very nice

1983 Scharzhofberger Spatlese
A little more fruit and depth of flavour than the preceding wine

1983 Wiltinger Braune Kupp Auslese
Delicious flavour with perfect balance, just a little more fruit acidity than the Scharzhofberger Auslese, but both were outstanding

1983 Scharzhofberger Auslese
A slightly fuller wine than the Wiltinger and truly splendid

For me, these two ausleses were the really exciting wines of this tasting and it took a long time to decide which I preferred. Although it was not quite so full flavoured, finally I liked the Wiltinger Braune Kupp best, because of its delightful finish

1983 Wiltinger Braune Kupp Auslese Goldkapsel
Masses of fruit and masses of flavour, much richer and a marvellous wine

1984 Scharzhofberger Eiswein
Rich and well balanced with tremendous style, but somehow there was the evidence of a less great vintage

1983 Scharzhofberger Beerenauslese
A great mouthful of heavenly flavour, sheer bliss!

1983 Scharzhofberger Eiswein
A huge wine, rich and majestic. What will this be like when it has had sufficient time to display all of its charms!

To taste the whole range of wines of a very fine vintage from this exceptional grower is indeed an unforgettable experience.

Having done our duty as it were, and what an agreeable one, we were invited to the next room to drink rather than merely taste some more fine wine. Since nothing could compete with the splendour of the 1983 Eiswein, we began with a 1967 Scharzhofberger Spatlese, even so the poor thing was pretty well overwhelmed.

1979 Scharzhofberger Auslese
Medium sweet, packed with fruit, a mouthful of flavour and a lovely finish

1971 Scharzhofberger Auslese
Another wine brimming over with fruit with an aftertaste which went on and on

1975 Scharzhofberger Auslese
Younger of course, but so complete, this was nectar!

1971 Scharzhofberger Eiswein
The grapes were picked as late as 18 January 1972. So rich and so perfectly balanced – sheer heaven!

It is seldom if ever that one has the opportunity to taste such great wines as these.

From that moment our good fortune deserted us. We had hoped to reach our hotel in Alsace before dark, but it was around 5.30 p.m. by the time this fabulous tasting was over. Finally, after various misadventures, we reached our destination having had no supper and all of us pretty tired.

FRIDAY 11 OCTOBER

No matter how many times one has been to the mediaeval town of Riquewihr, it is always an enchantment even in spite of the tourists. Our modest but comfortable hotel, le Sarment d'Or in the rue du Cerf, had been hard to find in the dark, but our late arrival was alleviated by the warm welcome of the management. The weather was glorious and a wonderful change from the gloomy skies on the Moselle.

Our first visit was to Paul Blanck in Kientsheim, very much a family affair which has continued through the centuries. Marcel Blanck makes the wine and the rest of the business is carried on with the help of brothers, sons and nephews. This thriving family enlarged their premises some 15 years ago when they modernised their method of making wine. Their vines grow on two splendid hillsides nearby called Furstenheim and Schlossberg, and on these there are a variety of soils to which the family pays great attention. For instance, the upper slopes of Furstenheim are chalky and particularly good for the *gewurztraminer* vine. From the top of this hill there is a splendid view across the plain towards the villages of Kientzheim and Ammerschwihr. The other slope, Schlossberg, stretches westwards towards Kaysersberg and there the soil is excellent for the *riesling* vine.

1. Christies' wine tasters

2. At Château La Mission, Haut-Brion, with Françoise Dewavrin before the sale to Château Haut-Brion

3. With David and Tim Sandeman in their office. Behind, a portrait of the late Patrick Sandeman, who in 1945 recommended me to John Harvey and Sons Ltd

4. Dr Bill Dick (left) and Hank Case (right) helping me decant

5. (Left to right) Mrs Maggie Dick, Dr Bill Dick, the author, Dr Charles Thomas and Jill Thomas

6. With Jean Paul Gardère, who has managed Latour since 1963 and made the wine

7. With Jean Paul Gardère and Geoffrey Jameson of Justerini and Brooks at a Château Latour dinner in London

8. The author

9. *In the cellar of the Ritz Hotel, London*

10. *The author samples another fine wine*

11. The entrance to one of the tunnels at a winery in Calfornia

12. *The members of the Council of the Wine Guild of the United Kingdom in Nantes*

13. *Château d'Issan Cantenac, Margaux. Proprietor, Madame Emmanuel Cruse*

1983 Riesling, from Furstenheim
A pleasant light wine with some acidity

1983 Riesling, from Schlossberg
Fuller, rounder with less acidity

1980 Riesling, from Furstenheim
As was to be expected a better developed bouquet and flavour

1983 Pinot Noir, from Furstenheim
Medium colour, pleasant bouquet, a light wine, but nice flavour
and balance, with just a little tannin

1983 Muscat
Dry with a pleasant fruity flavour, a trace of acidity

1982 Muscat
Full flavoured with less acidity

1983 Tokay Altenberg, from sandy soil lower down the slope
Fresh and attractive

1983 Tokay Altenberg, from the middle of the slope
A fuller rounder wine with more depth, very nice

1983 Gewurztraminer Altenberg, *cuvée particulaire*
A delightful flavour which fills the mouth. *Note:* This family
produced six different gewurztraminers in the 1983 vintage

1983 Gewurztraminer, from sandy soil
A lovely taste, lively and exciting

1983 Gewurztraminer Altenberg
A lovely rich flavour, quite delicious

1983 Gewurtraminer Furstenberg, Vendange Tardive
Still rather closed up but has more elegance. This should be magnificent in about five years' time

Although we had made an appointment, we got the impression of
being on a bottling line when we called on Madame Faller who
owns the neighbouring property. She was overwhelmed by
visitors, but eventually we were able to taste a range of her wines,
mainly of the 1984 vintage. Although there are exceptions of
course, this vintage cannot be described as very good. There
were, however, some attractive 1983s to end with.

1983 Riesling Vendange Tardive
Heaps of bouquet, a fairly rich wine with a lovely flavour

1983 Tokay, Vendange Tardive
A gloriously rich wine with a delicious flavour

1983 Gewurztraminer, Grains Nobles
Rich and concentrated and almost as full as a good sauternes, if one dares to mention that word in Alsace!

In the attractive town of Ribeauvillé there is a picturesque fourteenth-century tower with the traditional stork's nest on the top. Nearby are the premises of F.E. Trimbach, one of the great firms of the region. Founded in 1626, the business has thrived ever since and has been handed down from father to son. There are now two brothers, Jean who handles the wine and who was busy with the vintage and Hubert, who is responsible for the successful sale of Trimbach wines in the United States.

1984 Riesling, regular
Good fruit, a pleasant flavour but with a touch of the 1984 acidity, quite nice nevertheless

1982 Riesling Cuvée Frederic Emile, the wines under this label are produced from the firm's own vines
An attractive wine with a good varietal flavour. *Note* The crop in 1982 was enormous

1983 Riesling Cuvée Frederick Emile
A pleasant fresh bouquet, a whole gamut of flavours. More complex and fuller than the 1982 vintage. A fine wine which needs more time to develop

1978 Riesling, Clos St Hune
A shade darker and a most attractive wine, another gamut of flavours

1982 Gewurztraminer Reserve
Fuller and more fragrant than the rieslings, an attractive wine

1982 Gewurztraminer Cuvée des Seigneurs de Ribeaupierre, single vineyard
So rounded it filled the mouth with fruit and flavour. A fine wine, made from ripe grapes

1983 Gewurztraminer Cuvée des Seigneurs de Ribeaupierre
A complex wine giving a whole mouthful of lovely flavour, delightful

1976 Gewurztraminer Cuvée des Seigneurs de Ribeaupierre
Rich and full bodied, but by no means aggressively so, a proper
mouthful, but it could have had a little more acidity

1983 Gewurztraminer, Grains Nobles
Not yet ready for release, but amazingly full and rich, the taste
went on and on.

Our evening was altogether unusual for we had been invited to a
souper de vendange by the Blanck family in Kientzheim where
we sat at a long table in the company of the *vendangeurs*. The
kitchen was at the far end where the womenfolk attended to the
cooking and serving of the food. The meal was copious but fairly
simple, an excellent *soupe de vendange* to begin with, fried eggs
on spinach, chicken and the local Munster cheese. Marcel, who is
responsible for the wine making, produced bottle after bottle and
towards the end of the meal, as if by magic, Bernard, his brother,
brought out a whole range of *eau de vie* which he had made
himself: poire, framboise, kirsch, coing (quince), marc and so on.
In turn Bernard poured a small measure of each into a vast
engraved glass which he then turned almost upside down and
twirled it around so rapidly that not a drop was spilt. Once the
aroma was fully aroused this loving cup, as it were, was passed
around for each of us to sniff and to sip. I thought I had seen it all,
but for me this was an altogether new experience. The quality of
those *eaux de vie* seemed to be particularly good.

There was also a bottle of *eau de vie de lie* (lees) with which
we were invited to massage our hands and certainly it made a very
good friction. Bernard assured us that it proved an excellent relief
when used as a massage for arthritis and similar complaints. In
addition he assured me that if I were to drink five centilitres of
eau de vie first thing every morning, I would never again catch
'flu or similar complaints'. This might be worth trying!

SATURDAY, 12 OCTOBER

The journey to Hugel et Fils provided no problem because their
premises were virtually around the corner from our hotel in
Riquewihr. Our host was that outstanding personality of the wine
trade, Johnnie Hugel, who has done so much for the cause of the
wines of Alsace. There was a pleasant and unexpected surprise
when my friend Parks Redwine from Atlanta, Georgia, joined us
for the tasting.

1983 Pinot Noir Reserve Personnelle, one-third new casks;
two-thirds one-year-old
We were all surprised by the depth of this wine as well as by the

quality. *Note* Pinot Noir is a relatively new feature for Alsace and as the wines grow older, this innovation may become important

1983 Sylvaner
Medium light with a slightly earthy taste

1983 Pinot Blanc
A fuller wine with more depth

1983 Riesling
Medium dry with a definite varietal flavour, fresh and rounded with plenty of character

1983 Riesling, Cuvée Tradition
A finer bouquet, similar to the regular 1983 but with far greater depth, a very nice wine

1983 Riesling Reserve Personnelle
An even finer bouquet, with even more depth and complexity. Still rather closed up

1981 Riesling Vendange Tardive, Selection Personnelle J.H., with 14°
Delightful bouquet, a splendid wine of enormous character, much too good to spit out!

1976 Riesling Grains Nobles 16° 100 per cent noble rot
Charming bouquet, rich and superb, this is magnificent

1984 Gewurztraminer
Fruity flavour, spicy but difficult to appreciate after the preceding wines

1983 Gewurztraminer, Reserve Personnelle
A delightful flavour, plenty of character and a good finish. Fine quality.

1983 Gewurztraminer, Vendange Tardive
A very fragrant bouquet, well bred and full of charm, very good indeed

Johnnie Hugel informed us that most of the houses in Riquewihr were built between 1500 and 1600 during the years of prosperity for this region, one of those rare interludes when there was no war. The firm of Hugel has had to expand and, since no modern building is permitted, this has been carried out most skilfully underground. His own house was built by his father in 1925 and lies outside the town walls. During lunch, he produced a surprise for us, a 1948 Riesling Cuvée Personnelle, a remarkable wine whose age one would never have guessed. There must be some longevity connected with these wines of Alsace, because living in his house were his mother aged 86 and his mother-in-law aged 91 and both of them in excellent health. What a splendid advertisement for the wines of Hugel!

SUNDAY, 13 OCTOBER

We spent most of the day in Colmar, a town full of charm, especially the area around what is called 'Petite Venise' and the lunch at Schillinger with one star in the *Guide Michelin* came right up to expectations. This restaurant is worth a visit, likewise the Museum which is not far away.

MONDAY, 14 OCTOBER

The fine weather continued and with a good forecast, so it looked as though this promising vintage of 1985 was to be gathered in successfully. There was so much activity that it was difficult to progress along the country roads crammed as they were with vehicles of all kinds loaded with grapes. Although in places the slopes are steep, during the entire visit we did not see a single mechanical harvester, now so common in the Médoc.

Our first call was on the firm of Jerome Lorentz in the village of Berkheim, now an amalgamation of the two family firms of Jerome and Gustave Lorentz and which owns some 30 hectares of vines. We were told that around Berkheim there is the largest percentage of *gewurztraminer* vines, chiefly because the soil, composed mainly of chalk and clay, is particularly suitable for this varietal.

Pinot Blanc 1983
Pleasant bouquet, easy to taste with a nice fruity flavour

1983 Riesling, Cuvée des Templiers
A nice wine with plenty of fruit and flavour. This should be even better after another year in bottle

1983 Tokay
Good fruit and flavour with a nice finish, this too needs time to develop

1979 Gewurztraminer Reserve Kanzierberg
Lots of fruit and very nice

1983 Gewurztraminer Selection des Grains Nobles
An immense concentration of fruit and flavour. In due course, this should make a remarkable bottle

The notes on all these wines may appear unduly laudatory, but it must be remembered that not only was 1983 a very good vintage, but that great care had been taken to ensure that we visited some of the best growers. Undoubtedly there are other establishments of similar calibre, but in the four days available there was no time for more extensive investigation.

Our next visit was to a grower in Dambach called Louis Gisselbrecht where our host considers his 1985 vintage is going to be even finer than his 1983. He stressed that in this particular region with its preponderance of granite and gravel, the soil is especially suitable for the riesling vine.

1984 Pinot Blanc
Quite a surprise for this vintage, a wine with a lot of character

1984 Riesling, Gold Medal Colmar
A lot of flavour, good balance and a nice long finish, very good for 1984

1984 Riesling, Another growth but not yet bottled, also awarded a gold medal
Typical of its varietal, more lively and more complex than the other 1984

1984 Gewurztraminer Cuvée Reserve
An attractive bouquet, fresh, lively and delightful.
Note These were some of the best 1984s I have tasted, exciting with individuality

1983 Riesling, Gold Medal
Very fresh bouquet, light but lively and refreshing, very good

1983 Tokay, also straight from the *cuve*
A delightful flavour

TUESDAY, 15 OCTOBER

Our last morning and it was with some sadness that we left our little hotel in Riquewihr.

In Wintzenheim the family of Zind Humbrecht own some 30 hectares of vines; they sell only their own produce and buy no grapes whatsoever. They claim they were the first people in

Alsace to instal temperature controls for their vats. The father was busy attending to loads of grapes pouring in, so we were looked after by his son, a huge young man who is currently studying at the Oenological College in Toulouse. The latter told us that his family had been especially successful in 1984 with their *pinot gris* and *gewurztraminer* vines. The family felt that because of the drought, their 1985 vintage might be less good than 1983. Even so, in spite of some variation in quality the 1985 vintage might turn out along the lines of 1976. However, so far there had been few signs of botrytis whereas in 1976 there had been plenty.

1984 Riesling Herrenberg, from vines growing between
Turkheim and Wintzenheim on gravelly soil
An aromatic bouquet, full flavoured and quite attractive

1984 Riesling Braud, grand cru from a sandy soil
An attractive nose, a light but elegant wine and the difference in quality was discernible

1984 Riesling Rangen, grand cru from a volcanic soil
Quite full-bodied but there was too much acidity for my liking

1983 Riesling Herrenberg
A fruity bouquet, a nice flavour and much easier to taste than the sharper 1984s

1983 Riesling Clos Heuserer, limestone and clay soil
Typical aromatic bouquet, a wine of character

1983 Riesling Rangen, grand cru
An attractive bouquet, a fine well bred wine, superior to the Heuserer

1983 Riesling Braud, grand cru from old vines
Bouquet still closed up, but a distinctive flavour, more *nerveux* than the Rangen. *Note* These two rieslings were particularly good

1984 Pinot Gris Rangen, grand cru, 13.7°
One of the best 1984s I have tasted so far, less acidity and very easy to taste.
    Our host told us that their best 1984s had come from the *pinot gris* grapes

1983 Pinot Gris Rangen, grand cru, late harvest, 15°
Fatter, rounder, smoother, very good indeed

1984 Gewurztraminer Herrenberg
An aromatic bouquet, a little lighter but attractive nevertheless

1984 Gewurztraminer Hengst, grand cru, clay and limestone
soil
An over-flowing bouquet, just a little more acidity here but it is more lively, attractive and very good for its year

1984 Gewurztraminer Rangen, grand cru, late harvest, 15°
An even fuller wine with masses of fruit. Remarkable for its year. *Note* These seem to be among the best gewurztraminers of 1984 that we have come across

1983 Gewurztraminer Godlert, grand cru, late harvest, around
16°
A complex bouquet, quite rich with a delicious taste

1983 Gewurztraminer Hengst, grand cru
A lovely bouquet, rich and full of flavour, almost a dessert wine. This needs as much as from eight to ten years to develop

1983 Gewurztraminer Rangen, grand cru, late harvest, Selection Grains Nobles 16°
A lovely bouquet, rather rich with some residual sugar, delicious to taste!

1976 Gewurztraminer Hengst, grand cru, late harvest, 16°, 100
per cent botrytis
Medium golden colour, an exquisite aromatic bouquet, rich and full-bodied, yet fresh and lively, excellent

Our last visit was to the much respected firm of Leon Beyer in Eguisheim, a lovely village which is reputed to have a lower rainfall than anywhere else in France. Marc Beyer had prepared an interesting tasting for us and explained that his policy was to ferment all his wines right out which makes them appear drier than those of some of his competitors.

1984 Pinot Blanc
Fresh, clean with some acidity

Riesling Cuvée des Écaillers 1984
Smoother and easier to taste

1982 Riesling Cuvée Particulaire
Less acidity and a very nice taste

1974 Riesling Cuvée Particulaire
A pale golden colour, good fruit and flavour, just a touch of acidity

1983 Tokay Reserve
Fruity and full-bodied, needs time to develop

1982 Tokay Reserve
Easier to taste and very good to drink now

1979 Tokay Reserve
Lovely fruit, lovely flavour

1984 Gewurztraminer
Plenty of fruit, but also some of the 1984 acidity

1983 Gewurztraminer, Cuvée des Comtes d'Eguisheim
A fragrant bouquet, fairly dry but there is a delightful concentration of flavour, fine quality

1982 Gewurztraminer, Cuvée des Comtes d'Eguisheim
An attractive bouquet, an elegant wine with a lovely taste, this is a beauty

1967 Gewurztraminer, Cuvée des Comtes d'Eguisheim
A lovely fragrant bouquet, delicious taste with just a hint of sweetness

1983 Gewurztraminer, Vendange Tardive
Lovely bouquet and flavour, a fine wine with a great future

1983 Tokay, Selection Grains Nobles
A little less depth perhaps than the preceding wine and a little sweeter, considerable quality all the same

1983 Gewurztraminer, Selection Grains Nobles
A lovely bouquet, a fantastic depth of flavour and enormously rich, a masterpiece

In the past, merchants in England and so, I understand, in the United States, have always found it difficult to persuade their customers as to the undoubted merits of the wines of Alsace. One can only hope that this fine vintage of 1983, followed quickly by another good one in 1985, will help to spread the gospel of their charm and potential.

10

THE UNITED STATES
February 1986

In January last year we had been invited by Alan Hare, the President of Château Latour, to accompany him and his wife on a visit to New York, Washington, D.C. and Boston. The purpose of that visit had been to meet some of the people who distribute our wine, the press who write about it and at least a few of the members of the public who appreciate its quality. This visit was to be similar, but to Texas and California.

The first growths of Bordeaux are not inexpensive, so our object was to enable people to taste a range of vintages they would not normally see, to demonstrate how Latour can succeed in the off-years and to emphasise the quality of our second wine, Les Forts de Latour.

MONDAY, 3 FEBRUARY

Compared with the seething mass of humanity when we take the family on holiday in August, Gatwick Airport in February seemed calm and civilised.

In view of the weather to come, our arrival at Houston in a thunderstorm and torrential rain was not a good augury. However, our feelings were soothed by being met by Jim de George in his smart Rolls-Royce. It was Jim who had so kindly accepted to do the planning of our visit to Houston and Dallas and it is entirely thanks to him that everything went so smoothly.

TUESDAY, 4 FEBRUARY

An early start was necessary because there were 130 bottles to be uncorked and decanted in time for our first meeting at 10.30 a.m. With the help of an efficient team from the Remington Hotel, we managed to complete our task with some ten minutes to spare. There were about 100 people present drawn from the wine trade, the hotels and the press. The wines presented were as follows:

1978 Les Forts de Latour
A good dark colour, a robust bouquet, a wine with good balance and structure. Possible to drink now but will be much better over the coming five years.

Incidentally, in common with the other first growths, our policy has always been to release the *grand vin* for sale in the year after the vintage, but with this our second wine, it is kept back for a few years so that it can acquire some age in bottle before it is presented to the public.

The grapes which produce this second wine come from all the vines in the main vineyard which are under ten years old and from the outlying parcels of land called Petit Batailley and Pichon-Comtesse, from whose names their location can be deduced. At 20 years old, these vines are fully mature and naturally the quality of the wine made from them will continue to improve. The first vintage of Les Forts de Latour ever to be made was that of 1966. Thus, thanks to the elimination of the less good *cuves* from the *grand vin*, while it reduces the quantity, it has greatly improved the general quality.

1975 Les Forts de Latour
Very dark colour, a fine bouquet, this has a considerable depth of flavour, but because of its vintage, was a little harder and more tannic than the 1978

1970 Les Forts de Latour
An unusually dark colour, a concentrated complex bouquet, with considerable depth of flavour. This is good 'solid' stuff. Like many 1970s it is still somewhat severe and backward. No doubt it will be better in about five years' time

1982 Latour
A splendid dark colour, an immense bouquet, full of ripe fruit. A really huge wine which one can almost chew. There is enormous fruit and concentration and strangely enough it is agreeable to taste already, one day no doubt this will make a great bottle

1976 Latour
An attractive vintage which has matured early. A brilliant ruby colour, the bouquet sweet and gentle, the flavour, if less deep, is

delicious. Unlike most vintages of Latour when they are young, this 1976 is easy to taste and indeed already enjoyable to drink

1973 Latour
A good colour, but less dark than the others and the bouquet is soft and pleasant. There is less intensity of flavour, but it is fully mature and very nice to drink. While most of the 1973s are already dead and gone, this still bravely flies its flag. It is possibly the finest wine of this rather unreliable vintage

1971 Latour
A dark colour, the bouquet elegant and charming, there is a lot of fruit with even some richness in the flavour. This is ready to drink now but will continue to improve. After Pétrus, perhaps one of the most successful wines of its year

1970 Latour
A very dark colour, with the bouquet still firmly closed up. There is heaps of flavour and great quality lies under the heavy cloak of tannin. It has taken the 1961 Latour some 25 years to blossom into all its glory and I predict something similar will happen to this 1970

1967 Latour
A pretty garnet colour, a huge bouquet, fruity and deep. A lovely depth of flavour with some richness. A delightful wine which must be at its best now.

In the early days considerably more was expected of this 1967 vintage, but possibly because of unripe grapes, most of the 1967s developed an unattractive degree of acidity. However, there is none of that acidity in the 1967 Latour and after Pétrus it is possibly the best wine of its vintage. Another excellent 1967 is La Mission Haut-Brion

That evening Jim and Jane de George gave a splendid dinner party for some of the leading authorities of Houston. The guests were Mark Berman, Andre Crispin, Lenoir Josey, Frank Malone, Jean-Claude Robert, John Rydman, Robert Sakowitz, Michael Trabulsi and Kerry Wright. With this meal, we drank 1979 Haut-Brion Blanc, a fine example of this rare wine and 1966 Latour, dark colour, although still rather firm, a deep full-bodied wine. This needs another five or more years to reach its best.

1959 Latour
A bouquet which burst out at one and the flavour was excellent

1945 Latour
I must admit I have had better bottles but in spite of the tannin it was possible to see the underlying quality

The meal was rounded off by an excellent bottle of 1945 Taylor and what more can one ask.

WEDNESDAY, 5 FEBRUARY

Thanks to Jane de George we were able to spend an interesting morning in the Museum of Fine Arts where, since there was so much to see, we had to confine ourselves to the pictures. There were some fine Impressionists and I was delighted also to find some Western paintings by Remington.

Houston is deservedly noted for its splendid modern architecture, so Jane gave us the opportunity to see and admire some of those lovely tall buildings.

After lunch we paid a visit to two of the leading wine merchants, first to Spec's main store where John Rydman and Spec Jackson showed us some of their immense stock and then to Richard's on Richmond Avenue to meet again Dick Trabulsi and Henry Kucharzyk. This is a marvellous place, quiet and impressive and full of treasures. I was particularly tempted by a bin of 1982 Lafleur, their last dozen bottles of this rare wine, which so far as I know is no longer obtainable in London.

A formal dinner was held for about 80 people, the members of the main wine groups, such as the Commanderie de Bordeaux, the International Wine & Food Society, the Chaine des Rôtisseurs and so on. During the meal we drank the 1975 Les Forts de Latour which did not seem nearly so tannic with food and that was followed by the 1973 *grand vin*, now probably at its best.

THURSDAY, 6 FEBRUARY

No sooner had we arrived in Dallas than we were in touch with the staff of the Mansion Hotel concerning arrangements for the tasting and dinner that evening. There were many points to be covered concerning how many bottles to open, when to decant them and so on.

The afternoon was spent with John Roenigk, the local representative of the well-known importing firm, Chateaux and Estates. Later on, we called on three of the leading retail establishments, Sigel's, Red Coleman's and Marty's. At Sigel's I met an old friend, Victor Wdowiak, whom I first met when he was in charge of the wine department of Nieman Marcus and that must be some 25 years ago.

The procedure for the tasting and dinner was similar to the previous night in Houston and again some 80 or so wine enthusiasts were present. The *pigeonneau* which accompanied the 1975 Les Forts de Latour was particularly good, as good as any I have ever had in the great restaurants in France.

FRIDAY, 7 FEBRUARY

Apart from the weather, this all too brief visit to Texas is proving most enjoyable. Although very cold with a biting wind, we consoled ourselves with the thought that it was probably much worse at home; February in England can be pretty grim.

The morning passed rapidly with a tasting and lunch at the Mansion Hotel for the trade and press. It seemed that the two most popular wines were the 1971 and the 1967, neither of which are fashionable years. There is a tendency everywhere to go for the great vintages, but I felt we were proving the point that Château Latour succeeds also in the years which are not so good.

That afternoon we drove to Fort Worth where we visited a huge retail store called King's and then made our way to Marvin Overton's house, Foxcroft Farm, outside the city. A dedicated authority, Marvin is known to have one of the finest collection of wine in the country.

The dinner which he and his wife Sue had prepared for us was so splendid it could really be called a feast. Among the fortunate guests were Jim and Jane de George, Joe Glicksman, John Roenigk, Tom and Lou Ann Lipscomb and Joy Rothwell. For long Joy was a good friend and loyal supporter of the late André Simon and for many years a pillar of strength on the Committee of the International Wine and Food Society in London. Very much to our loss she now lives in Houston.

As we arrived at the table, we found that Lou Ann Lipscomb had designed and painted for each of us a wonderful menu, a worthy record of this exceptional meal. Those menus bore the imposing title 'Texas Sesquicentennial Comet Year Celebration with Chateau Latour'.

With generous portions of caviare from the Sacramento River, smoked salmon and other temptations, our host had cooled no less than four different bottles of old champagne. Most of us drink our champagne when it is around ten years old and younger, but there are a number of connoisseurs who like it much older when of course it has become a rarity and hard to find. As expected, the colour becomes darker and the wine tends to lose some of its sparkle, but as it ages, it acquires an attractive biscuity flavour.

Unfortunately, the Moet et Chandon 1949 had given up the unequal struggle, but the other three, Heidsieck Dry Monopole 1945, Piper Heidsieck 1945 and Salon le Mesnil 1949 were all in fine fettle. If anything, perhaps the 1949 Salon was the best of the three, still full of vigour and flavour.

A feature of this meal that was particularly attractive was that each course was served on a different set of fine old china. It began on a high note, delicious cream of broccoli soup with Blandy's Verdelho 1900! Madeira always goes so well with soup and what better than this delectable 1900. When I was a young man, there was plenty of lovely old madeira around and how sad it is that it has now become so scarce. Fresh jumbo lump crab-meat followed and with it our host served a bottle simply called Graves 1875. Considering its age it was remarkable that the colour was so pale and the wine so young. It had come from Christie's so we shall never know its origin, but we were intrigued to know where it could have been kept for it to be in such good condition.

With wild mushrooms from France, we drank Ch. d'Yquem 1911, Comet Year. Although somewhat frail, and it had lost most of its sugar, surprisingly the colour was unusually pale. We wondered how this could be when more famous vintages of the great wine such as 1921, 1929, 1937 and so on are often a dark amber.

It was now the moment for the claret which was to embellish the roast duck and what a range Marvin had decanted for us. The first pair, Latour 1949 and Latour 1945, were extraordinary. Sometimes with the 1949 Latour I have found a little too much acidity for my particular taste, but there was none of that here – it was the best example of this 1949 that I can remember. The 1945 was equally successful, a fine full-bodied robust wine which now must be almost at its best.

The second pair were served with the cheeses – American Blue, Wisconsin Mild Cheddar and Wisconsin Colby. The label Château Latour Comet Year 1911 had engendered expectations, but alas 'anno domini' had stepped in and conquered. Most of the fruit had disappeared and acidity had taken its place. The other claret, the 1900, was of interest because this was the last vintage of Latour to have been made entirely from pre-phylloxera grapes. A 'senior citizen' of course, but there still remained a lovely density of flavour. Unquestionably this could be described as a memorable bottle.

Our feast was by no means over because with a Parker County, Texas Pecan Pie, for which the nuts had come from Marvin's ranch, there were two vintage ports to compare and both of them of the splendid 1945 vintage. Although both had been in Marvin's cellar for the past 15 years, I think the Warre must have been moved around a bit before its final resting place, because the colour was paler than the Taylor and some of the brandy was coming through. The Taylor, dark of colour, masculine and magnificent, was sheer bliss.

The final treat, a cognac, Hine Grand Champagne 1945 evoked memories from my past, for it had been landed, matured in wood and bottled by Harveys of Bristol. When I joined that firm after leaving the army in 1946, I found their purchasing of table wine had been somewhat unimaginative so I set about trying to improve matters. Among the things to which I introduced them were firms such as Hine, Delamain and Frapin for their cognac. English landed cognac was a matter of pride for our fine old wine firms; it was much sought after by connoisseurs and it is sad that it has almost become a thing of the past.

SATURDAY, 8 FEBRUARY

The wind was very cold so we were glad to get into the Museum where we spent most of the morning. Later on, John Roenigk entertained us at a Mexican restaurant where some of the appetizers were so peppery they almost lifted the roofs off our mouths.

SUNDAY, 9 FEBRUARY

Glorious weather at last (this was to be our only really fine day) and how fortunate that it should coincide with our arrival in San Francisco. As this was Jill Hare's first visit to this exciting city, we spent the morning seeing the sights along Fisherman's Wharf where luckily the crowds were less oppressive than usual. We lunched at Aliotos by a window overlooking the rows of fishing boats and it was fortunate for us that the season had just started for the famous Dungeness crab. With this we enjoyed an excellent bottle of chardonnay, 1983 Sonoma Cutrer les Pierres. This winery has only been established for a short while but already it has gained a reputation for its chardonnay, similar in a way to the reputation of Domaine Leflaive of Puligny-Montrachet.

As we were soon to find out, our visit had been organised most efficiently by Caryl Saunders. Although ostensibly a business occasion, the dinner at the Stanford Court Hotel for some 90 people was more like a private party. So many of my old friends were present that it was impossible to talk to them all. The food was unusually good, beginning with the local Olympia oysters as well as caviare. With these we drank some excellent 1981 Louis Roederer Crystal Champagne. The wild mushrooms *à son flan à l'echalotte* were outstanding and amongst these was a local speciality called the hedgehog. As may be imagined all this went very well with the 1975 Les Forts de Latour. This meal was also embellished by some 1979 Lafaurie Peyraguey, a gift from Chateaux and Estates as well as another champagne from Louis Roederer, their Carte Blanche. This, being slightly sweeter, married very well with the dessert. I am aware it is unfashionable to admit one likes sweet champagne, but at the end of a meal, it is often more suitable than a drier wine.

MONDAY, 10 FEBRUARY

In the early morning, we paid a visit to John Hogan, who had moved his business, John Walker & Co., to attractive new premises on Sutter Street. His array of magnums and larger bottles of fine claret and red burgundy was impressive.

The tasting and lunch for the trade and press was another enjoyable occasion because once again a large number of old friends were present.

There is no doubt that the Stanford Court on Nob Hill is a lovely hotel. Directed by Jim Nassikas, it must be one of the finest in the country. As we drank our aperitifs that evening, we watched the cable cars as they clanged their way up and down the steep hills and so were able to capture some of the romance of this scintillating city.

TUESDAY, 11 FEBRUARY

We arrived in Los Angeles just in time to make arrangements for the tasting and dinner at the Biltmore. This hotel, decorated in the style of days gone by, has immensely spacious public rooms and, as it was built in 1923, it is now the oldest on the West Coast.

THURSDAY, 13 FEBRUARY

Alan and Jill Hare were about to leave for Atlanta, Georgia, but on the way to the airport we called at Wally's on Westwood Boulevard, one of the leading retailers. Steve Wallace then drove us to the Beverly Wilshire where who should we see but Christian Bizot, the head of Bollinger Champagne. As Christian said, we have to come to the United States to meet, because the last time had been in New Orleans.

There was a disappointment because Bob Vaillancourt, who had invited me to a lunch at the Beverly Wilshire in honour of Jean-

Michel Cazes, had suddenly had to fly to Mexico. Nevertheless, I found myself in the good hands of Jim Craig and a lot of other old friends. Among them were that illustrious hotelier Hernando Courtwright, Web Hansen whom I have known since about 1960, Bob Myerson and John Masterson. We enjoyed a very good 1980 cabernet sauvignon from Beaulieu Vineyards and two clarets from Bordeaux.

1961 La Gaffelière
Beginning to turn a little brown but it had a lovely bouquet, a fine rich rounded wine, still at its best

1961 Lynch-Bages
A darker colour, full bouquet, strong and powerful and a lovely mouthful of wine

FRIDAY, 14 FEBRUARY

At 8.30 a.m. Steve Wallace collected us to take us to a breakfast he had arranged at the Regency Club so that some of his friends could meet Jean-Michel Cazes. Among those present were Miklos Dora, who looks after the affairs of Mouton-Rothschild in the United States; also Tom Jones who lives in the attractive district of Bel Air where believe it or not the value of land is worth $4 million for 2½ hectares!

Tom has a large property here which includes a valley with steep slopes and in this hilly area he has planted quite recently some 1.4 hectares of vines, which with land of that value can be no more than a hobby. Unfortunately, he has already lost all his *chardonnay* vines through Pearce's disease, a malady which fortunately has not yet been transplanted to Europe.

Our original plan had been to go straight to the Napa Valley, but unexpectedly we had received an invitation from Bipin Desai to attend his tasting of the 1945 vintage and such an invitation was impossible to refuse.

Bipin has been mentioned in these notes before, for he is the remarkable man who organises the finest claret tastings I have ever attended. Among those at which I personally have had the honour to be present have been 132 examples of the 1961 vintage, some 40 or more vintages of Château Latour and a similar number of Château Lynch-Bages. So for me, this range of such an exceptional vintage was a culmination of the most important vintages of bordeaux since the war.

The first half of this event took place that evening at the Century Plaza Hotel and the principal guests were Jean-Michel Cazes and Michael Broadbent. There were many old friends among the 50 or so participants, so for Prue and I it was also a delightful social occasion. Besides the usual French and Canadian enthusiasts, there was a new feature caused by the presence of half a dozen of the great collectors of wine from Germany. It would seem, therefore, that these tastings are attaining some international status.

1945 has always been regarded as one of the great vintages of the century, but because the wines were so hard, it took years before they were ready to drink. Owing to severe frost on three successive days, 1, 2 and 3 May, the crop that year was greatly reduced, but as the weather throughout the following summer was unusually fine, the vines were able to lavish all their bounty on their few remaining bunches of grapes. The only disadvantage was a shortage of rain which caused the grapes to have very thick skins. Thick skins produce a lot of tannin, consequently the 1945s have been very hard and all too slow to develop.

The proceedings began with four wines from Saint Estèphe, none of which was outstanding; in fact this was possibly the weakest group.

The assessments are my own for this 1945 vintage tasting.

Saint Estèphe
Montrose
Medium colour, and showing its age. A curranty bouquet, plenty of fruit, but rather dry and it was marred by its acidity   14.5/20

Lafon-Rochet
Darker colour and a sweeter nose, slightly rounder but this too had a sharpish finish   15/20

Cos d'Estournel
A good colour and a more robust bouquet, there was also more fruit and depth, but it was not outstanding   15.5/20

Calon-Ségur
A darker colour, with a brownish tinge. Although this may have had less elegance, it had quite a lot of fruit and certainly was more robust than the others. The best preserved of these four   16.5/20

After this somewhat disappointing beginning, the red graves were more reassuring.

Red Graves
Haut-Bailly
Very good colour, a nice fruity bouquet, a pleasant taste with even a hint of sweetness   16/20

Haut-Brion

A splendid colour and a much deeper bouquet. Altogether more robust with a fine depth of flavour. Very good indeed 19/20

Latour Haut-Brion

Good colour, something odd about the bouquet, powerful in fact almost aggressive, a wine without much charm 15/20

La Mission Haut-Brion

Very dark colour, a restrained bouquet, a big fruity well balanced wine, still a little firm 16.5/20

Note I remember much better examples of this when I used to stay at the *château*

Domaine de Chevalier

Good colour, pleasant bouquet, medium body, spoilt for me however by a rather fierce finish 15.5/20

Saint Emilion

Ausone

A fine dark colour, a deep attractive bouquet, plenty of fruit, but a trace of acidity at the finish. A little disappointing for so august a *château* 16.5/20

Cheval-Blanc

Dark colour, a fine full bouquet, massive fruit with a delightful sweet finish. One of the finest wines of the whole tasting. 19/20

Note This is interesting because half of the crop developed volatile acidity so this has always been a suspect wine. We were lucky on this occasion

La Gaffelière

Medium colour, a well bred fragrant bouquet, a complete wine with a delightful almost sweet flavour. 17.5/20

Note The attractive quality of this wine was a surprise for all of us

Grand Corbin Despagne

Medium colour, an attractive bouquet, long in the mouth with a very nice flavour. Another pleasant surprise 17.5/20

Clos Fourtet

Good colour, the bouquet a little oxidised, plenty of fruit, but spoilt by a rather astringent finish 14.5/20

I gained the impression that everyone had been looking forward to tasting the pomerols. The colour of this group was noticeably darker than the two previous ones. Although there were a number of highlights among them, there were also some disappointments. Perhaps we had been expecting too much.

The pomerols of 1945 have nostalgic memories for me. Owing to wartime restrictions, the first year we British wine merchants were allowed to travel abroad was 1947. It was then that Edouard Cruse introduced me to the wines of Pomerol and opened my eyes to their possibilities. It was also thanks to him that I was able to buy for my firm Harveys of Bristol the first four wines in the following group. It must be admitted though that they were purchased with a view to consumption within 15 years or so and not at 40 as they were now!

This was at a period when the wines of Pomerol were scarcely known on the English market. So far as I remember most firms restricted themselves merely to buying wines like Nenin or Gazin. Pétrus was almost unheard of, chiefly I suppose because most merchants bought their wines through the big *négociants* in Bordeaux, none of whom handled this wine. I tried in vain to buy the 1945 and 1947 vintages of this *château* and finally tracked the 1949 vintage down through a firm in Libourne. At that time it was considerably less expensive than the four first growths.

Pomerol

La Croix de Gay, bottled by Harveys in Bristol
Dark colour, a slightly 'tarry' bouquet, not a big wine but it had an attractive fruity taste. There was a sharpish finish though, so clearly it has not lasted the course   15/20

L'Enclos
Dark colour, a nice vinous bouquet, plenty of fruit with a fine depth of flavour and it finished well. A success, with plenty of charm   17.5/20

Lafleur
Very dark colour, a fine rich bouquet, still firm and vigorous
                                                                       17.5/20

La Fleur-Pétrus
Dark colour with a hint of tobacco on the nose, a lovely full-bodied, rounded wine. Excellent   18.5/20

La Fleur-Gazin
Pale colour with a suspect bouquet, thin and disappointing 14/20

La Pointe
Good colour, again a somewhat suspect bouquet, medium body with some astringency   14/20

Nenin
Dark colour, pleasant bouquet, sound all through, but not exciting   15.5/20

Pétrus
Magnificent colour, a delightful sweet bouquet, a wonderful wine with enormous depth of flavour which filled the mouth. May continue to improve even further   19.5/20

Trotanoy
Dark colour, a lovely fragrant bouquet, plenty of body with a delightful slightly sweet flavour. Still has some tannin to lose, a remarkable wine   19/20

Clos l'Eglise
Very dark colour, fragrant bouquet, well made, well knit with quite a lot of tannin   18/20

Clos René
Good colour, fruity bouquet, an attractive wine with plenty of charm and a slightly sweet finish. At its best and probably needs drinking   17.5-18/20

Vieux Ch. Certan
Good colour, a bouquet reminiscent of currants, but it lacked charm and did not stand up to its predecessors   15.5/20

FRIDAY, 14 FEBRUARY

The second session began during a downpour of rain which was so bad it could have interrupted the tasting. The large room where this took place was below ground and owing to a broken or overflooded drain above, the water began to cascade down through about a dozen outlets in the ceiling. Happily these were at one side of the room, but the sound of the water descending into numerous buckets tended to distract our attention.

Margaux and Haut-Médoc
Brane-Cantenac
Good colour, an attractive rather opulent bouquet with quite a rich taste. The finish was also good   17.5/20

Cantenac-Brown
Good colour, but a doubtful bouquet. Altogether thinner and sharper than the Brane-Cantenac, disappointing   14/20

Kirwan
Medium colour, a pleasant fragrant bouquet, a nice fruity wine with both sweetness and charm. Probably at its best now. A pleasant surprise   17/20

Malescot
Dark colour, a full attractive bouquet, a wine with a good base, perhaps a little dry and severe on account of the tannin   16/20

Margaux
The wine in one bottle had broken up completely, but the other had a fine colour and an attractive bouquet. Although not outstanding for a first growth, it was well balanced and, as to be expected, well bred   17.5/20

Palmer
Dark colour, an attractive rich bouquet, full-bodied, but spoilt by its astringency, a disappointment   16/20

Rauzan-Gassies
Good colour, an attractive bouquet and a nice depth of flavour but a trace of acidity nevertheless   16/20

Rausan-Ségla
Good colour, a fruity bouquet, a very nice taste, but too much acidity for my liking.   15.5/20
Note A number of the participants preferred this to the Rauzan-Gassies

Latour du Mons, from a magnum
Good colour, a nice flowery bouquet, the flavour rich and attractive. Probably because of its large bottle this had kept better than most, a fine effort for a *cru bourgeois*   17/20

Cantemerle
Medium colour, a pleasant rich bouquet, good fruit and flavour with a nice finish   17/20

La Lagune
Dark colour, fruity bouquet, some fruit, but excessive acidity
14/20

Latour-Carnet
Good colour, a smell of currants, medium to light body, pleasant   15.5/20

There was nothing outstanding in this group, not even the Château Margaux. All the same, there were the two pleasant surprises, the Kirwan and La Tour du Mons.

Saint Julien

Beychevelle

Dark colour, a distinguished bouquet, plenty of fruit and a nice depth of flavour, better than expected   17/20

Branaire-Ducru

Colour turning brown, a 'chocolate' bouquet, good fruit, spoilt by its sharp finish   14.5/20

Ducru-Beaucaillou, from a magnum

Dark coluor, an oldish bouquet, quite a big wine which finished well   16.5/20

Ducru-Beaucaillou, bottle

Similar bouquet and flavour, but with less body. It should be remembered that this *château* had been through a bad period and for me at any rate, it was not until the 1955 vintage that the quality really began to improve   15/20

Gruaud-Larose

Very dark colour, a full fairly powerful bouquet, lots of fruit, well bred with a good depth of flavour. Seemingly more alive than many others   18/20

Langoa-Barton, bottled in Bordeaux

Good colour and bouquet just a little oxidised, still has some fruit   15.5/20

Léoville-Barton, bottled by Corney & Barrow, London

Good colour, a nice cedar nose, very nice fruit and flavour 16.5/20

Léoville-Barton, bottled by Cockburn & Campbell, either in London or Edinburgh

A paler colour, good fruit but some astringency   15/20

Léoville-Lascases

Good colour, a fine fruity nose, still rather firm, but complete with a good depth of flavour. A fine wine   18/20

Léoville-Poyferré

Good colour, a fragrant bouquet, medium body, but some acidity   15/20

Talbot
Dark colour, distinguished bouquet, good fruit and flavour and it finished well. As with the Gruaud-Larose alive and vibrant   18/20

Pauillac
Batailley
Dark colour, a nice rich bouquet, good fruit and a very nice flavour and finish. A success   17.5/20

Grand-Puy-Lacoste, from a magnum
Very dark colour, a doubtful bouquet, plenty of fruit but spoilt by its acidity   15/20

Lafite
The colour too pale, but a distinguished bouquet. Lovely fruit with masses of breeding, handicapped by its acidity   17/20

Latour
Dark colour, a powerful bouquet, a lot of fruit and flavour, probably at its best now. There was some variation between the two bottles; for the better bottle   19/20

Lynch-Bages
Dark colour, good fruit but too much acidity   15/20

Mouton-d'Armailhacq
Good colour, a pleasant chocolatey nose, plenty of fruit spoilt by distinctly sharp finish   14.5/20

Mouton-Rothschild
A lovely dark colour, a fine cedary bouquet, a fine, full-bodied wine, packed with fruit. *Un grand seigneur*   19.5/20

Pichon-Baron
Good colour, lovely bouquet, fine flavour with a nice finish. Better than expected   17.5/20

Pichon-Lalande
Good colour, full bouquet, alive and vibrant, but again some acidity   16.5/20

Three Different Bottlings of Pontet-Canet
Bordeaux Bottling
Good colour, bouquet, showing some age, lots of fruit with some sweetness as well as a trace of acidity   15.5/20

Château Bottling
Good colour, a rather tired bouquet, but a delightfully sweet
flavour, the best of the three   17.5/20

French Bottled
Good colour and bouquet, but sharp and unattractive   14/20

According to my tasting notes at home, this Pontet-Canet used to
be so much better 20 years ago.

Bipin Desai is to be congratulated for assembling together such
an impressive array of wines from what has now become a rare
vintage.

As I was a guest, it ill-behoves me to look a gift horse in the
mouth, but frankly I had expected more from this wide range of
the 1945 vintage. All too frequently the words acidity and astringency crop up in these notes. My general impression was that in a
number of cases the tannin had outlived the fruit.

Had this event taken place some ten years ago, many of the
wines might have presented themselves in a better manner, but
then we did not have the remarkable Bipin Desai on the scene to
organise such an historic event! Ten years ago the tannin might
have been more aggressive and the acidity less evident, so what
one wins on the swings, one loses on the roundabouts!

Unfortunately, in order to catch a plane to San Francisco, we
had to leave before the end of the deliberations, but I have heard
there was some quite lively discussion.

It was teeming with rain as we arrived at Oakland airport, so
the drive to the Napa Valley took longer than usual. On arrival at
Bella Oaks we were just in time for a glass of champagne before
dinner in the company of such old friends as Bob and Dottie
Adamson, Narsai and Veni David and Charles Myers, all of them
vineyard owners. Among the dishes was stuffed racoon, the meat
was very dark and not too attractive, so no wonder no one recognised what it was.

With 'crab Imperial' we drank a nice 1981 Rutherford
Chardonnay, but thereafter all the wines had come from Charlie
Myers' own vineyard. The first was a 1985 Zinfandel, almost
'nouveau' in style, then 1973 Harbor Shenandoah Valley Zinfandel,
a wine with a good depth of flavour and 1982 Harbor Cabernet
Sauvignon, Spring Lane. Finally we had a very good single vineyard
vintage port, the 1970 Quinta do Cachao, the property of Taylor
Fladgate.

SUNDAY, 16 FEBRUARY

The rain had teemed down incessantly all night and the downpour continued through the day. We are used to rain in England, but I have never seen anything so heavy or so continuous as that. Among the guests for dinner that evening were Robert and Margrit Mondavi, Louis and Liz Martini and Jack Davies. Our host Barney Rhodes served his guests' wines in turn. Jack Davies' 1977 Schramsberg Reserve, 1983 Robert Mondavi Chardonnay Reserve and two interesting zinfandels from Louis Martini, the 1979 Sonoma Special Selection Monte Rosso vineyard and a magnum of 1974 Special Selection from the same source. Which we preferred was a matter of choice, the 1979 fresh and charming and the 1974 with greater depth of body and of course more serious in accordance with its fine vintage. The delicious Cockburn 1955 vintage port needs no extended comment.

MONDAY, 17 FEBRUARY

The heavy rain continued and in consequence many roads were blocked and the vineyards were becoming flooded. We had been bidden to lunch at Stag's Leap by Warren and Barbara Winiarski, but since the road was impassable, we met at Mustard's, a nice restaurant on the Napa Road and we only just managed to get through. Warren had brought along with him his excellent 1979 Cabernet Sauvignon, Cask 23.

Bob and Dottie Adamson had planned a big dinner party for us that evening, but half of the guests were unable to come because of the weather. In his usual thoughtful manner, Bob Adamson had set out several wines made from grapes from his own vineyard, but which had been vinified and bottled by different wine makers. There were a couple of chardonnays totally different from each other and three cabernet sauvignons all of the same vintage, but all with their own individuality. One has to come to California to find comparisons like this.

TUESDAY, 18 FEBRUARY

The weather had been so overcast that this was the first time I had even seen either a cloud or the sky since we left Los Angeles. This storm turned out to be the worst for over 100 years with a general rainfall of 55 cm and in places up to 70 cm. The Russian River had overflowed and flooded the village of Guerneville where the entire population had had to be evacuated and only 16 km from Bella Oaks, a part of the town of Napa was under 60 cm of water.

Joe and Alice Heitz were flooded out, so our invitation to dine with them had to be cancelled, nor were they able to get to Bella

Oaks. By luck, Milt and Barbara Eisele of Eisele Vineyard, Calistoga, were able to join us. In the absence of Joe and Alice, Barney produced the three 1981 cabernets recently released from the Heitz Vineyard.

1981 Bella Oaks, bottled June 1985
The colour brilliant but not very dark, the wine on the light side but very fruity and ready now

1981 Heitz Cabernet Sauvignon, the regular bottling
A darker colour, full of fruit and flavour with good depth. A relatively inexpensive wine of impressive quality

1981 Martha's Vineyard, bottled April 1985
Very dark colour packed full of attractive flavour, still very immature

WEDNESDAY, 19 FEBRUARY

While the downpour had lessened, it was still raining most of the time. Owing to the weather, Louis Martini had brought a vehicle which stood high enough off the road to negotiate reasonable flooding. In fact, on our way to dine with Marsai and Veni David in Berkeley, we passed extensive flooding in the area around Napa. During the journey, Louis told us that 24 hectares of his vines at Healdsberg were under water. He added that he had been receiving telephone calls from all over the country, but in reality, the vines had suffered little damage.

The dinner proved to be a meal of gastronomic interest for to begin with there were three kinds of caviare which Narsai and his son had prepared at different times and with different methods. With these he served two vintages of Schramsberg, the 1975 and the 1973. There were mixed views, but because of its greater depth, I personally preferred the older wine. Then came some very good sturgeon, a fish one seldom encounters in England. This sturgeon had come either from Washington State or Oregon and this accounts for the availability of caviare in this neighbourhood. With this we compared two vintages of chardonnay from Sterling.

The vegetables with the veal chops were most unusual, snow peas and sugar snap, a new kind of pea bred from snow peas and beans; there was also some very thinly sliced green cactus. All of this had been prepared by Narsai who is a noted chef with his own television programme from San Francisco. Had I been Louis Martini, I would have been proud of the three cabernet sauvignons. First of all, the legendary 1968 vintage, a dark colour with a lovely flavour which I would have mistaken for a much younger wine. The 1958 vintage had a paler colour and to begin with I thought it had too much acidity, but then all sorts of delightful flavours began to break through. The last wine, the 1940 vintage was remarkable, a good colour and fine all through. Here indeed was an example of how well good California wine will mature in bottle.

THURSDAY, 20 FEBRUARY

A delicious lunch with Bob and Margrit Mondavi who live on a hilltop in what can only be described as a kind of fairy palace. Beautifully designed, there are splended views in all directions and there can be few prettier places than the Napa Valley. However, on this occasion all one could see down below were flooded vineyards. The other guests were Milt Eisele and Mr and Mrs Jay Corley, the proprietors of the Monticello Vineyard, in fact we began the meal with a nice 1983 chardonnay from that vineyard. Thereafter the wines were Bob's, a very drinkable 1981 Pino Noir Reserve, and Opus One 1981 and Opus One 1979. Bob pointed out that he had made his 1981 to be both ready to drink early and to keep for many years and it was certainly very good to drink now. The 1979 had a darker colour, a bigger wine perhaps with more tannin. Although very different both wines were extremely good.

At seven o'clock at Bella Oaks the guests began to arrive for an anonymous tasting of 1966 clarets and those participants were the Heitzes, Tim and Dorothy Mondavi, Andy Lawler and two people from Christian Brothers, Brother David Brennan and Ron Batori, the Vice President. The Cheval-Blanc emerged as easily the best and full details of this tasting are included in the chapter about the 1966 vintage.

FRIDAY, 21 FEBRUARY

At long last, the rain had stopped and the sun even was beginning to break through. Joe Heitz called to take us to see the considerable damage the storm had done to his recently acquired vineyard alongside Conn Creek. The torrent had changed the course of this small stream and had swept away two of his reservoirs and valuable equipment had been washed to the bottom of the creek; in addition half a road had been eroded away. The general damage to the flooded vineyards had not been too serious but those growers whose vines were close to the rivers and creeks had suffered extensively and, of course, since it was an 'Act of God' there would be no claims for insurance. The growers' lot is not always as happy as it would seem.

11
BORDEAUX
March 1986 – The Final Fling

A few comments on the vintage of 1985. This recent succession of fine vintages is becoming almost embarrassing, so much so that the good ones at the end of the last decade have now been out-shone by what has been going on in the 1980s.

Admittedly, the present decade began on a somewhat muted note, but although light and short lived, many of the 1980s have developed early and have been delightful to drink. The good quality of the unfortunate 1981 vintage has been eclipsed by the brilliance of the 1982s, and so far it has had little opportunity to spread its wings, but its turn will come. The even better 1983s have also been overshadowed by the 1982s, the latter made from very ripe grapes, a phenomenom hitherto virtually unheard of in Bordeaux, a fact which helps to make it a kind of freak vintage.

The failure of the pomerols and the Saint Emilions helped to give the 1984s a poor reputation, but were it not for the spate of successes from Bordeaux, the médocs of 1984 would have been more appreciated; one day these too will find a useful place on the market, meanwhile they are difficult to sell.

Now we have *un embarras de richesses*, the Comet Year of 1985. In order to form an accurate assessment of a new vintage it is better to wait until the wine is about a year old, however a fairly good impression of its potential can be formed during the spring following the harvest. First of all I think the vital statistics may be of interest here.

In spite of slightly less favourable conditions than in either 1982 or 1983 the flowering of the vines was successful. The month of July was warm with a little more rain than usual with August cool and dry. The first half of September was warm and sunny with the second even finer and scarcely a drop of rain fell during the entire month. As a matter of interest during the past

30 years there have only been four Septembers which were equally warm, 1958, 1959, 1961 and 1964 but none of these was so dry as 1985. The original date for the harvest had been 23 September. However, the grapes had not ripened sufficiently so this was postponed until the end of the month. As the magnificent weather continued throughout the harvest, the grapes were ripe and in perfect condition.

It was not difficult, therefore, to predict an exceptional vintage. There were problems during the fermentation on account of the heat, but those were easily overcome by the *châteaux* with up-to-date cooling systems. The colour of the 1985 is dark and intense, the bouquet exceptional. The structure of the wine is good but different from that of 1982 when if anything the grapes were over-ripe. The style and quality is similar to that of 1983 and perhaps even finer. The crop was very large with some over-production especially from the younger vines. Rigid elimination of the less good *cuves* was essential and those proprietors who were not zealous over the selection of their *cuves* were not so successful.

These are some of the wines I was able to taste during a very short visit:

Richotey, Fronsac
An amazing colour, not much bouquet yet, good fruit and structure

La Dauphine, Fronsac
Promising bouquet, very good fruit and body

Canon de Brem, Canon-Fronsac
Lovely fruit and body with some depth

Canon Moueix, Canon-Fronsac
A lovely mouthful of wine with depth

Grand Pontet, Saint Emilion
Pleasant bouquet, full of charm and fairly forward

Le Prieuré, Saint Emilion
Well made with a good flavour

Belair, Saint Emilion
Bouquet closed up, marvellous fruit and flavour with a fine finish, excellent

Rouget, Pomerol
Medium body with plenty of fruit

Le Gay, Pomerol
Beautiful bouquet, a splendid wine with an excellent finish

Haut-Batailley, Pauillac
Good colour, medium body and full of flavour

Grand-Puy-Lacoste, Pauillac
Dark colour, bouquet still closed, a fine well made wine

Ducru-Beaucaillou, Saint Julien
Very dark colour, rich well bred bouquet, a fine concentrated flavour, plenty of tannin, full of promise

Gloria, Saint Julien
Pleasant bouquet, not a big wine, but has depth and a nice flavour

St Pierre, Saint Julien
Very dark colour, bouquet still closed, well balanced with good concentration, rather good

Les Ormes de Pez, Saint Estèphe
Good colour, attractive with a nice finish

Haut-Bages Averous, Pauillac
Splendid colour, more depth with a fine flavour

Lynch-Bages, Pauillac
A splendid colour, a great mouthful of wine. This is a beauty

Potensac, Ordonnac
Very dark colour, ripe bouquet, lots of attractive flavour, rather good

Clos du Marquis, Saint Julien
Very dark colour, a good 'solid' wine with a good finish, one to buy

Léoville-Lascases, Saint Julien
Very dark colour, well bred bouquet, lovely style and breeding, extraordinary quality, will make a great bottle

Pichon-Lalande, Pauillac
Colour almost black, concentrated nose, masses of fruit, considerable depth of flavour, a really fine wine

The wines which stood out from the above were: Belair, Le Gay, Grand-Puy-Lacoste, Ducru-Beaucaillou, Lynch-Bages, Léoville-Lascases and Pichon-Lalande. One could not fail to receive a favourable impression and can only hope the price of this vintage will not get out of hand as it did with the 1982.

12
FINE CLARET
Some 1966s

After the 1961 vintage, which is in a class all on its own, 1966 is considered to be the best of the decade. The problem with 1966 has always been an excess of tannin and in consequence some of the finer wines of this good vintage are only now becoming enjoyable to drink.

On account of its reputation, it was hoped and indeed expected that once the tannin had worn off, many of the 1966s would turn out very well. Thus for years it has been a vintage we have been looking forward to. Unfortunately it does not seem to have happened quite like that, because, as may be seen from the following tasting notes, too large a number of the well-known *châteaux* are showing more acidity than is altogether desirable.

The following notes have been compiled from three tastings, two of them in 1984 and the last in 1986.

The London Tasting, 18 October 1984, Joseph Berkmann
at Les Jardin des Gourmets

L'Angelus, Saint Emilion
Medium colour, good fruit, pleasant taste, almost ready

Grand-Barrail-Lamarzelle-Figeac, Saint Emilion
Dark colour, good fruit, medium body, some acidity and could have more charm

Nenin, Pomerol
Dark colour, fairly full-bodied, pleasant, almost ready

Smith-Haut-Lafite, Graves
Dark colour, good fruit, medium body, some acidity and could have more charm

Pape-Clément, Graves
Good colour, good fruit and flavour, well balanced, rather good

Domaine de Chevalier, Graves
Medium body, good flavour, rather nice

Haut-Bailly, Graves
Good colour, plenty of fruit, good flavour, well balanced, very good

La Mission Haut-Brion, Graves
Very dark colour, a huge wine, packed with fruit and promise. Not at all ready, but one of the best

Fourcas-Hosten, Listrac
Dark colour, fruity and full-bodied with lots of flavour, but less distinguished. Still backward

Gloria, Saint Julien
Medium body, a delightful flavour, very good

Cantemerle, Macau
Medium colour, has fruit but is too sharp and lacks charm

Croizet-Bages, Pauillac
Paler colour, good flavour and nicer than the Cantemerle

Mouton-Baron-Philippe, Pauillac
Good colour, fruit and body

Batailley, Pauillac
Good colour, lively and rather nice

Haut-Batailley, Pauillac
Sharpish and lacking charm

Lynch-Bages, Pauillac
Dark colour, full-bodied, full-flavoured, very good in spite of a suspicion of acidity at the finish

Talbot, Saint Julien
Good colour, well made and rather nice

Branaire-Ducru, Saint Julien
Dark colour, lots of fruit and a nice finish

Beychevelle, Saint Julien
Dark colour, lots of fruit and body, well balanced and very good

Giscours, Labarde
Medium colour, plenty of fruit, pleasant

Malescot, Margaux
Good colour, more feminine with an attractive flavour and plenty of depth

Calon-Ségur, Saint Estèphe
Medium colour, good fruit and flavour, very good

Léoville-Poyferré, Saint Julien
Good colour, has fruit and body, but spoilt by a sharpish finish

Durfort-Vivens, Margaux
Good fruit, well balanced, pleasant finish

Lascombes, Margaux
Paler colour, trace of acidity, quite nice

Brane-Cantenac, Margaux
Good colour, medium body, a little disappointing

Cos d'Estournel, Saint Estèphe
Good colour, plenty of fruit but still very hard

Gruaud-Larose, Saint Julien
Good colour, masses of flavour, fine depth and very good

Pichon-Lalande, Pauillac
Good colour, complete, solid, excellent

Léoville-Lascases, Saint Julien
Medium colour, has quality and finesse, nevertheless a little disappointing

Ducru-Beaucaillou, Saint Julien
Good colour, plenty of depth, lovely fruit and flavour, very good

Palmer, Margaux
Dark colour, deep, full-bodied, rounded and delightful, the best of all

Margaux, Margaux
Dark colour, medium to thin body, disappointing

Latour, Pauillac
Dark colour, great depth of flavour, has weight and tremendous quality, still very backward

Lafite, Pauillac
Brownish colour, severe, lacks generosity

While in most cases the tannin had diminished, in at least nine instances out of the above 35 there was an excess of acidity and the result was disappointing. Of course, with wine of this age account must be taken of the natural variation between one bottle and another and also how well the wine has been stored, but this proportion is higher than I, for one, would have expected.

The Knoxville, Tennessee Tasting, 10 November 1984 at the home of Dr F. Killifer

Cos Labory, Saint Estèphe
Browning a little, medium body, but is too sharp

Langoa-Barton, Saint Julien
Browning, medium body, also rather sharp

La Lagune, Ludon
Good colour, slightly acetic bouquet, has some depth, but again too much acidity

Montrose, Saint Estèphe
Good colour and bouquet, a lovely flavour with a good finish

Lynch-Bages, Pauillac
Complex if earthy nose, medium body, a lot of fruit, with a hint of sweetness, most attractive

Léoville-Lascases, Saint Julien
Good colour, a rather muted bouquet, well bred with plenty of fruit, but a trace of acidity

Ducru-Beaucaillou, Saint Julien
Medium colour, an intense perfumed bouquet, good fruit with an attractive flavour, the best so far

Margaux, Margaux
Good colour, good if subdued bouquet, good fruit with some depth, marred by its acidity

Lafite, Pauillac
Medium colour, a trace of sharpness on the bouquet, plenty of fruit and flavour, but there is too much acidity

Haut-Brion, Graves
Good colour, a rather pointed bouquet, plenty of fruit and flavour, but again too much acidity

The results on this second occasion were even more disappointing, there were only three really good wines out of the eleven. As it turned out, five of the *châteaux* were represented at both of the early tastings and with four of these *châteaux* the results were consistent – disappointing that is for Léoville-Lascases, Margaux and Lafite and very good for Ducru-Beaucaillou. In so far as Lynch-Bages is concerned, there was a hint of acidity at the London tasting, but none whatsoever in Knoxville. This can be attributed perhaps to indifferent storage, because at a tasting in Los Angeles in April 1985 when 38 vintages of Lynch-Bages were tasted, two bottles of the Lynch-Bages 1966 had been opened and both were in excellent condition.

The Bella Oaks Tasting, Napa Valley, 20 February at the home of Dr B.L. Rhodes

Mouton-Rothschild, Pauillac
Good colour, a delightful bouquet, medium body with a pleasant finish in spite of a little acidity

Palmer, Margaux
Good colour, fruity bouquet, nice flavour and a good finish, but not outstanding. This may have been owing to a poor example

Haut-Brion, Graves
Dark colour, pleasant bouquet, a lovely big, quite powerful wine with a fine finish

Ausone, Saint Emilion
Good colour, a full bouquet, soft, sweet and rounded, rather good

Pétrus, Pomerol
Very dark colour, but a little browner, a fine rich bouquet, full-bodied and well made, a lovely wine

Latour, Pauillac
Dark colour, a rich bouquet, good fruit, but still some tannin – spoilt by its acidity

Cheval-Blanc, Saint Emilion
Dark colour, fine bouquet, still some tannin, but rich, rounded and splendid

Lafite, Pauillac
Good colour, with a brownish tinge, elegant, distinguished and well made, but not outstanding

Margaux, Margaux
Vinous bouquet, rather lean and it could have more charm

Ducru-Beaucaillou, Saint Julien
Good colour, a roasted bouquet, fine and robust with a good finish

All of the wines of this last group had been bought through Christie's during the previous three years and were tasted anonymously.

The Cheval-Blanc was easily the most popular with the group, after that in second place equal came Ausone, Margaux and Latour.

13

DOMAINE BOTTLED WHITE BURGUNDY

Apart from champagne, it must be admitted, I suppose, that in so far as we British 'stick in the mud' wine enthusiasts are concerned, our two main addictions are white burgundy and red bordeaux. There are of course diversions, or dare one say 'disloyalties', but in the main we seem to favour those two particular wines.

Quite deservedly, an enormous fuss has always been made over the red wines from Bordeaux. The evidence is there for all to see; lectures, articles, books galore and still it goes on. Thanks to all this information good claret is relatively easy to select, but it is by no means so easy to find good white burgundy.

There have of course been changes in the trade over the past 50 years and among the chief advances for red bordeaux have been the obligatory *château* bottling and the general improvement in oenology. It is highly unlikely we shall ever see again such tannic vintages as those of 1928, 1945 or even 1961, nor let us hope such disastrous years as those of 1963, 1965 and 1968. On the whole Bordeaux has not let us down.

How sad it is that the same cannot be said of red burgundy where over production and other reasons have helped to diminish the over-all quality of the red wine. Some allowance must of course be made for this district, situated as it is so much further north and so far away from the mellowing influence of the sea; certainly the climatic conditions are more severe and consequently the great vintages less frequent.

Well I remember before the war when wine lovers used to lay down red burgundy as enthusiastically as they did claret; the devotees of burgundy were fantastically loyal to what at least one of my friends used to call 'the true faith'. It was of course a different 'animal' in those days, but that is another story. Unless one includes 1976, there have been only two really good vintages in the past decade, 1971 and 1978, but it does seem that few enthusiasts are laying down red burgundy, whereas there is a host of supporters for claret. For instance, the new man on the scene, the investor, is only interested in red bordeaux.

Although at least some steps are being taken to retrieve 'the red situation' in Burgundy, the bright star in the firmanent on the Côte d'Or is surely the white wine; maybe not everyone will agree, but for many of us this is the finest white wine in the world. Happily, and again there may be some who will disagree, neither the quality nor the reputation of white burgundy has been allowed to deteriorate in the same way as it has in the case of red. Indeed it is safe to say that thanks to greatly improved methods of oenology and generally better equipment, the white wine from Burgundy is as good now, if not better, than it has ever been before.

There has certainly been a great improvement in Britain since white burgundy has been bottled on the spot. Until fairly recently both red and white wine was despatched in cask from Burgundy and Bordeaux and was subject first of all to the hazards of the weather while in transit. Then on arrival in England, all too frequently there were strikes by dockers as well as the ordeal of passage through Customs where wine was treated like any ordinary commodity and no topping up of the ullaged casks was permitted. So no wonder that by the time the poor stuff was put into bottle a lot of it, and especially the white wine, was oxidised.

The majority of English bottlers took a pride in their work and much of it was excellent, but the dice were loaded against them. Now that it is bottled at the *domaine* or at least in Burgundy, those particular worries can be forgotten.

Broadly speaking, white burgundy can be placed in two categories: the wines from the *négociants*, some of which are exceedingly good, and those from the *domaines*, or single growers. Most of the wines from the *négociants* have necessarily to be blends because they have to satisfy the demand of a world-wide market. The quality then depends largely upon the reliability of the firm in question; while a number of *négociants* are first rate, others definitely are not so good. *Négociants* claim that through blending the faults of individual wines are eradicated and this may be true. In any case, however good it may be, a blended wine does not usually have the individuality and the character of one from a single *domaine*. It must be admitted that the quality of the latter is dependent on skill and other factors which can vary from grower to grower and in addition the quantity available is usually limited.

One of the subtle changes that have been taking place on the Burgundian scene is the emergence of the individual grower both for red and white wine, but more perhaps for the latter. Instead of, as in the past, selling their produce to the *négociants* when very young, a number of important growers have installed up-to-date equipment and are handling the wine themselves, incidentally thereby making more money. If at times their produce is hard to find, they do none the less supply wine with plenty of character and originality.

On the whole, the producers of white burgundy seem to fare better with their vintages than those for the red and this has certainly been the case over the past decade. For instance, when the climatic conditions have not been really suitable for the *pinot noir* vines, they are often more favourable for the *chardonnay*. It is of course the recent vintages of white burgundy which are primarily of interest. Both 1978 and 1979 were very good, especially the former, 1980 was average with, however, a few fine wines; 1981 was very good an 1982 still better.

Since the excellent 1978s have disappeared from the market and the 1979s are now somewhat scarce, Jasper Morris, the English representative of Comte Lafon, that fine grower in Meursault, arranged an anonymous tasting for a few of us of some of the more recent vintages. Incidentally, among those tasting was a visitor to London, Dr B.L. Rhodes, who planted the vines of Martha's Vineyard in the Napa Valley and who is reputed to have one of the finest palates on the West Coast, or anywhere else for that matter.

No 1983s were included; there are notes on this fine if irregular vintage in the chapter on the visit to the Côte d'Or in April 1985.

1980 Meursault, Clos de la Barre, Comte Lafon
A good but perhaps a rather obvious bouquet, good fruit, well balanced with a pleasing finish, rather good   Placing Equal 4th

1982 Puligny-Montrachet, Les Combettes, Jacques Prieur
A fairly restrained bouquet, perhaps a little more depth than the Clos de la Barre, as well as a little sweeter, fresh, fruity and fairly forward   Placing Equal 4th

1982 Meursault, les Perrières, Jacques Prieur
Fresh bouquet, fruity with a pleasant finish   Placing Equal 7th

1980 Puligny-Montrachet, les Combettes, Leflaive
Quite a big wine with masses of fruit, delightful flavour, fine quality   Placing 2nd

1981 Puligny-Montrachet, Leflaive
Bouquet fresh and fruity, a nice clean wine, fairly full-bodied and well balanced   Placing 3rd

1981 Puligny-Montrachet, Clavoillon, Leflaive
Rounded with lots of fruit and flavour, easy to taste and rather good   Placing 6th

1981 Chassagne-Montrachet, Marc Colin
The bouquet less attractive than some of the others, quite full-bodied though, in fact quite a mouthful and a nice finish. Good even though it was placed seventh   Placing Equal 7th

1980 Puligny-Montrachet les Pucelles, Leflaive
A powerful wine with heaps of fruit and flavour, first rate quality
Placing 1st

1981 Puligny-Montrachet les Folatières, René Monnier
Medium body, less charm and quite high acidity   Placing 9th

1981 Chassagne-Montrachet Morgeot, Marc Colin
Quite full-bodied, but much harder and has less charm
Placing 10th

The order of placing was pretty well unanimous and it was as well perhaps the labels had been hidden, otherwise one might have suspected we all had a bias towards the Domaine Leflaive. As it was, the two examples of the 1980 vintage, of admittedly not quite so good a year, may have benefited from that extra twelve months in bottle. It was odd, however, that we all preferred the straight 1981 Puligny-Montrachet to the 1981 Puligny-Montrachet Clavoillon.

14
POMEROL WITH A LITTLE HISTORY

How encouraging it is to see that a genuine interest is at last being taken in the wines of Pomerol, a district hitherto so neglected by the English trade. I personally was lucky to be introduced to these delightful wines soon after I had left the army.

By now, it will be forgotten how for the first two years after the war while all our cellars were still empty, all the Government permitted us to buy from Bordeaux was some very ordinary stuff under a neutral label and at an unduly elevated price. Although grossly overpriced by the Bordelais *négociants* at least it was an improvement from the Algerian red which we had been glad to accept after the successes of the Eighth Army in North Africa.

It may also be forgotten that no one was allowed to leave the country until 1947. Food rationing was still very much in force, so you can imagine my pleasure to be able to go to France once again and to eat some good food. My previous visit to Bordeaux had been during the summer of 1939 when war was imminent.

As far as wine is concerned the Germans had behaved correctly during the Occupation, the cellars in Bordeaux had not been emptied and there were still some good bottles around. Some of the shortages were still severe, for example I saw quite a lot of the quite good 1943 vintage still in barrel owing to the acute lack of bottles and a scarcity of corks. It was a fairly light vintage in any case and after some four years in wood some of those poor 1943s had lost much of their fruit and colour.

When I paid my respects to the all important firm of Cruse on the Quai des Chartrons, Edouard Cruse invited me to spend a day with him in Pomerol, a district of which I was woefully ignorant; he warned me I was going to be surprised. We duly set out, probably in one of those rather spectacular pre-war Citroëns and in the company of Monsieur Giovetti, a well-known broker for the district.

The morning was spent visiting various *châteaux*, in fact most of them were little more than farmhouses of one kind or another whose names until then I had never heard. Among them were La Grave Trigant de Boisset, La Croix de Gay (and what a 1947 this was), L'Enclos, La Conseillante, Gazin and Lafleur. A table had been reserved for us at La Plaisance in Saint Emilion and to prove his point, Edouard had brought along with him to accompany our lunch a bottle each of 1929 La Grave Trigant de Boisset and 1929 La Croix de Gay. At that time the heavenly 1929 vintage was at its summit and such was their perfection, I still remember those bottles distinctly. Of course I became completely hooked and, packed with tannin as they were, I ordered hogs-heads of all the above mentioned of the 1945 vintage as well as L'Enclos, Lafleur, Gazin and Le Gay.

With my appetite whetted I returned the following year to buy the 1947 vintage of all these wines and in addition Vieux Château Certan, L'Evangile and La Fleur-Pétrus. In my opinion 1947 had been the finest vintage for the wines of Pomerol since the war and remained so until the 1982s came along. Even so, with all the advantages of improved vinification and so on, the 1982s will have a job to surpass the quality of those lovely 1947s.

It is really only during the last ten years or so that the district of Pomerol has become more generally accepted and one of those who have been preaching the gospel is John Armit, the former managing director of that fine firm in the City of London, Corney & Barrow. In December 1985 he arranged a tasting for a few Pomerol enthusiasts of some of the better wines of the 1981 vintage. 1981 was in fact a good all round vintage, but it has been overshadowed by the glamour of the 1982s and all the hoopla that went with them.

Some of the Pomerols of 1982, an anonymous tasting

Latour-Pomerol
A full quite rich bouquet, a fine full-bodied wine with a lot of character

La Fleur-Pétrus
A lovely bouquet, rounded and concentrated, a good mouthful of flavour, a fine wine, with tremendous style

Trotanoy
Very good bouquet, a lot of fruit and well balanced, a little less rounded than the La Fleur-Pétrus

Pétrus
A splendid rich bouquet, full-bodied with a marvellous flavour

Vieux Château Certan

Attractive bouquet, medium body, but more tannic, lacking depth and charm

Gazin

Attractive bouquet, good fruit and flavour, medium body

L'Evangile

Paler colour, good fruit and body, still immature, a fine wine nevertheless

Lafleur

Medium colour, lots of fruit and a lovely flavour

La Conseillante

Fine bouquet, a huge wine, full of fruit and concentration, with perhaps just a slight lack of elegance. This should make a fine bottle all the same

La Grave Trigant de Boisset

Attractive bouquet, medium body with a lot of fruit and such a delightful flavour

Certan de May

Lovely bouquet, well balanced with masses of fruit and fine flavour, a lovely wine

With the possible exception of two wines, the quality throughout was excellent and those enthusiasts who have been wise enough to put some of these wines aside will not regret it.

15

HARD NUTS TO CRACK!

I feel sure there is no need here to go into all the physical details of tannin, but this new phrase 'tender tannin', new at least to me, which has been used in connection with the 1982 vintage, has led to some thoughts on the subject of tannin in general.

Within my own experience there have been quite a number of very stern and austere vintages, which have taken far too long to develop. Beginning with the decade of the 1920s, there were at least two. First of all there was that good year of 1926, but for all too long the wine was as hard as nails. Well I remember, because my pre-war firm Block, Grey & Block had bought a number of 1926s and as late as 1939 could not sell them because of their tannin, although doubtless later on there was little difficulty in disposing of those wines during the wartime shortage. Those 1926s, originally so dry and resistant, did not really begin to come round until the vintage was nearly 30 years old and then like the sun beginning to peep through the clouds, at last the sweetness and charm began to emerge through the layer of tannin. The Latour which had been so austere in its early stages, began to blossom around 1966 and has continued to improve ever since. Of all the vintages lying in the private cellar below the *château*, this has been one of my favourites.

Another extremely tough nut to crack was the notoriously severe 1928 and that took 30 or more years to mature, by which time many people had given up all hope and had drunk up all their remaining bottles. One of my roles during my days with John Harvey & Sons was to sell wine to the Colleges at Oxford and Cambridge. Before the war, King's College, Cambridge had laid down a large quantity of the 1928 Latour, and in the early 1960s I remember the Fellow of the College in charge of the cellar complaining it was undrinkable; so it was. I recommended that he kept it and hope he did.

In order to celebrate my eightieth birthday in June 1984, the proprietors of Château Latour gave a splendid dinner for 50 people at the *château*. The two vintages of Latour which were served were 1961, of which more later, and the 1928. The latter was simply magnificent and, as a number of authorities present remarked, the finest wine they had ever tasted. Wonderful as it now is, from a practical point of view, one should not have to wait over 50 years before a wine becomes enjoyable to drink!

The next hard vintage was 1937, for which there had been such high hopes in the early days. When I was in Bordeaux in July 1939 the *négociants* were enthusiastic and predicted a great future for it; this was wishful thinking no doubt after a decade of such dreadful vintages. As it happened, I believe most of that vintage was consumed by the Germans during their occupation of France. Certainly there was little left to be shipped to England after the war and that was just as well. According to my tasting notes, the few 1937s in my possession only became ready to drink once they had reached about 30 years of age, but by that time in too many cases the tannin had outlasted the fruit, so their early promise was never fulfilled.

The 1945s followed much along the same lines; it was a fine vintage, but overwhelmed by its excessive tannin. As recently as 1981 the 1945 Latour was still backward and to quote my notes from the last time I tasted it 'a concentrated typical Latour bouquet, a glorious flavour, true Pauillac. Still some tannin, but the wine improved enormously after half an hour in the glass.' A year later, however, when I had an opportunity to compare the Mouton against Haut-Brion, both of them great bottles, there was no mention of tannin. Regrettably it is not possible to expand much further except that with great good fortune I still have one or two magnums of Talbot and they are splendid. Patience is rewarded, but all the same I have had to wait some 40 years to enjoy this wine.

The fine 1952s were completely overshadowed by the charm of the 1953s and only now are they fulfilling their early promise. I had bought the 1952 Latour long before I became associated with the *château* and the wine remained so hard and obstinate that some ten years ago, stupidly as it now transpires, I sold the five cases in my cellar. Now, of course, the wine is remarkable, powerful and masculine admittedly, but with so much fruit and such a lovely flavour – how I regret my lack of patience!

Most of the 1957s were severe and unattractive to say the least and I would place them more or less in the same category as the 1937s. Had it not been for all that tannin, this vintage might have been a little more amenable. Even so, the 1957s suffered a dreadful handicap, for the vines had only had a year in which to recover from the frost of February 1956, the worst for 200 years. Lynch-

Bages was among the better wines.

Another bird of the same feather is 1961 – after a hot summer, the grapes had less juice than usual in relation to their skins and the latter were simply crammed with tannin. Most claret lovers are at least old enough to be cognisant of the quality of this great vintage. Of course, after 25 years some 1961s are ready to drink, but others certainly remain too hard to display their full splendour. For instance, it has been a shame so far to drink the Latour which faces a fantastic future, similar perhaps to that of the 1928 Latour. What more can one say than that!

The other tannic vintage of the 1960s is 1966. While the tannin of some of the 1966s had begun to wear off, not all of them have emerged as well as we had hoped. In its place, in a number of cases, some unwelcome acidity has become evident.

During all these years there has been a slow but steady improvement in the culture of the wine coupled with the advance in the art of vinification, so never again, it seems, shall we see such exceptionally hard vintages as 1945, 1937 and 1928. For example, hard as they were, because of the advance in oenology, etc. since the end of the war, the 1961s were not quite so resistant as they might well have been. Even then all was still not resolved, because after some 15 years we are still waiting for some of the fine 1970s to come round and unveil their charm. Hopefully in this case the tannin will not outlast the fruit.

The most recent tannic vintage is 1975 which, although I was not among them, was considered by a number of people to be superior to 1970. There is indeed a lot of tannin in the 1975s, but that tannin does not seem so 'lethal' as that of say 1945 or 1928.

Had it not been for the improvement of oenology generally, the 1982 vintage could well have been harder than it is. In fact, it is the first time I have heard of the term 'tender tannin'. Thanks to the grapes being riper than usual when they were gathered, one could actually enjoy drinking one or two of the lesser 1982s in their extreme youth – up to date, a rare experience.

One of the burdens the *châteaux* proprietors had to bear in the past was the fear of rain, both before and during the harvest, resulting in rotten grapes and the rot could spread quickly. Thanks to the new special sprays for the vines which eradicate much of the risk of *pourriture*, the growers can delay the picking until their grapes are really ripe and with fully ripe grapes the tannin is not quite so aggressive.

It may help here to quote an example which is pertinent to Château Latour, known always for the slow development of its wine. During the past few years certain authorities have been asserting that since the recent vintages from this *château* have appeared less tannic, perhaps the manner of making the wine has been changed? In fact, there have been no changes whatsoever in the way the wine is being made, the difference is that thanks to these modern sprays, it has been possible to leave the grapes on the vines until they were riper than in the past, hence the softer style of wine.

Now that the *château* proprietors have the advantage of these special sprays one can hope perhaps that the wine of future vintages will resemble more that of 1982 rather than that of 1970. There may thus be fewer hard nuts to crack than in the days gone by.

16

A BRIEF SURVEY OF THE DECADES OF THIS CENTURY

It is a sobering thought to realise I have had a personal association with seven of these decades, because when I joined the wine trade in 1934 the only claret we had to sell were the vintages of the 1920s.

The greater part of this survey was written in 1981 and before the good years from 1981 to 1985 had come into being. At that time it looked to me as though the 1970s had the makings of 'the decade of the century', but as things are developing, that of the 1980s looks like being a strong contender for this title.

There are now four vintages left from 1986 to 1989 inclusive when, goodness knows, anything can happen to the weather. Even so, the odds are in favour of better quality owing to the improvement in viticulture and oenology.

Some fresh horror may raise its ugly head, but for the time being at least we must be grateful for the new sprays which seem so successfully to combat the *pourriture*, that long standing scourge in the vineyards of Bordeaux. Alternating rain and heat have always caused the grapes to rot and frequently have forced the growers to pick their grapes before they were altogether ripe. Thanks to these sprays, the grapes can be left on the vines even in rainy weather until they are much riper and that can make a considerable difference to the ultimate quality of the wine.

It is forgotten how desperate was the crisis for the *châteaux* proprietors and even of the first growths at the beginning of the century. At Château Latour, for instance, the *domaine* could scarcely pay its way and so serious was the financial situation that the owners, and they were not alone in this, were forced to make an unfavourable contract with some *négociants* in Bordeaux to sell the five crops from 1906 to 1910 at a fixed price. In addition, such was still the lack of confidence in the new grafted vines, that they had to agree not to plant any more grafts until the termination of that contract.

This meant that no replanting with the new grafted vines could begin seriously at Latour until at least 1910 and was soon to be interrupted by the outbreak of war in 1914. Meanwhile the poor pre-phylloxera vines continued to die all too quickly.

In order to produce fine quality in any good vineyard, a healthy proportion of old vines is essential, but these adverse circumstances could only cause a diminishing percentage of venerable vines. Climatic conditions apart, this may well have affected the quality of the wine during the early years of the century. Indeed there could have been precious few pre-phylloxera vines of any age, so if the example of Latour is anything to go by, the replanting with grafts between 1900 and 1920 must have been intermittent and in any case, few of those grafted vines would have been old enough to produce the required quality. All the same, thanks to the two exceptional vintages of 1928 and 1929, that decade ended in a blaze of glory. Incidentally, such were the depths of the economic crisis by 1931 that good as they were, some merchants had difficulty in disposing of their stock of 1929s! A chastening reminder perhaps for the present day investor.

I think we can discount the dreadful 1930s, although like clutching at straws, there was some enthusiasm at the time over the 1934s. I remember I had very much looked forward to enjoying some of the 1934s after the war, but they never really lived up to their promise.

There is little doubt the 1940s suffered from the ravages of the war, although some of the 1943s were light but pleasant, owing to the shortage of bottles many of them had to be kept for too long in cask. The 1945 vintage was magnificent of course and so was 1947 for the districts of Pomerol and Saint Emilion. 1949 was welcomed by a fanfare of trumpets, but not too many of the 1949s reached perfection.

The decade of the 1950s opened with an abundant crop of light, agreeable but shortlived wines which were almost absurdly inexpensive. We sold the Cheval-Blanc and La Mission Haut-Brion (English bottled of course) for nine shillings a bottle, that is under 50p present day, but of course inflation has to be taken into account. 1951 was a poor year, 1952 very much better, but impregnated with tannin; indeed some 1952s like Lynch-Bages, although very good, are still rather on the defensive. 1953 was a sheer delight, but relatively shortlived; according to my notes these wines were really at their best when around ten years old, but what a delightful best! 1954 was indifferent, while 1955 produced a copious crop of good but not really great wine. This was the watershed as it were for cheap claret, the last vintage we were able to buy inexpensively. Subsequently, prices were to rise first because of the great frost of 1956 and then from the effect of the newly fledged American demand.

The disaster of 1956 was caused first of all by the frost in February, the worst for 200 years, which literally devastated the vineyards of Pomerol and Saint Emilion, and later by bad weather during the summer. Although the weather was better in 1957, many of the vines were still suffering from the frost of the previous year. There were one or two successes, like Lynch-Bages and La Mission Haut-Brion, but in general the 1957s were austere and uncharitable.

At least this decade ended on a high note with the much finer vintage of 1959, of which Lafite and Haut-Brion are such splendid examples.

The vintages of the 1960s are a mixed bunch, alternating from the heights to the depths. It began with a lesser year which, although shortlived, was not too bad in its day. For instance, while it lasted the 1960 Château Palmer was a delight and the Latour is still good, especially from a magnum.

1961 we all know about, one of the great successes of the century. To begin with, the 1962s were not sufficiently appreciated but they were the ugly ducklings which turned into swans. This vintage was not destined for a very long life, but in its heyday, the 1962s gave immense pleasure to a great many people.

Except for one or two wines, 1963 was pretty well a disaster. In 1964 we had the drama of the rain during the vintage in the Médoc, but it was quite successful for the wines from Pomerol and Saint-Emilion. The less we say about 1965 the better!

In spite of their intense tannin, there were great expectations for the 1966s, so the disappointment has been all the greater. There is, of course, a good proportion of excellent 1966s, but in a number of cases there remains too much acidity for enjoyment.

1967 proved to be a damp squib. Made from unripe grapes, this is another vintage which did not come up to expectations. Pétrus was easily the most successful, followed by Latour.

1968 was the third catastrophe of this irregular decade which literally fizzled out with the indifferent vintage of 1969.

Now we come to the 1970s and what is unusual about this decade is that there was only one really bad vintage, one which admittedly plumbed the depths. For although 1974 and 1977 are not much to write home about, they were not absolutely disastrous like 1963, 1965 and 1968.

The 1970s started off in fine fettle with one of those golden years which occur all too seldom and which yielded a very large crop of excellent quality. It is rare for such quality to accompany a large harvest and it was not until some time later that sceptics could accept it had actually happened.

After a late spring, the conditions throughout the summer and autumn were pretty well ideal; in consequence just before the picking began the vines were festooned with bounteous bunches of the most magnificient looking grapes. This was also a particularly good year for the *merlot* vines, hence the success in the districts of Saint Emilion and Pomerol. In fact it was a success in all districts. The wines had a lovely colour, an attractive bouquet and a fine full-bodied flavour. A drawback and quite a serious one has been the tannin which has persisted for longer than one had hoped. In common with many others no doubt, the writer made the mistake of drinking his lesser 1970s too soon and only now are these beginning to come into their own.

Possibly the most enjoyable 1970s to drink at the moment are the lesser growths of Saint Emilion and Pomerol. If you can keep your finer wines for a few more years, your patience will be rewarded, but at my age, I wish they would hurry up!

Both for size and quality the crop of 1971 was overshadowed by its copious predecessor; few vintages offer such a cornucopia of plenty as did 1970. Happily the weather was fine at the time of the harvest, but unlike 1970 there was a shortage of *merlot* grapes and among the médocs there was also some irregularity. Under such circumstances, a skilful merchant can be of more use to one than a knowledge of *châteaux* names.

On the whole the districts of Pomerol and Saint Emilion, especially the former, were more successful than the Médoc. Even so the Latour continues to increase in stature. The 1971s have had the advantage of developing faster than the more robust and tannic 1970s, but most of them should be drunk before too long.

The 1972 vintage – oh dear! In spite of good weather during the harvest, thanks to wretched climatic conditions during most of the summer, the grapes had no chance to ripen and the result was some of the most unattractive young wine the writer has ever had the misfortune to taste.

When I tasted these horrors during the summer of 1973, I was appalled by the price the growers were asking for them. With my long experience of the wine business both in England and the United States, I tried to warn some of them by quoting the Biblical parable of 'the Gadarene swine', but found that very difficult to translate into French. Of course, a year later, over the precipice they did go! By now a few of the more successful 1972s, if we can call them such, have lost some of their sharper edges, but this is a page better left unturned.

The portents for 1973 had been propitious – until a cold spell; then it began to rain in September, to such an extent that the grapes swelled almost to bursting point. In consequence the production was a vast one mainly of rather pallid washed out wines, low in acid as well as tannin. Here indeed was a test for the wine makers and those who were not ruthless in discarding their unsatisfactory *cuves* produced a thin anaemic liquid.

The successful 1973s, namely those with a good colour, although perhaps on the light side, but with feminine charm, have proved useful. More successful for the Médoc than either Pomerol or Saint Emilion, many 1973s have been delightful to drink. One of their assets was early maturity and if their role was a fairly modest one, the impact was agreeable. This has never been a vintage to keep, but as my twins were born in 1973 I put aside two cases of double magnums of Latour for them; I am hoping the wine will last the course until they are 21!

The 1974 vintage – The weather throughout the summer did little to encourage enthusiasm and the harvest was gathered during intermittent showers. Quite a large crop was thus born under unfavourable circumstances. However, in spite of their original unpopularity, these awkward, somewhat angular wines have been producing a few agreeable surprises.

1974 cannot be placed among the good years, yet in due course it may have something more to say for itself. From early days the quick maturing 1973s displayed their feminine charm, whereas the more masculine 1974s of a deeper colour and more depth were edgy and altogether less appealing. It has been a more difficult vintage to assess, but now that they have lost their youthful brashness, some are pleasant to drink. Possibly some of the most successful 1974s came from the Graves district, wines like La Mission and Latour Haut-Brion.

I have never thought, as I believe some people did, that 1975 was a better vintage than 1970, but of course time will tell. After a very hot summer, the yield was small and the grapes had very thick skins. This was another occasion when the *merlot* grapes were in excellent condition, the result being an all round success: a beautiful dark colour, a fragrant bouquet, full-bodied wines with heaps of fruit, but slow to mature. At the moment the finer 1975s are closed up and undeveloped. At a major tasting held by Sotheby's in 1984, the wines from Margaux and Saint Emilion were a little disappointing, whereas those of Pauillac, Saint Estèphe and Pomerol were excellent.

It could be many years before the greater 1975s are ready to drink and treasures such as these should not be touched for some time to come.

1976 – From the bursting of the buds at the beginning of April until the middle of August, the weather was exceptionally fine, warmer and drier than usual. Luckily the vines were saved from the ill effects of possible drought by some rain in August, with more in September. The vintage began ten days earlier than usual on 15 September and, in spite of occasional nocturnal rain, the weather was reasonably good. The production was large and equal more or less to 1973 with the quality satisfactory in all districts.

While not quite so dark, nor so deep and full-bodied as the 1975s, they formed a delightful contrast. They had a rich, fruity flavour combined with charm and finesse. Many were enjoyable to drink within three or four years of the harvest. This has been a most useful vintage and one to be enjoyed while it was young. Among the médocs, the Lafite was the most successful.

In accordance with nature, when the vines burst into leaf earlier than usual, inevitably they are subject to damage from spring frosts. Some years, of course, there are few if any, but misfortune certainly struck in 1977. Successive frosts wrought havoc among the vines, especially the more forward *merlot* plants. Cool weather persisted thus causing a late flowering and it was prolonged.

Heavy rain followed during July and August engendering cryto-gamic diseases among the vines. In places the land became so waterlogged as to prevent the use of tractors for the necessary preventive measures. Then came the finest September for over 100 years, the ground dried up and the vines recovered some-what, so that in those vineyards which were well cultivated, if the crop was not large, at least the vines were healthy.

The vintage began later than usual on 3 October and was gathered in under good conditions. In spite of the rather desper-ate beginning, the shortage of *merlot* grapes and the fact that some of the *cabernet sauvignons* were not completely ripe, the quality of the wine could at least be described as reasonably correct. 1977 has been called *une année jalouse*, in other words a year of irregular quality, dependent upon the date of picking and the efficiency of individual vinification.

The wines lacked body, but at least matured early and were inexpensive. Had it not been for vastly improved methods of vini-fication, this could well have been another of those disaster years.

1978 was the 'miraculous vintage' and I think I can claim responsibility for this epithet. It is certainly deserved anyway because until as late as 12 August the weather had been so appal-ling that hope of making even drinkable wine had almost been abandoned. Thence onwards, however, the sun reigned supreme and that, accompanied by uncomfortably warm nights, helped to ripen the backward grapes. While the *merlots*, etc. were of a good size, the *cabernet sauvignons* were very small, with thick skins and all too little juice. As districts go, this could just be described as a good all round year, but more successful for the médocs and red graves than elsewhere.

The 1978s have a lovely dark colour, an attractive bouquet with a good depth of flavour. There is some tannin, but it is not nearly so aggressive as, say with the 1975s. While the classified growths and better *crus bourgeois* of the Médoc have turned out well, considerable care must be exercised over the selection of the lesser wines, many of which, especially among the *petits châteaux*, can be sharp and of a feeble colour. No doubt most of the 1978s have already been drunk in the restaurants of Bordeaux, but it is better to give those in your cellar plenty of time to mature.

More rain fell during March, April and May of 1979 than in any comparable period since 1946! The buds burst about two weeks later than usual and fortunately, for the second year in succession, there was little or no frost. Continuing poor weather set the vines back further, yet even so there were already signs of a large crop. A fine July enabled them to catch up in time for a late flowering around the 20th of that month.

The retarded flowering was responsible, however, for the third late harvest in succession and under such circumstances there is always the danger of the weather deteriorating, as indeed was to happen in 1980. July was warm and dry, but August disappointing; more sunshine would have been welcome. The weather remained fine during the vintage, but without the splendid sunshine and general warmth of the previous year; the *merlots* were fully ripe, but the *cabernet sauvignons* would have benefitted from more maturity.

Thanks to the climate, unripe *cabernet sauvignons* have often been the besetting sin of the Médocain vintages, of which 1967 was an example. So far as I am aware, 1979 was the last vintage before the introduction of the new 'anti-*pourriture*' treatment, so let us hope this will be the end to all that!

That there was going to be an abundant crop was evident, but at the time of the vintage there was little or no excitement regarding the quality. As it turned out, more wine was made in the Médoc than any vintage since the war.

This vintage may never be in the class of *une grande année*, but it was satisfactory in all districts nevertheless, especially those of Pomerol and Saint Emilion. It is safe to say the 1979s have a good colour and an attractive bouquet, coupled with plenty of fruit and flavour. Since they have less tannin than the 1978s, they should be ready to drink sooner.

From the above, I think it will be agreed that the 1970s have at least a claim to be one of the best decades so far of this century. Undoubtedly the 1980s have made a most auspicious beginning, but with four years still to go, they have yet to fulfil themselves, and what will happen during the 1990s is in the lap of the gods.

It will be interesting to assess the matter more fully and at a more correct moment, that is after the turn of the century. That will be someone else's problem, but a younger person unfortunately by the law of nature will not have had personal experience at least of the 1920s and 1930s.

17

BACK TO THE CAVE MEN

A title such as the above probably conjures up an image of our forebears the ancient Britons painted with woad and clad in fur skins rather than the very latest twentieth-century trend in California where, strangely enough, there is indeed a return to the caves.

The wine industry of California, if one can describe it in such blunt terms, was started around the middle of the last century by either Italian or German families who had emigrated recently from Europe. Fortunately for those wine makers, their arrival had coincided with the period just after the vast railroad system had been completed from coast to coast. Thousands of Chinese had been imported, as it were, to undertake the heavy work.

Some of the winemakers' storage problems were in part solved by this cheap labour for, among their other tasks, the growers employed those Chinese to excavate long tunnels (an immensely arduous task) deep into the solid rock of the hillsides of the Napa Valley so as to facilitate the proper storage of their wine in a temperature which was both cool and constant. Some of the early tunnels were dug in the 1860s and more of them later on in the 1880s.

This was by no means a new idea as indeed for centuries wine has been stored in caves under the town of Saint Emilion near Bordeaux and some of that excavation dates back to the time of the Roman occupation. There are of course no real extremes of temperature in Bordeaux, even so, with their minimal variation throughout the year, those cool cellars in Saint Emilion had proved ideal for the storage and maturation of young wine. How much more valuable then could similar cellars be in the Napa Valley where in summer the temperature can at times rise above 38°C!

After the last war, the demand for Californian wine was still meagre and although it may be difficult to believe now, there were less than a dozen wineries established in the Napa Valley. The revival and expansion of the business did not really begin until the decade of the 1960s and among the early pioneers were Jack and Jamie Davies who, in 1965, bought a defunct vineyard and winery near Calistoga which had been founded originally by Jacob Schram in 1862.

Apart from the good soil and situation, this vineyard was chiefly notable for the fact that the writer Robert Louis Stevenson used to stay with his friend Jacob Schram and wrote some of his books there. Naming the property Schramsberg, the Davies set about producing a high class sparkling wine made under the *methode champenoise* and soon the label was to become famous. At that time, however, the winery was very small and one of the features of one's visit was to be shown a curiosity, i.e. the tunnels hewn into the rock by those Chinese labourers a century before and which were now being returned to their former use, the storage and maturing of wine.

The decade of the 1960s proved to be a teething period for modern Californian oenology when lovely air-conditioned wineries full of gleaming stainless steel fermentation tanks were beginning to spring up almost like mushrooms in the Napa and Sonoma Valleys and indeed elsewhere in California. Meanwhile the rock tunnels remained more or less a pleasant kind of historic anachronism.

Thanks to the oil wells in Texas and elsewhere, fuel had always been considerably cheaper in the United States than in Europe, so these up-to-date plants were not too expensive to run and all went well until the energy crisis erupted which resulted in a dramatic increase in the cost of upkeep. The cost of air-conditioning, etc. had suddenly become a serious added expense and inevitably this was to cause a change of thinking. So instead of being useful curiosities to show to visitors, these tunnels, the few that there were that is, suddenly assumed added importance and appeared as a major asset.

Since then the expansion of the wine business has been simply enormous and still continues and this has meant enlarged premises as well as still more wineries. Now, about a decade later, it is not only the actual cost of the building that has to be considered but the cost of maintenance has also to be taken into account, for to keep a large building cool during the summer in California is a very different proposition from one, say, in France.

In the meantime, the wines of Schramsberg had been slowly but steadily gaining eminence and two American Presidents have taken this particular wine with them on official visits to China, first Mr Nixon and more recently Mr Reagan. Faced with the need of expansion, Jack Davies had to decide whether to build another large warehouse or to extend considerably his old cellars deep in the rock. The cost of employing people to hack out further tunnels by hand would, of course, have been prohibitive. However, since there had been such a vast improvement in mining machinery during the past few years, perhaps an extension of his cellars in the rock was no longer totally out of the question.

After making enquiries he heard of a mining engineer named Alf Burleston who had equipment, made incidentally in Britain, which would be suitable to delve tunnels or caves in the living rock. Now that the initial cost of the operation is a thing of the past, the cost of maintenance should be minimal henceforth. Jack Davies claims his cellars are now as big and as efficient as any of the famous ones around Rheims and Epernay in Champagne.

Schramsberg was but the forerunner of the new trend for tunnelling, the next to follow suit was Carmenet in the Sonoma Valley, a relatively new vineyard belonging to Chalone Incorporated. The glycol-cooled fermentation tanks are housed in an attractive very modern looking beehive type of building and the caves have been hewn into the rock immediately behind. The tunnelling began in 1982 and was finished the following year. The main areas remind one somewhat of the caves in Saint Emilion, in extent about 45 metres deep and 9 metres across. The temperature remains constant at 14°C throughout the year.

Another operation reaching completion is near Yountville where Mr S. Anderson, a dentist from Los Angeles, has employed Mr Burleston to burrow into the rock of one of the small hillocks which rise out of the level of the valley. With the help of a well-known architect he had achieved some beauty as well as practicability. His caves are 6 metres wide and at 5 metres, higher than most. Already these caves are proving highly satisfactory.

This particular winery demonstrates another new trend, a concentration on only two wines, chardonnay and a very good sparkling wine. What a contrast with only 20 years ago when every winery used to produce and sell half-a-dozen different varietals!

Thinking along similar lines are the directors of the important Rutherford Hill Winery on the west side of the Napa Valley. This winery has been so successful that extra storage space has been essential. In spite of the fact that hewing out new cellars in the rock would cost in the neighbourhood of some $2 million, in view of the saving of energy and to obtain the necessary humidity and stable temperature, it was considered worth while.

The drilling here commenced during the winter of 1983 and was by no means finished by the summer of 1984. In this case, the rock was volcanic and the plan more ambitious, i.e. to accommodate 6,500 barrels. As there was a lot of water around, visitors had to don rubber boots as well as miners' helmets. Owing to different geological conditions there had been some complications, blue clay had been encountered so the original plan had to be altered to where there was pure rock. In addition, because of the rock formation the tunnels here had to be less wide, at $3\frac{1}{2}$ metres and 4 metres high, but longer, up to 76 metres. Here the Alpine Miner drilling machine was on the spot and looked more like some prehistoric monster!

Another mining operation envisaged probably for the future is at Stag's Leap Wine Cellars where Warren Winiarski has made such a reputation for quality that his winery has expanded again and again. He says his next move will have to be cellars drilled into the hillside by his winery.

It would appear, therefore, that the improvement in calibre of mining machinery has changed the thinking of some of the growers and has revived the concept that caves in the rock, as an economic alternative for the maturing of wine, is not merely a flash in the pan.

18

VINTAGE PORT

I have always loved this wine and so have an urge to write about it. There are of course, two kinds of port. One is the more universal wood port which has been matured in cask and that includes ruby, tawny and vintage character, all of which should be consumed soon after bottling. In fact, it should be remembered that wood port does not improve once it has been put into bottle.

Also under the heading of wood port, there is a fairly recent but important development from Oporto which is to produce a late bottled port, a vintage wine which instead of being bottled after the customary two years, is matured for a longer period in cask. This late bottled vintage port, as it is called, has become exceedingly popular in England. Although similar in style, it is not so expensive and is easier to handle, it does not have to be laid down for years nor does it need decanting before serving.

The other kind is vintage port and a vintage is only declared after the climatic conditions have been particularly favourable. The wine is bottled after two years in cask and thereafter is matured in bottle from ten to 20 years, according to the calibre of the vintage. As it matures vintage port throws a crust, or heavy sediment, and so has to be decanted before serving.

Unlike the Bordelais and the Burgundians who produce a vintage every year, the port shippers are more discriminating in their outlook for they only declare a vintage on an average of three times in each decade. Vintage port has been popular in Britain since the introduction of the cork and the cylindrical bottle, roughly that is since the beginning of the nineteenth century.

Conditions have changed considerably since I was a young man; it was then the custom to lay down a pipe of port (roughly 55 dozen) following the declaration of a good vintage and it was usual also to lay down a similar quantity on the birth of a son. Sadly, all too often there was not much left of that pipe by the time the boy had reached his 21st birthday, most of it having already gone down his father's throat! Unfortunately, my father died when I was a child, but my uncles taught me to appreciate, if not to drink, this splendid after-dinner beverage when I was a schoolboy and it has been an abiding joy ever since.

I have a friend, now aged 75, who is still enjoying the remaining few dozen of the fine 1924 vintage which he inherited from his father. He, in turn, has laid down vintage port, if not perhaps in the same quantity, for his son and his grandsons. This may sound like male chauvinism, but in England at any rate, men have been more fervent in their addiction to this nectar than their womenfolk.

Apart from all other considerations, when the port is on the table, there is the pleasure to be had by comparing one vintage with another and indeed the wine of one shipper with another, for the style can and does vary. At times, of course, one has the added treat of actually comparing an example of say the 1963 with another wine of that excellent vintage. Also there is the fun of trying to guess the vintage that one's host is presenting.

Besides consumption at home, the great institutions have always been noted for their port. For instance, after a good year, it has been the tradition to lay down some vintage port at the Colleges of Oxford and Cambridge, for the Benchers of the famous Inns of the legal profession and the Clubs along St James's Street and Pall Mall in London.

One of my more agreeable tasks is to act as wine consultant for the Ritz Hotel in London where, as is right and proper, quite a lot of vintage port is consumed. To emphasise the interest taken, there are some 20 wines on the list and of vintages extending all the way back to the venerable Taylor 1924. As the annual consumption amounts to some 150 dozen, necessarily we have to keep hundreds of dozens maturing in the cellar. Among these are examples of some of the most outstanding vintages since the war, namely 1945, 1955, 1963 and 1977.

The consumption in the hotel is mainly by the glass and until recently a 1966 was being served. Normally, this would be followed by a 1970 but since the 1970s have not yet quite reached their best, the wine being used is Warre 1975, admittedly a less good year, but one which is relatively more forward and ready to drink. In time to come no doubt, this procedure will be repeated, e.g. list the 1980s, the 1982s or even the 1983s before that other exceptional vintage 1977, in order that the latter may reach the point of maturity it will so richly deserve.

Although not quite of the calibre of either 1963 or 1977, the 1970 vintage is very good and while it is possible to enjoy it now, it will be so much better in a few years' time. It is generally agreed that the great vintages for port reach their zenith at around 20 years while less serious ones *vide* 1975, can be consumed earlier. That delightful entertainer, the late Maurice Chevalier, used to sing so charmingly 'thank heaven for little girls', so we in turn can be grateful for the little or at least lesser vintages of port.

How lucky we are to have such a splendid vintage as 1977 maturing in store for us, a vintage which has claims to be the greatest since 1927 and with such excellent intervening years as 1945, 1955 and 1963, that is saying quite a lot.

In these days, few of us live in houses with a fine cellar underneath, but we still do our best. Indeed, all is not lost, for at least in London we are fortunate to have several firms with good bonded cellars who keep our port for us under excellent conditions.

In my own case, I am down to my last few bottles each of the 1960 Croft, Fonseca and Warre. Although as a vintage 1960 was not quite of the calibre say of 1955 or 1963, the 1960s have been and still are delightful to drink. I have not yet touched my Croft 1963, but have been unable to resist some of the delectable Fonseca. In reserve, I have a respectable quantity of Dow 1970 and Warre 1977, but fear some of this may have to be sacrificed to help pay for the children's education. Now I find I am unable to restrain the urge to put aside a little 1983, but that will be for the children to enjoy when they have grown up. As may be seen, I am too weak to resist the desire to lay down good vintage port, although I am aware that as an investment red bordeaux of a good year is perhaps a better proposition. After the temptation of so many good vintages recently from Bordeaux, the purchase of the 1983 vintage from Oporto becomes a strain on one's resources!

While for centuries it has been the custom for the British to lay down port soon after a vintage has been declared, so far as I am aware this is still unusual in the United States. In fact, with exceptions of course, the laying down of wine in the USA seems only to have become more general with the advent of the exceptional 1982 vintage from Bordeaux. Admittedly there are problems about laying down vintage port. As with red bordeaux it has to be stored in a cool constant temperature, but unlike red bordeaux, once the crust has formed, it does not like to be moved unduly, for with every move, the less good it becomes.

One does not hear of this so much nowadays, but in the wine trade before the war, when we were considering the purchase of a parcel of port (that was the term we used), we always inquired the history of the wine in question and if it was found it had been moved several times, the purchase did not take place. Heaven knows how one is to ascertain the history of a vintage port once it has been shipped across the Atlantic, so for the purist, provided he has a really good air-conditioned cellar and can afford it, it is better perhaps for him to lay down his vintage port before it has formed the crust. In that case, the following notes may be of interest to a would-be buyer.

Not long ago I was fortunate to be invited to a tasting of a number of wines of the 1983 vintage held by the ancient and much respected firm Corney & Barrow in the City of London and among those present were leading members of the wine trade, including Ben Howkins, the author of a recent useful book on port. We were asked to give points from one to ten and the wines were presented anonymously.

Some of the Wines of the 1983 Vintage

Quarles Harris
A nice wine with a good fruity flavour, perhaps a little on the light side

My points 6/10

Taylor
A massive wine, packed with fruit, has considerable depth and is very good

My points 9/10

Smith Woodhouse
A nice creamy wine with plenty of fruit, perhaps a little light

My points 7/10

Warre
Good fruit and very well made, fine quality

My points 8/10

Gould Campbell
Medium body with a very nice flavour

My points 6/10

Dow
good fruit, but a harder fiercer wine, or so it seemed

My points 6/10

Fonseca
A fine rich wine with a lovely flavour

My points 8/10

Cockburn
A nice rich mouthful of fruit, plenty of tannin and very good

My points 8/10

Graham
A fine big, sturdy wine with a tannic finish

My points 8/10

Very young port is difficult stuff to taste; it carries such a punch that it is not easy to pick out the salient points. Although naturally there was some variation of style and character, the above wines were all good.

According to the combined group result, the Taylor came first, second equal, Warre, Graham and Fonseca, fifth equal Smith Woodhouse, Cockburn and Quarles Harris, eighth Dow and ninth Gould Campbell. As may be seen, my findings were roughly the same, except that I placed Cockburn higher. I found it hard to make up my mind between the Warre, the Graham and the Fonseca. While not a really outstanding vintage like 1977, the 1983 is certainly a good one and is definitely worth laying down for the future.

As touched upon earlier, it has taken a long time for the ambrosial attraction of vintage port to be recognised in the United States, a wine which to my biased British palate is the finest postprandial potion of them all.

It is now nearly 20 years since I first began to lecture on wine in the USA for Les Amis du Vin. The subject was usually red bordeaux, and when now and then I happened to mention vintage port, there was virtually no response; few people had heard of it, let along tasted it. Then slowly over the years there would be a question or so, until one happy day I was asked to give a lecture. It is a delightful topic for any speaker, but it was a revelation on those rare but cheerful occasions when this nectar was the subject that few if any of those present had ever tasted it. The conversions were easy to make and it made me wish I had some to sell.

There are of course a number of connoisseurs who have fine cellars of port. To give but one example, some years ago a friend in California arranged for me a tasting of no less than 12 vintages of Taylor Fladgate and all from his own cellar. I very much doubt whether such a feat could be emulated in Britain.

At the moment there is an awakening interest and one can only hope this will not have the same dire result as when, around 1960, American buyers began seriously to purchase red bordeaux. The inevitable outcome was that ever since the price of claret has continued to go through the roof!

This burgeoning interest in the USA provided a delightful experience for me in September 1984, when I was invited by David Sandeman, the scion and chairman of that historic firm (founded 1790), to accompany him to New York for the launching of his Sandeman's Founders Reserve Port, a delectable vintage character wine based primarily on the 1977 vintage. As those in the know will be aware, 1977 is possibly the greatest vintage for quality in the past 50 years. The prime interest of that launch was to satisfy the new demand and also to help educate the beginner, at the same time avoiding, for him, the complication of all the laying down and eventual decanting; in other words, 'French without tears'.

During those brief but most enjoyable days, I was fortunate enough to taste a number of wines the details of which may be of interest to some of the port 'cognoscenti'. For the sake of convenience here those wines have been assembled together, but they were in fact tasted on three occasions. The first was for some of the leading New York merchants among whom were Sam and Michael Aaron of Sherry Lehman, Peter Morrell of his own firm, Don Zacharia of Zachy's, Jack Lang of 67 Wine and Spirits and Bill Sokolin also of his own firm. The second was with some of the members of the Circle of Wine Writers including Eunice Fried, Doris Tobias, Alexis Bespaloff and Peter D. Meltzer. The final tasting took place on the 106th floor of the fabulous Windows on the World restaurant for a wine club under the aegis of the able Kevin Zraly and arranged by Ray Wellington and his efficient staff.

At that time the last vintage to be declared by the Shippers in Oporto had been 1980. If not perhaps of the quality of the exceptional 1977 or the 1963, this is certainly a good year and people have compared the 1980s with the 1960s. The 1960s may be a little past their best now, but they have been most agreeable to drink over the past ten years.

1980 Robertson
Good colour, plenty of fruit and flavour, lacks perhaps a little 'grip', but should be ready comparatively early

1980 Sandeman
A fine dark colour, not a very big wine, but supple and elegant. This should make a good bottle, from 1993 onwards

1980 Warre
Very dark colour, powerful and full-bodied, still fierce with youth, fine quality, but should take quite a long time to mature

1980 Graham
Very dark colour, another big wine, heaps of fruit, a little less agressive perhaps than the Warre. Lovely quality and will also take a long time to develop

1980 Sandeman
Dark colour, a fine powerful wine which is still imbued with some of the fire of youth

1977 Sandeman
A fine dark colour, still very strong and powerful, an excellent example of this outstanding vintage. Will probably need another 15 years before it is ready to drink. What a vintage this is!

1970 Sandeman
Dark colour, a fine powerful wine which is still imbued with youthful vigour, will need some years to reach its zenith

1966 Sandeman
Good colour, still youthful but has heaps of fruit and good flavour. Well developed, in fact is agreeable to drink now, even so will continue to improve

1963 Sandeman
Very dark colour, a fine full-bodied wine with almost twice the depth of the 1966. A worthy example of a great year

1958 Sandeman
A much paler colour and on the light side, this needs drinking but still has plenty of charm. 1958 was never a great vintage and it was a surprise to find this had kept so well

1940 Sandeman
A dark tawny colour, lighter and drier than the preceding vintages, still attractive but definitely showing its age.

Note 1940 was the first vintage to be bottled in Oporto, because of the war. Prior to that, all vintage port had been bottled by the wine trade in Britain

For those who are interested, there are a number of excellent books on this fascinating subject, useful ones have for instance been written recently by Wyndham Fletcher, George Robertson, Sarah Bradford and Ben Howkins. All of these are well worth reading.

Besides the Sandeman's Founders Reserve, there is now a fairly wide selection of late bottled port on the US market and a limited but slowly increasing choice of vintage port. Over the centuries, each great House in Oporto has developed its own individual style and after that it is really a matter of personal taste and what is available in your local store. In my early days in the wine trade a good description for a full-bodied port was 'it had a grip of the gob' and once you have tasted a good vintage character wine you will understand what that somewhat unusual expression means!

There are a number of Oporto firms who export to the US market whose produce is hardly ever encountered in Britain, so I can speak little of those. Among those which are the most popular in Britain, however, are Taylor, Graham, Fonseca, Warre, Croft, Sandeman, Cockburn, Dow, Martinez, Gould Campbell, Quarles Harris and Tuke Holdsworth. Some of those specialise in big robust wines and others, like Sandeman, concentrate on elegance and finesse. It is all a matter of one's personal taste.

Having to wait some 20 years before you can drink your vintage port may appear somewhat daunting, all the same, my advice to the beginner is to buy a couple of dozen of the outstanding vintage of 1977, the good 1980 or the even better 1983 which have recently come on the market. Do not delay because at the moment they are not too expensive and then you must forget about them for a while. When another good vintage comes along buy that as well and before you realise it, you will have a small but nice collection for future enjoyment.

Meanwhile during the time your little hoard is maturing, enjoy some of the late bottled vintage port which is readily available. Alternatively, if you are not prepared to wait so long, there are good but earlier vintages, around the 1975s which are coming along nicely and sooner than expected and the 1970s which should be ready before too long.

If it is any consolation to those readers of more mature years, I myself have laid down 20 dozen of the exceptional 1977 vintage and if I am not around to drink it, it will be there for my widow and son to enjoy and yes, my daughter too! Hope springs eternal in the human breast.

19
THE UNITED STATES
May and June 1986

TUESDAY 27 MAY

What a journey – from the time my first plane left Heathrow until the second arrived in Louisville, Kentucky, it had taken just over 12 hours. It was a relief, therefore, to settle down at the comfortable Seelbach Hotel. Built in 1905, this had recently been completely refurbished, but retains a nice turn-of-the-century atmosphere.

My previous visit to Louisville, some eight years ago, had been a rushed affair, so it was nice to have a little more time to spend with this congenial Chapter of Les Amis du Vin. The present director is Anne Joseph whom I had met in October 1985 while visiting the Faller vineyard near Mittelwihr in Alsace. In fact, the presence of Anne and her husband was the one bright spot on one of those rare occasions when one's reception at a vineyard had been displeasing.

WEDNESDAY 28 MAY

At around 80°F the change in temperature was definitely noticeable after the poor spring we had been having in England and where all the flowers in my garden were about three weeks behind in their development.

At nine o'clock Anne Joseph and Judy Haas came to collect me to take me to a Horse Farm, an establishment which in England we would call a Stud Farm. I should know, for I was born at Chilwick near St Albans where my father managed the Stud. Judy is a former director of this Chapter of Les Amis du Vin; on my previous visit, she had been the cause of my being created a

Kentucky Colonel, the nearest thing to any senior rank I ever achieved during my six wartime years with the Welsh Guards.

Although during my life I have had little to do with racing, I have a strong family connection with Newmarket where I spent many a holiday during my youth. It was, therefore, of particular interest for me to be taken into the very heart of the American racing community around Lexington. The countryside was unexpectedly lovely and, after recent rain, both the grass and the trees were a luxuriant green. Before leaving home, my twelve-year-old daughter Harriet had asked me if the grass of the Blue Grass Country was really blue; I can now assure her that it is as green as green.

Our rendezvous was at the Jonabell Farm which only a week before had been visited by our Queen. Set in beautiful surroundings this is a splendid estate of some 800 acres. There we saw several famous stallions, a number of broodmares, foals of all ages and yearlings galore. It is here that the yearlings receive the necessary handling in preparation for the Sales. The visit awoke memories of my distant youth and was of the greatest interest.

The wine tasting that evening had for its theme the *crus bourgeois* of the 1982 vintage, but actually it did not quite turn out like that because instead of the 1982 Château Larose Trintandon, the suppliers had sent the 1980 vintage. In fact, this proved somewhat of an advantage so as to demonstrate the contrast between the two years.

1980 Larose Trintandon, Saint Laurent
Definitely a lighter colour than all of the 1982s and as was to be expected, a good deal lighter in style. Clearly not destined for long life, it was nevertheless soft, easy to taste and pleasant to drink. Here we had a good example of this originally rather maligned vintage which has proved so useful for present consumption.

1982 Coufran, St Seurin-de-Cadourne
This vineyard is unusual for the Médoc because of its very large percentage of *merlot* vines. The colour was dark and after the 1980 the extra weight in the mouth was immediately noticeable. The flavour was soft, rich and rounded. There was plenty of tannin, but it was not aggressive, an attractive wine

1982 Greysac, Begadan
A wine one comes across more in the USA than in England. A good colour, a nice full flavour with plenty of fruit. The serious *cabernet sauvignon* element was evident here after the softness of the predominant *merlot* of the Coufran

1982 Poujeaux, Moulis

Very dark colour, here again one had the impression of very ripe grapes. This more generous wine has a lovely flavour

For me this 1982 vintage is somewhat of a freak, because in my now long experience in the wine trade, it is perhaps the only one which was made from such ripe grapes. It has been compared, correctly perhaps, with California, where owing to the hot climate the wine is nearly always made from ripe grapes and at times over-ripe ones, whereas in Bordeaux, because of the *pourriture* which can spread like wildfire, all too often the grapes have to be gathered before they are fully ripe.

1982 Gloria, Saint Julien

A fine dark colour, not quite so rich and luscious as the Poujeaux, but there was greater elegance combined with a lovely flavour

This tasting was a further proof of the remarkable quality of the *crus bourgeois* of the 1982 vintage.

1982 Camensac, Saint Laurent, Fifth Growth

The only classified growth in the tasting and although the group did not agree, for me the extra breeding was apparent. A dark colour and a wine clearly made from ripe grapes, it had plenty of charm combined with a very nice taste. There was some tannin so it should keep well and improve further

On a show of hands, the two favourites were the Coufran and the Poujeaux and that was understandable. I personally preferred the Gloria and the Camensac.

Later on, about 50 of us dined in a private room in the hotel and the wines were all from California. To begin with a nice 1981 Chardonnay from Acacia, then two cabernets. The first 1981 William Hill was for me still too young and the 1981 Beringer Reserve was more agreeable to drink although there was still some tannin.

THURSDAY 29 MAY

Luckily the weather had improved for this was to be a busy morning. At ten o'clock Bob Haas drove me to his home in Glendale, a charming estate on the outskirts of the city. Judy, his wife, has always been mad on horses and has founded her own driving club. There she was in her surrey, a nice looking Morgan in the shafts, a breed emanating I believe from Vermont; it was truly a picture.

Bob Haas had warned me that I was going to meet an old friend but kept the name secret and who should arrive but Kay Bullet, formerly Kay Stammers, a Wimbledon champion in the 1920s. I first met her when I joined the Welsh Guards at the beginning of the war and at the time she was married to a brother officer. At 72 she is as beautiful as ever. We clambered up into the surrey and Judy took us for a drive through the Glenview Estate where there are some splendid houses. The drive reminded me of my boyhood when cars were few and far between.

The Bullets must be one of the oldest families in Kentucky for they have been established there since before the State was created. The early part of the house was built in 1786 and the rest in 1810. Her husband Tom owns some 800 acres on which there is not only a polo field, but his own steeplechase course. Other reminders of the past were the small house by the swimming pool which at one time had been used as a kitchen for the slaves, and nearby there were two other houses now occupied by members of the staff but both of which had formed part of the slave quarters.

I am grateful to Les Amis du Vin for providing two such delightful days.

Later that afternoon I arrived in Pittsburgh to spend a few days in the hospitable hands of Ray and Barbara Syzmanski. Ray used to be in the computer business, but has now followed the dictates of his heart by becoming the local agent for the Majestic Wine Company. We dined at the Common Plea, an unpretentious looking restaurant which inside belied its outward appearance. Some times in the past I have had the good fortune to eat soft shelled crab, but never better it seemed than on this occasion. With this we began with an attractive chardonnay, the 1981 Clos du Bois Calcaire, a success attributable to Frank Woods, and that was followed by an excellent 1978 Chassagne-Montrachet Premier Cru from the good house of Leroy.

FRIDAY 30 MAY

A quiet day which was just as well because my jet lag was at its worst. Very noticeable though was a violent thunderstorm during which 3 ins of rain fell within the space of two hours. Later, we went to watch the Pirates of Pittsburgh playing baseball against the Dodgers of Los Angeles. The huge stadium was barely filled, but then it has a capacity of 50,000 people. I found baseball much easier to understand than American football. In my now distant youth I had played enthusiastic rugby all over the West Country at home, but it did little to help me comprehend American football. From a blinkered British spectator's point of view, each team seems to spend too much time in conference instead of getting on with the game.

SATURDAY 31 MAY

A welcome change in the weather with the temperature over 80°F. Guy Corsello took me to visit an impressive feature, the recently completed Pittsburgh Plate Glass building in the centre of the city. It is a sensational building of black plate glass edged with a silver looking framework. Modern gothic in style, it has a vast tower and the only comparison I could make would be something like Salisbury Cathedral. We then walked to the point where the Mononahela and Allegheny Rivers meet to form the gigantic Ohio. There lie the remains of Fort Pitt, constructed I think by the British in the eighteenth century. Nearby there is a fascinating museum concerning the history of that period which had me fully absorbed. Later Ray Syzmanski had organised a tasting of 13 vintages of Château Latour and it was attended by some 16 enthusiasts.

Château Latour

The weather had been unusually hot during the summer of 1976, but the prospects of a great vintage were dispelled by some inclement weather before the harvest. The result was an attractive wine, but one which lacked concentration. Although the 1976s may not be destined for long life, they have had the advantage of developing early.

1976
Good colour, plenty of good fruit and flavour, with no excessive acidity and well forward in its development   15/20

The crop of 1975 was considerably smaller than that of 1976, but if tannic the quality on the whole was very good. Some people initially considered it superior to 1970, but I was never of that opinion. Thanks to their heavy tannin, the successful 1975s are developing slowly and should live for a long time.

1975
Darker colour than the 1976, there is masses of fruit, but this particular wine is still very immature. It has much more depth than the 1976 and although firm and closed up, there is great potential

17/20

At the time, I called 1974 the rainbow vintage, for after constant showers at the time of the vintage, there always seemed to be a rainbow in the sky. 1974 can definitely be described as one of the off-years. Although masculine in style, the young 1974s had many rough edges and in their youth tasted far less well than the more attractive and more feminine 1973s.

1974

Quite a good colour, plenty of fruit, but just a small trace of acidity. This has lost some of its awkward corners and happily is smoother than it was a few years ago. It gave the impression that it would continue to improve (but perhaps my marking is ungenerous)

13/20

The prospects for the vintage of 1973 were altogether favourable until it began to rain in September. The rain was so continuous that some of the grapes even began to burst. The result was a pale coloured diluted wine which proved a test of the ability of the *châteaux* proprietors. Where they did not eliminate rigorously, the wine they produced was anaemic and insipid with little keeping power. In contrast, the successful growers produced a light but attractive wine, feminine in style and it matured early. By now most of the 1973s are dead and gone.

1973

Good colour, good fruit with an attractive flavour, there is no tannin of course, but it is alive and full of vigour as well as very easy to drink. Probably at its best now and possibly the most successful wine of its year

14/20

1971 was an irregular vintage for the wines of the Médoc, but more successful for the districts of Pomerol and Saint Emilion, especially the former. Many of the médocs developed relatively early so unfortunately some of them are beginning to go downhill.

1971

A good dark colour, full of fruit and flavour and well balanced. There is still some tannin so this wine should continue to improve. Excellent now and after Pétrus possibly the best of the year

16.5/20

If not quite so good as 1961, 1970 was a great vintage and for all districts. It is one of those rare vintages when an abundant crop was allied to considerable quality. The *merlot* grapes were very ripe. Unfortunately though, the *cabernet* grapes in superb condition had an excess of tannin in them. In consequence, the 1970s have taken an unconscionable time to develop and many of them are still not ready to drink.

1970
Very dark colour, a fine rich almost massive wine. Still tough and robust with excessive tannin. If attractive to drink now, this is nevertheless a great wine and one which may take from five to ten years to soften up

19/20

Another tough, tannic vintage is 1966. Certainly a fine year, but one from which we may have expected more than it could give. Thanks to excessive tannin it has taken a very long time to develop. In a number of wines the tannin has outlasted the fruit, but the successful 1966s are very fine indeed.

1966
A fine dark colour, still firm, but there is a lovely rich underlying flavour. This should make a splendid bottle by say 1990

18.5/20

All the portents for quality in 1964 were favourable, but those growers who, hoping for even riper grapes, delayed their picking of the *cabernet sauvignons*, were caught by the rain which commenced on 8 October and never ceased until it was too late. In consequence there were some disasters in the Médoc. At Latour, by luck or good judgement, and I think the latter, the last load was brought in on the morning of 8 October.

1964
Good colour, good fruit and an attractive flavour with plenty of charm. A lighter wine naturally than the 1966, but it has a good finish. It is recognised to be the finest of the médocs

17/20

Owing to heavy frost, the crop of 1961 was greatly reduced but thanks to excellent weather subsequently, the 1961s have a wonderful concentration of fruit and flavour. Owing to their heavy tannin, they have taken a long time to develop. While some of the less successful wines have begun to go downhill, the others are superb and like the Latour need some years yet to reach their best.

1961
A very dark colour, a superb concentration of bouquet, body and

flavour. The intensity of fruit is remarkable. In due course this may become as magnificent as the 1928 Latour is at present

20/20

There was a huge crop in 1955 and the quality if not great, was certainly very good and especially for Latour. This was the last vintage from Bordeaux when the wine was inexpensive. After the disastrous frost in February 1956, the worst for 200 years, the price began to rise and spiralled even further thanks to the American interest which began with the fine 1959 vintage. Since then the price of red bordeaux has been on an ever continuing upward trend.

1955

The colour beginning to turn brown, good fruit and flavour and probably at its best now. All the same I have had many much better bottles of 1955 Latour than this one. *Note* The Latour is possibly the finest wine of this vintage and a good bottle would rate higher than 15.

15/20

Although not long lived, the 1953 vintage has given enormous pleasure. When the 1953s first appeared on the market I wrote that they were so attractive they could charm a bird off a tree. Others may not agree, but in my opinion, the 1953s were at their heavenly best when they were young. In my tasting notes written between 1967 and 1971, although they were very good there were signs that they were losing something. Many are still very good, especially from a magnum, but for me it was their youthful charm which was so delightful. With the exception of Latour, all of the first growths were outstanding. Latour was an ugly duckling and never as good as the others. It has taken years to find the reason and I believe the answer is that an unusually large amount of wine was made at Latour in 1953 and the management was not sufficiently rigorous in eliminating the less good *cuves*. In its favour, the longevity of Latour has enabled the 1953 to stand up well to the test of time.

1953

Good colour, browning a little. Still a great deal of fruit and flavour and tasting better than ever before, a pleasant surprise

17.5/20

1949 was hailed originally as a great vintage. At Harvey's in those days from time to time we used to taste our 1949s and wonder when they would come round. Later on, a number of them developed an unattractive acidity. The masterpiece of the vintage, of course, was the Mouton followed closely by Lafite. Occasionally I have had a really good bottle of Latour, but often for me at any rate, its excellence was marred by some acidity at the finish.

1949
Good colour, lots of fruit, a very nice taste and a good finish. One of the better bottles and a pleasant surprise

18/20

Later, a few of us went to dine with Guy and Pat Corsello. I have written before of the lovely food one eats in their house and that evening was no exception. We began the meal with an excellent bottle of 1979 Puligny-Montrachet Clavoillons from Leflaive, but the 1961 Margaux which followed was too lean and ungenerous and thus disappointing. The evening ended on a high note with a fine bottle of 1963 Fonseca and what more can one ask?

SUNDAY 1 JUNE

A very hot day, the temperature rising to 90°F, but luckily it began to cool off by the time the Syzmanskis' guests arrived for a barbecue. These were Guy and Pat Corsello, Henry Block and Richard Gray.

These are some of the wines we tasted:

1978 Chassagne-Montrachet 1er Cru, Leroy
This wine has already been mentioned

1971 Reiler Mullay Hofberg Riesling Auslese, Rudolf Muller
It is some time since I have had the good fortune to drink a moselle of this great vintage and what a treat it was

1982 Groth Cabernet Sauvignon
A new winery for me but because of its distinguished label it made a good impression. A big, full-bodied wine, packed with fruit. An example of the powerful California style

1980 Chappelet Cabernet Sauvignon
A fine well balanced wine and such a contrast from the more massive cabernet from the Groth winery. The majority of us preferred it too

1982 Callaway Sweet Nancy
Rich and sweet, but without much substance

1976 Château Guiraud, Sauternes
This tasted almost dry after the Sweet Nancy, or was it because of the strawberries and cream? All the same, there was far more depth and, dare I say it, quality

1915 Setubal J.M. Fonseca, Moscatel
This veteran was in a squat-shaped bottle in a kind of wicker basket and, from what one could see of the glass, the stain from the wine had made it opaque. What a *bonne bouche* and what a treat to finish such a meal. So delicious was it that, although the wine had been decanted, we even drank the lees that had been left in the bottle! After the first sip, it seemed like a fine old madeira, but what an introduction to Setubal, a wine of which I have little or no knowledge. Rich and glorious, this was sheer nectar.

An interesting story is attached to this particular bottle. A few years ago, while on his morning round, a newspaper boy found a strange but full bottle which had been left out with the garbage. He told a local resident whom he knew and the latter went to collect it. Ultimately this stranger telephoned Raymond Syzmanski and offered it for sale and taking a risk, Ray paid him $35. As has been seen, it was a gamble which paid off.

MONDAY 2 JUNE

A decided change in the weather, from great heat a drop to a distinctly more comfortable temperature.

The main purpose of my visit took place at the Hyatt Hotel in Pittsburgh. Thanks to Ray and his committee, this Chapter has had a run of success ever since it was founded some eight years ago. The success culminated at a recent Convention of the Society when Pittsburgh was declared The Overall Chapter of the Year 1985. No mean feat when one considers there are some 400 Chapters across the country. The tasting covered a broad spectrum of recent vintages.

1982 Château du Glana, Saint Julien
A pleasant bouquet, not a big wine, but there was plenty of fruit. There was a slightly saline taste which I quite liked. This should mature reasonably early

1982 Château Gloria, Saint Julien
The bouquet still rather closed up. A lovely flavour though, rich and concentrated with a gentle tannin, a success

1981 Château Beychevelle, Saint Julien
A distinguished bouquet, but although correct and classic, there appeared to be a slight lack of generosity

1980 Château Pichon-Lalande, Pauillac
The bouquet on the light side, but pleasant. Elegant and well balanced with a good finish and ready to drink

1979 Château de Pez, Saint Estèphe
A more mature bouquet, quite full-bodied with a lot of fruit. A little coarser maybe, but a nice mouthful of wine nevertheless

1979 Château Mouton-Rothschild, Pauillac
Dark colour, the lovely cedar bouquet of Mouton. A classic well bred wine with both style and character. Even so it could have had a little more amiability. This may have been an off bottle

1978 Château Giscours, Margaux
A very dark colour, a fine concentrated nose, a delightful rich flavour, a wine one could almost eat. For me and all the group, the best of the evening

1976 Château Cos d'Estournel, Saint Estèphe
The colour turning from red to brown, a light bouquet, with medium to light body but with plenty of charm. Probably good for a few more years yet, but not destined for a long life

TUESDAY, 3 JUNE

Ray Syzmanski drove me from Pittsburgh to Silver Spring in Maryland. It was a pleasant change from the everlasting aeroplane and in fact the four hour journey did not take much longer when one considers the waiting at airports and so on. In any case, it was a pleasant drive through the Alleghenny mountains which otherwise I would never have seen.

On arrival at Wines Ltd. in Silver Spring, I found three old friends, Marvin Stirman, Doug Burdette and Alfio Moriconi. And upstairs in the office of Les Amis du Vin were Celeste Maier, the general manager and Kevin Moran, the Director of the Washington Chapter of Les Amis du Vin.

For all too short a time I was to be the guest of Marvin and Phyllis Stirman who recently had added a splendid deck area together with a swimming pool behind their house. It was to be my first swim of the year.

Doug and Gene Burdette came for dinner as well as Henry and Alice Greenwald, all of whom have been mentioned in my earlier diaries and the wines we enjoyed must be recorded.

My eyes opened wide when I saw the label on the apéritif, the 1982 Château de Rozay, for as may be gathered from the account of my last visit to the Rhône Valley, I have a penchant for the too rare wines from Condrieu.

The first claret was a delicious bottle of 1970 Château Palmer which is now ready to drink and possibly approaching its best. I asked my host what he could possibly produce to follow it, but he accomplished this without ado with excellent bottle of 1961 Château La Mission Haut-Brion, approaching its best and with a fine future ahead.

Both Marvin and Henry Greenwald are devotees of vintage port and together have acquired a notable collection of old vintages. So the crown of that evening was a superb bottle of Graham 1945, need one say any more!

WEDNESDAY, 4 JUNE

My wedding anniversary, another reminder of how lucky I am. In fact, June is a special month for me because my birthday is on the 9th, but this year alas the latter was to be spent mostly in an aeroplane.

Never before have I had an opportunity to visit the Capitol and it was thanks to Sander Vanocur, the senior correspondent of ABC News, that I was able to do this properly. On that fine morning he led me through the Senate and the House of Representatives to lunch with Tony Coeghli, a Representative for the State of California. As with our House of Commons in London, the kitchen is not renowned for its cooking, but I found the traditional bean soup very good, even on so hot a day.

About 60 members were present for the meeting of the Washington D.C. Chapter of Les Amis du Vin, including the President Ron Fonte and the dynamic Joe Schagrin who is doing so much for this excellent organisation. It was an evening when we had to have our wits about us – a blind tasting to compare some of the finest cabernets from California with two red bordeaux included. This is what happened.

Ridge 1981

A fine dark colour, a fruity rather toasted bouquet, a fine wine with plenty of flavour with the right amount of tannin. A little too massive perhaps for my European palate

16/20

William Hill, Gold Label 1981
The colour a little browner, a pleasant bouquet and flavour, lighter in style

15/20

Charles Krug 1980
Medium colour, curranty fruit in the bouquet, an attractive rich flavour, a lot of tannin

17/20

Château Lascombes, Margaux, 1981
.: pretty colour and a very nice nose, medium body with a lovely balance and a nice finish. A very good wine which I have to admit I did not pick out as from Bordeaux

18/20

Château Tartiguière 1981, Bordeaux
Medium colour, quite nice, but by no means great. At least I recognised this as from Bordeaux!

13/20

Martha's Vineyard 1981
A very dark colour, a fine bouquet, packed with fruit and flavour but because of its youth still too massive and overpowering

17/20

Opus No. One 1981
A lovely colour, medium body, distinguished and well bred. For me the best of all and mistakenly I wrote down Lascombes! This shows the value of a blind tasting

19/20

Finally, without having to guess, there were bottles of Château Latour 1981 which in some ten years' time should become a beauty. It had a lovely colour and although immature, there was a lovely depth of flavour.

THURSDAY, 5 JUNE

The main event of the day was the dinner party at the Stirmans' house. The guests were Eddie Sands, the owner of the flourishing wine business Calvert Woodley, Henry and Alice Greenwald, Dr Market, a surgeon and Fiske Tasker, a collector of fine furniture.

Our first wine was Mick Grgick's 1983 Chardonnay which has a well deserved reputation. Then three reds followed:

1970 Cos d'Estournel, from a magnum
Nothing like ready to drink and not nearly so pleasant as the 1970
Palmer we had enjoyed two nights before

1971 Latour, also from a magnum
Rich and delightful. In a magnum this has years of good life ahead
of it

Latour 1966
An example of how good this vintage can be. Although still rather
firm and resistant, the power and distinction were evident. A
wine which needs patience, for one day one hopes it will unbend
and blossom

1978 Chateau Gris, Nuits St Georges
By no means ready to drink, but one could see how good this will
probably become in about five years' time. It made me wish I had
bought more for my own cellar when I had the opportunity

Henry Greenwald had brought along a rather special bottle of
1865 Bual but unfortunately it was too fierce and fiery. Happily
the Taylor 1935 made up for this disappointment, a big plummy
wine. Looking a gift horse in the mouth, right from the beginning,
I personally have always preferred the 1934s to the 1935s. At the
time, a big fuss was made of the 1935 vintage because that was
the Jubilee Year of King George V.

Henry's disappointment over the Bual was made up for by his
1865 Old Liqueur Grand Fine Champagne, which although dark
of colour was good but again I must be critical. When I was a
young man, the words Old Liqueur often appeared on the labels
of more expensive cognac and in times gone by caramel was used
occasionally to darken the colour in order to make the contents
appear old and I remember in London before the war, there was
quite a lot of doubtful cognac on the market.

FRIDAY, 6 JUNE

I caught an early plane from Baltimore to San Juan, my first visit
ever to the Caribbean area. There I was met by Luis Rodriguez,
the Director of the local Chapter of Les Amis du Vin and at lunch
we were joined by a lawyer named Francisco Acevedo, the President of another vinous society La Cofradia Puertorriquena del
Vino who together were responsible for this exciting invitation.

From a first glimpse it was a lovely island with a lot crammed
into an area of some 100 by 30 miles. The vegetation is tropical,
very green and luscious. One could not help being amazed by

the trees, many varieties of palm of course, the pretty flamboyants with their orangey red flowers and the ubiquitous blueish purple of the Queen of the Flowers, and many other flowering trees and shrubs too numerous to mention. All of these provide an exotic splash of colour.

My first engagement in this tropical region was a tasting at the home of Domingo and Tita Pagan who lived in a splendid house up in the hills near Caguas. The large patio where the tasting took place overlooked a long swimming pool. On the white walls were lizards waiting to snap up the moths which were attracted by the light. Also climbing the wall over a decorative pool were huge snails which, I was told, are edible. All of this was accompanied by a great clamour, not unlike the song of birds. This din was made by what must have been a myriad of minute frogs called coquis, indigenous to the island. Seldom seen, they make an astonishing noise.

As it transpired our tasting was somewhat over-ambitious, the subject matter being pre-war burgundy and burgundy is not noted for longevity. All of the wines had come from our host's air-conditioned cellar. In fact the first wine was a bit of an outsider because its source was Rioja!

Castillo Ygay 1934, Special Reserve, Marques Murrieta
The colour was pale but the bouquet quite complex. It was a complete surprise, still full of fruit and in full command of its faculties and quite remarkable considering its age. It lasted in the glass for about 20 minutes before fading away

1927 Charmes-Chambertin, Ropiteau Frères
Pale colour, but an agreeable bouquet. There was fruit and body, but it lacked generosity and soon began to die in the glass

1938 Corton, Dr Barolet made by an *eleveur* called François Marienat
Although the colour was pale, this was the wine of the evening. An attractive bouquet with a remarkable depth of flavour. Considering 1938 was nothing special as a vintage, the quality was astonishing

This wine evoked memories, because I had had a lot to do with the appearance on the scene of the Dr Barolet Collection. Dr Barolet, a batchelor, had inherited pre-war wine from his father who had been a small but clearly discriminating wine merchant based in Beaune. After the doctor's death, the entire cellar had been brought by a firm called Henri de Villamont in Savigny-les-Beaune. One morning in London I received a call from my broker friend, Louis Jacquemont from Burgundy, to say there was a wonderful cellar and would I come at once. It was indeed fabulous and full of wine of the vintages of 1919, 1923, 1933, 1934 and so on.

I shall never forget that cellar, it seemed like entering an Aladdin's cave. The fungus, or whatever it is that covered some of the bins, was over 30 cm deep and in places I had to plunge my arm through to reach a bottle. After tasting some of these marvels I telephoned Michael Broadbent in London and subsequently the first sale of these wines took place at Christie's. Later on, a large part of this cellar was distributed on the American market.

Three more venerable wines followed, a 1929 Pommard, a 1929 Pommard Charmots and a 1934 Clos Vougeot, but they were all too old. Undeterred, our host produced three bottles of the 1970 vintage:

1970 Romanée-Conti
Good colour, a fine bouquet, but rather light and not very exciting. It may have been a bad bottle

1970 Pichon-Baron, Pauillac
A well bred wine, but spoilt by some acidity at the finish

I did my best to restrain our host from opening a bottle of Latour 1970 for although the potential is enormous it is still so immature it is almost disagreeable to drink now.

1980 La Mission Haut-Brion
Full-bodied with heaps of fruit and very good for its vintage, this overshadowed the 1980 Pétrus which was served alongside, good as the latter was

Following a delicious meal prepared by our hostess Tita Pagan, the men repaired to the cellar to share a bottle of 1963 Fonseca which tasted every bit as good as it does at home. On an island with a climate as warm as this, I was surprised to find such a strong interest in vintage port. At home in England we hesitate to open bottles of vintage port during our so-called summer, so clearly air-conditioning must add a new dimension to its consumption.

SATURDAY, 7 JUNE

After such a long day and the late night that followed, it was not surprising I suppose to wake up feeling a bit tired. Nevertheless, at ten o'clock Luis Rodriguez collected me and then showed me round the old part of San Juan which happily has retained its old Spanish atmosphere and is still unspoilt.

The attractive narrow streets are paved with the cobblestones which had been used for ballast in the Spanish galleons which sailed from Spain to pick up the cargoes of gold and silver from the New World. We visited the fortresses with which the Spaniards had defended the island, the first, San Cristobel and the second, El Morro. The latter guarded the entrance to the harbour. In 1595 El Morro had helped to repulse Sir Francis Drake and his fleet which had arrived hoping to plunder the gold and silver lying at a smaller fort farther inside the harbour. The Spaniards had also sunk a line of ships across the entrance in order to prevent the English from getting into the harbour. Finally, Drake had to withdraw with heavy losses.

Close to the entrance, one can see part of a ship which sank in more recent times and I was told it is crammed with lobsters which dare not leave because of the multitude of sharks which it seems have a partiality for them. In turn, owing to the rapacity of the sharks, the fisherman are also unable to catch the lobsters. Thus the latter live in comparative safety. As for bird life, instead of the inevitable seagulls, the birds here were mainly albatross.

It was well the sightseeing finished in good time, because by the time we had reached the house of Francisco Acevedo it had begun to rain in torrents, so much so that for a good hour we were unable to leave. No time was wasted, however, because Francisco opened first a bottle of the excellent Krug non vintage and then a bottle of 1973 Beaulieu Vineyards Private Reserve, the latter being a lovely wine. Francisco's house lies on a slight slope and the rain was so heavy that it was at least 1 inch deep as it poured down the road. When finally we decided to leave, rain or no rain, the roads lower in the town were awash, all the traffic was held up and at places the water was over 12 inches deep. Such are the tropics.

At last we arrived at La Casita, a small restaurant across the bay but by that time the other patrons had long since departed. The proprietor specialises in cooking fish so we had a delicious meal. I was introduced to tostones, special to Puerto Rico which are locally-grown plantains, deep fried in a special manner and with these we ate conch, shrimps and lobster. The shellfish was enlivened with a hot spicy tomato sauce. The main dish was very fresh red snapper with more grilled lobster.

My generous hosts, Francisco Acevedo, Jose Luis del Dias Villegaas and Dr Dolfin Bernard had put their heads together and had brought with them some of the treasures from their cellars.

1983 Château Grillet

The noted wine from Condrieu was good, but from memory I

preferred the 1982 Château de Rozay which Marvin Stirman had given me in Washington D.C.

1976 Montrachet, Domaine Fleurot Larose
A delightful rich flavour which filled the mouth. Well bred and of excellent quality

1980 Château Montelena Chardonnay, 13.5°
Also quite rich and certainly rather sweet. Just a little too full for my own taste

Although this was a simple restaurant, with such good fare and such good company, we could scarcely fail to enjoy ourselves.

The evening tasting at the Swiss Chalet restaurant had been organised jointly by the Ponce Chapter of Les Amis du Vin and the Cofradia Puertonniquena del Vino and the theme was a comparison of Chardonnay with white Burgundy. As it turned out the contest was a little one-sided, because it would appear that for various reasons it is difficult to obtain all the best burgundies in Puerto Rico. So apart from the Puligny-Montrachet les Folatières, the white burgundies had to take on a top flight team from California.

Meursault Charmes 1984, Bouchard Père et Fils
A nice pale colour, a pleasant flavour, but rather dry and with too much acidity. 1984 was not a very special vintage on the Côte d'Or

My points 14/20

Chassagne-Montrachet 1983, Drouhin
Pale colour, quite a sweet wine but with an attractive flavour. A good example of the 1983 vintage which produced so many rich rather luscious wines without much acidity

My points 15.5/20

Puligny-Montrachet les Folatières, Bouchard Père et Fils
Pale colour, with a lovely flavour, the breeding stood out

My points 18.5/20

Corton 1982, Bouchard Père et Fils
A deeper colour, plenty of fruit and flavour and a nice hint of sweetness, but somewhat disappointing for a wine with this name

My points 16.5/20

The Challenge from California
Jordan 1982
Quite a big wine, pleasant, but there was a strike which is hard to explain

My points 15/20

Stag's Leap Wine Cellars 1983
Good colour and a very nice flavour, well balanced

My points 17/20

1983 Grgich Hills
Good colour and bouquet, a very nice taste with some interesting facets

My points 17.5/20

Sonoma Cutrer 1983
Good colour and bouquet, a fine well made wine

My points 18/20

There was some disagreement over the best wine of the evening, but finally the Puligny-Montrachet les Folatières emerged just ahead of the Sonoma Cutrer. Otherwise the California chardonnays were more popular and, I felt, rightly so. One has to remember that California chardonnays are more potent and usually a little sweeter than their burgundian equivalents and this gives them an advantage on an occasion such as this.

The combined members of these two groups were certainly the noisiest I have ever come across as well as some of the nicest and merriest and that is saying a lot with Les Amis du Vin, whose members are noted for their 'bonhomie'. It was a delightful evening.

SUNDAY, 8 JUNE

As well as the torrential rain on the previous day, there had been even more downpours, so it was just as well this particular morning remained fine when Luis Rodrigues drove me to the El Yunque area, named after a benign Indian god and up into the rain forest. The only other rain forest I had visited had been in Kenya, but that one had been full of wild animals. This one, if far less dangerous, was of equal beauty.

On our way up the mountain we called on Dr Hector Hernandez, a dermatologist, who has created an amazing tropical garden around the house. Besides many varieties of luxurious palm and fern trees (the latter abound in this forest) there were bananas, plantains, coconuts and a fruit called guanabana, or soun-sap, which provides a refreshing if rather solid drink. The giant ferns were as tall as trees and I was told they only grow here and in the forests of Guam and Brazil, that is where there is an average rainfall of over 300 ins. I also saw for the first time veromellia, a parasite plant which grows on the trunks of fern and other trees, and has no roots in the soil.

Driving further up the mountain, we saw giant clusters of tall bamboos and large bushes, almost shrubs, of Impatiens which in England is better known as the busy lizzie; here it grows wild by the roadside. Our final destination was one of the old Observation Towers, built around 1600, high up on the mountain and from whence the view was certainly magnificent. In the sixteenth century the Spaniards had found their gold from the rivers and streams of this mountain.

Printed on the number plates of many of the cars in Puerto Rico are the words 'Isla del Encanta', well for me at any rate, this had been a visit of enchantment.

The final event of this brief but busy visit took place at the lovely house of Margarita Godoy. A group of enthusiasts clubbed together to buy a remarkable cellar which came on the market and they had already met on a number of occasions to enjoy the contents. Arranged by Margarita Godoy and Perez Coira, this was the ninth or tenth event and the quality of that cellar can be assessed by the calibre of this tasting.

Some Vintages of the Domaine de la Romanée-Conti

1965, from a magnum

So poor a vintage that it is no longer included in the vintage charts! A pale brown colour, Domingo Pagan described the bouquet as the smell of old library books. It was definitely thin, but it had retained its fruit and in spite of some acidity was infinitely better than I or anyone else present would have imagined. However, it soon began to fade in the glass

14.5/20

1974, from a bottle

The colour darker brown, but this was watery with a rough finish, the product of a poor vintage, although one bottle was better than the other

12/20

1973

A brown colour, with just a hint of ruby, a fairly pronounced *pinot noir* bouquet. This was not a big wine, but it had an attractive flavour and a pleasant finish and was richer than the previous wines. By far the best so far

15/20

1967, from a magnum

Again a brown hue. There was plenty of fruit on the nose, but it lacked depth and attraction

14/20

1972

A better colour, and although the bouquet was somewhat reticent, this had lovely fruit and a fine depth of flavour. Happily there was none of the usual acidity attributed to this vintage. Still youthful with plenty of room to mature. One bottle was better than the other, but this was fine quality

18.5/20

This restored our faith because as one member of the party had stated, the first four wines had hardly been worthy of the great name of Romanée-Conti.

1970, from a magnum
A dark colour and a pronounced bouquet, good flavour with a delightful finish. *Note* Considerably better than the bottle at Domingo Pagan's house two nights before

17.5/20

1976
A pretty ruby colour, an attractive bouquet smelling of herbs. A delightful deep flavour with masses of fruit. A heavenly wine whose flavour filled the mouth. Both bottles were good

19/20

1971, from a magnum
A pretty colour, and an aroma of violets. The flavour was both full and deep. A glorious bottle to culminate the evening

19/20

The supper which followed was set in romantic surroundings, for Margarita Godoy lives up in the mountains near Caguas where the vegetation is tropical just like that of the rain forest I had visited that morning. There we ate our meal accompanied by the almost deafening chorus of the coquis. These, believe it or not, begin to sing at precisely the same moment every evening.

MONDAY, 9 JUNE

An early rise to catch a plane to Los Angeles and it took nine hours from airport to airport. What a way to spend one's birthday.

My hosts in Glendale were Mr and Mrs Kenneth Doty. For some time, Ken Doty has been the director of the very efficient Glendale Chapter of Les Amis du Vin and this is associated with an equally efficient retailer, Red Carpet Wines.

This proved to be a busy day for no sooner had I arrived than guests, a number of whom were old friends of mine, began to assemble for a glass of California Champagne. Later some of us went to dine at Gennaro's, a local and very good Italian restaurant. There we drank two wines our host had made himself, a chardonnay and a merlot and they made me wish I could do as well myself.

TUESDAY, 10 JUNE

We paid a call on Red Carpet Wines which is managed by Phillip Simon and owned by John Vincenti. Their range of fine wine is remarkable. Lunching later with these two at another good restaurant, the Phoenecia, we compared the Simi Reserve Chardonnay 1983 with the Long Vineyard of the same year. I personally preferred the Simi.

Since the Glendale Chapter is the most senior of the Los Angeles area and is very active, it was not surprising that over 120 members were present at the tasting. The theme proved to be sensational.

The 1983 Vintage from Bordeaux

Beychevelle, Saint Julien

Dark colour, very good fruit and flavour, even so it could have had more charm

Lynch-Bages, Pauillac

Dark colour, a lovely flavour and packed with charm, a most attractive wine

Pichon-Lalande, Pauillac

An even darker colour, although still immature, there was a fine depth of body, its quality stood out

L'Evangile, Pomerol

Also very dark, rich and delightful, an example of a really good pomerol

According to a show of hands, the Lynch-Bages was the most popular of this group, with the Evangile a close second.

Cheval-Blanc, Saint Emilion

Good dark colour, a delightful wine with considerable style and breeding

Haut-Brion, Graves

Good colour, some tannin still to lose, but a fine, well balanced wine

Margaux, Margaux

A marvellous colour, an explosion of fruit and flavour, as well as a wonderful depth of body. A very fine wine

Mouton-Rothschild, Pauillac

Very dark colour, that lovely Mouton bouquet and flavour, excellent quality

Latour, Pauillac

Very dark colour, fine bouquet with a remarkable depth of flavour

On the show of hands, the Margaux was the favourite of this group with Latour not far behind. Imbued with prejudice as I am, if one can judge from this tasting, I have a feeling that the Latour will turn out very well in the long run.

The *bonne bouche* was the lovely 1983 Château Rieussec from Sauternes and what a good vintage 1983 is for that district. Were it not for the fact that they have been overshadowed by the richer and more luscious 1982 vintage, I am sure the quality of these splendid 1983s from Bordeaux would have received far more acclaim.

As a final treat, Don Schliff, who is noted for his collection of vintage port, invited us to his home. True to tradition, in his cellar he proceeded to nip off the neck of a magnum with a pair of heated tongs. The 1948 Graham has always been a glorious wine, so imagine what it was like from a magnum! What a tragedy it was that so few firms shipped this exceptional vintage.

WEDNESDAY, 11 JUNE

I arrived in San Diego feeling tired; it may have been a build-up from the constant travelling, but more I think, owing to jet-lag and disturbed rhythm of sleep.

The San Diego Chapter is directed by two doctors, one of whom, Dr Lee Jaret, was my host and the other was Dr Sandy Shapiro. During an excellent meal at a restaurant Tambo d'Oro, Dr Jaret produced a treasure from his own cellar, the 1978 Puligny-Montrachet Champ Canet, Etienne Sauzet. 1978 was one of the best vintages for white burgundy for many years, but it has been a long time maturing and in fact it is only now approaching its peak. As a lover of white burgundy, in my cellar at home I have bottles and magnums of this fine vintage of various wines of Etienne Sauzet, Comte Lafon, Louis Jadot, Louis Latour and Domaine Leflaive. This may sound like boasting, but what is the point of collecting fine wine if one is unable to talk about it!

Seldom have I attended a more interesting tasting. There were ten wines in all, the 1982 and 1983 vintages from five *châteaux* and all of them were served anonymously. The wines were served in pairs and all we were told was the names of the châteaux, but not which was which. The rest we had to sort out for ourselves and it was no easy task.

I was aware that on an occasion such as this, my total loss of smell would be a grievous handicap.

An Anonymous Tasting of the 1982 and 1983 Vintages
First Pair Château Lynch-Bages, Pauillac
1983

Good colour, but with a hint of brown, rich, rounded with a pleasant hint of sweetness, a charming wine

16/20

1982

Similar colour, more massive with a lovely flavour and a very good finish

17/20

Second Pair Château La Lagune, Ludon
1982

Very dark colour, a splendid full-bodied wine with a fine full finish

17/20

1983

Dark colour, good fruit, but marred for me by some acidity

13/20

Third Pair Château Cheval-Blanc, Saint Emilion
1982

Very dark colour, rich, rounded and delightful, very great quality

18.5/20

1983

Dark colour with a hint of brown at the edge, good flavour and well balanced. Another fine wine

18/20

Fourth Pair Cos d'Estournel, Saint Estèphe
1983

Dark colour, excellent fruit and flavour, coupled with a nice rich finish

18/20

1982

An unusually dark colour, the taste sweet and charming, for me the most attractive of the evening

18.5/20

Fifth Pair Château Mouton-Rothschild

1983

Good colour, has good fruit, but more acidity than I would like

14/20

1982

Fine dark colour, much richer and rounder and altogether better

18/20

According to a show of hands, the points given to the various wines were as follows: Lynch-Bages 1983 13 points, 1982 8 points; La Lagune 1982 14 points, 1983 8 points; Cheval-Blanc 1982 18 points, 1983 16 points; Cos d'Estournel 1983 6 points, 1982 22 points; Mouton-Rothschild 1983 19 points, 1982 25 points.

When finally the identity of the bottles was revealed, I was delighted to find that I had got all my vintages right and, apart from confusing the Cos with the Mouton, the *châteaux* as well. I am still unable to understand the acidity in the Mouton 1983, I have never before noticed acidity in this wine and indeed had tasted it as recently as the previous evening. I can only put this down to bottle variation. According to my notes made at the time, I had erroneously attributed the fourth pair to Mouton, expecting what I considered the better pair to be the first growth! Ah, well!

At the risk of boredom, I must explain that some four years ago I was involved in an horrendous motor accident in France, when sitting in the right-hand seat at the back. I was ejected through the other door and woke up in hospital some five hours later. Owing to a hit on the head, my loss of sense of smell ever since has been total, a grievous thing to happen to someone in the wine business. However, it does seem that since then I may have been developing other faculties with my sense of taste.

Without wishing to be boastful, I understood I was the only person present at that tasting to achieve so satisfactory a result. I have mentioned this in order that it may give some reassurance to those like myself who have suffered a similar misfortune.

THURSDAY, 12 JUNE

My last visit to Barney and Belle Rhodes in the Napa Valley had been three months before in March when, after 23 ins of rain within three days, there were floods everywhere. Now I was to have ten days in the sunshine to catch my breath as it were and to see more California wine.

On Highway 29 there is an extremely popular restaurant called Mustard's which is packed from the time it opens at 11 a.m. until it closes at midnight. Reservations have to be made days ahead. The food is both excellent and inexpensive and all the wine on the extensive list comes from the Napa Valley. In fact, one finds wines here which are difficult to obtain or are unobtainable elsewhere. During dinner that evening I was to come across one of those unobtainable wines, the 1982 Howell Mountain from the Dunn Vineyard. This, I gather, has been receiving considerable acclaim. I have to admit I was disappointed, it was altogether too much of a good thing, a wine more suited to a tasting competition than to be enjoyed with food.

FRIDAY, 13 JUNE

A pleasant new restaurant called Knickerbocker's has recently been opened at Freemark Abbey near St Helena and there I lunched after a meeting of a group of wine growers, among whom were Barney Rhodes of Bella Oaks, and Chuck Carpy and Laurie Wood, both directors of Freemark Abbey. The meal was notable for the four cabernets which Chuck Carpy had brought from his own cellar.

1970 Freemark Abbey Bosche
Very dark colour, an exciting taste with lots of fruit and a delightful flavour

1970 Heitz Martha's Vineyard
Dark colour, very good flavour, more robust and with greater depth

1970 Souverain, Lee Stewart
A shade browner, smoother than the others and very easy to drink. Probably at its best now

1970 Robert Mondavi, unfiltered
Dark colour, lots of fruit, a more powerful wine with a slightly fierce finish. This needs more time to mature

By consensus of opinion, we placed them in this order: Heitz, Freemark Abbey, Souverain and Robert Mondavi. There has been some discussion about the longevity of California cabernets, well at 16 years three of the above were in great form. The only one to be showing any signs of age was the Souverain.

My old friends Milt and Barbara Eisele came to dinner. Their Eisele Vineyard, bottled under the J. Phelps label, is deservedly among the leading cabernets of the Napa Valley. Also present were Warren Winiarski, his daughter Kasia who helps him run his winery and Mr and Mrs Jack Cakebread. This was a meal which featured mainly European wines, two of which stood out. The 1959 Lafite, which was a treat for I have not tasted this for some time, and the 1959 Cos d'Estournel. No wonder the Lafite 1959 has such a great reputation, nevertheless the Cos stood up to it well with greater depth perhaps but less distinction.

The meal ended with pistachio nuts and a delectable bottle of 1960 Quinta do Noval Nacionale. For those who are unversed in the lore of vintage port, the Nacionale is produced from a very small area of pre-phylloxera vines, the quantity made is minuscule, consequently the Nacionale is extremely rare.

SATURDAY, 14 JUNE

Jack Cakebread's vineyard has increased considerably in size since I called on him some ten years ago and he now has a lovely new winery which has recently won an award for architecture. He has handed over the day-to-day management to his son Bruce while he attends to the agriculture and acts as a consultant for other growers. Lunching with father and son, we drank an excellent 1981 chardonnay and an equally good cabernet sauvignon of 1978. The Cakebread wines are consistent in style and this is a winery to watch.

I do not know whether it was caused by the floods three months before, but this year the luxuriance of the vines was notable and especially those of the *sauvignon blancs.*

The Rhodes drove me to dine with Milt and Barbara Eisele, whose wineyard is near Calistoga. As I have mentioned before, Milt is one of the most respected growers in the Valley. Our fellow guests were Joe and Alice Heitz and Eleanor McCrea whose Stoney Hill Vineyard is so well known. These are some of the wines we enjoyed:

1981 Chardonnay Trefethen
A good colour and a very nice flavour

1976 Cabernet Sauvignon Joseph Phelps Insignia, Eisele Vineyard
A splendid colour and a wine packed with fruit. As there was still some tannin this should be at its best around 1990 or perhaps later

1982 Pinot Noir Robert Mondavi

Quite a rich wine and ready to drink now. I used to wonder about the future of the pinot noirs of the Napa Valley and here was a good example of the progress that has been made

TUESDAY, 17 JUNE

A cooler day with some clouds in the sky. We spent the morning with Ric Forman whom I first met when he was the wine maker at Sterling and that must be some time ago. He now has a small new winery which he has created on the hillside overlooking the Silverado Trail with a good view of St Helena. He had to blast tons and tons of rock in order to build his house and the winery. His vines are now seven years old and he hopes to produce about 1,000 cases of chardonnay and 1,200 of cabernet sauvignon. I liked the style of his 1985 chardonnay and in due course his cabernet sauvignon should also be very good.

It is always a pity to visit California without at least one glimpse of San Francisco. My wish was to be granted because the Rhodes had made reservations for a meal, called a 'dinner with the winemakers', arranged by Robert Mondavi and the Vichon Winery at the Fairmont Hotel. Vichon has recently come under the Mondavi umbrella, but with the firm intention that its wines would maintain their own individuality.

1984 Vichon Chevrignon, a blend of 50 per cent each *semillon* and *sauvignon blanc*

A little bland perhaps, but fresh and agreeable. We felt it might have been better as an apéritif, whereas the 1982 Mondavi Fume Blanc was better with the seafood. There was a stronger varietal flavour and a fuller taste

Two chardonnays followed with a very good consommé:

1984 Robert Mondavi Chardonnay

A typical California chardonnay, for my taste it could have had a little more fruit acidity

1984 Vichon Chardonnay

Alert, vibrant and more exciting and for me the better of the two

With the lamb, the 1982 Mondavi Cabernet Sauvignon was served, a pleasant bouquet, heaps of fruit, later in the meal with the cheese an attractive touch of sweetness emerged. This should continue to improve.

In fact the two best wines had been reserved for the cheese course:

1982 Mondavi Cabernet Reserve
A fine wine with an attractive quite rich finish

1982 Opus One
A fine dark colour, it was smoother with a lovely rich flavour, a wine which undoubtedly will continue to improve

WEDNESDAY, 18 JUNE

My hospitable hosts had planned another dinner party to which they had invited more of my friends, Ruth and Stanley Burton, Ron and Sheila Light, Haskell and Rae Norman, Eleanor McCrea and her twin sister Mary Wheeler. The food was delicious, a platter of mixed shellfish to begin with, and really tender lamb to follow.

As may be gathered, Barney has a remarkable cellar, remarkable on account of impeccable selection over the years. With his usual generosity, he had asked me if there was anything particular I would like to try, either old vintages from France or from California. I am glad to say I had the good sense to choose the latter for I felt it would be of interest to find out how the noted 1974 vintage was progressing. So far as was possible our host based his theme for the evening on that year and to start with was even able to produce a 1974 George Goulet Cuvée du Centenaire. With the shellfish we compared two chardonnays:

1974 Heitz
A pale golden colour, the more full-bodied of the two but very nice

1974 Stoney Hill
A very pale colour considering its age, a lighter style and in very good condition. Eleanor McCrea had every reason to be proud of this

Then came the main feature of the evening, four cabernets of the successful 1974 vintage. All of them had a superb colour and for the first ten minutes were served anonymously.

Martha's Vineyard
Heaps of fruit with a fine depth of flavour and still quite a lot of tannin. My only criticism of this wine was it was a bit too dry, so I placed it third

Mount Veeder

A pleasant wine with plenty of fruit, but it was lighter than the others and thinner, so I placed it last. According to that bottle at any rate, this could be the only one of the four which may not keep well

Trefethen

Very good flavour, it has such charm as well as depth that I placed it first, but I was one of the few to prefer it. At least I was consistent, because I had liked this wine immensely when the 1974 vintage first came on the scene and had five cases shipped to England. From time to time this particular wine had been enjoyed at our Zinfandel Club dinners in London

Phelps Insignia

Although for me this did not have quite the depth of the Trefethen, it was a delight, lovely fruit with an attractive hint of sweetness

As was to be expected, these wines evoked considerable discussion and with regard to general preference, the final outcome was in this order: Phelps, a short head in front of Martha's, Trefethen and Mount Veeder.

We were all mystified by a magnum decanter which appeared on the table, a wine with a very nice taste and very easy to drink which turned out to be Louis Martini's 1974 Zinfandel.

It would seem difficult to follow such a galaxy of stars, but not from Barney's cellar. The 1931 Quinta do Noval proved to be a rare treat; 1931 must surely be the greatest vintage for port of this century. Well I remember my sorrowful experience of this particular wine during the late 1930s. At that time Hitler was invading country after country and business in the English wine trade was so bad that my firm could not even sell this wine! In fact much of it was used to invigorate the blend of our Vintage Character Port!

THURSDAY, 19 JUNE

My one regret concerning this visit to the Napa Valley was that Francis and Françoise Dewavrin were in Paris. A close friendship with this particular family dates back over 20 years, first of all with the genius among winemakers, the late Henri Woltner, then his brother Fernand and later with the Dewavrins, because Françoise is the daughter of the last named. The French Napoleonic Code can cause all kinds of problems in families, so some years ago the Dewavrins decided to up-sticks and move to

California. They sold their forest in Les Landes near Bordeaux and ultimately La Mission-Haut-Brion. Their more recent story is of such interest that I am going to repeat it at length.

Some five or six years ago, they purchased a defunct winery some 500 metres up on Howell Mountain where the last wine had been made in 1940 and subsequently the land had been allowed to return to nature. Originally, the vineyard had been established in 1877 by two French *vignerons* called Brun and Chaix and the named the property 'Nouveau Médoc'. In 1886 they completed the construction of a large three-storey winery built solidly of stone, so once again this is serving its original purpose.

With its special micro-climate, this rolling land on top of Howell Mountain appears to provide a remarkable setting, especially for the production of the *chardonnay* grape and already some of the vines are five years old. The first vintage 1985 is now maturing in new oak casks.

The Dewavrins have chosen a good team with Ric Forman as the consultant, Ted Lemon as cellarmaster and René Rondeau to handle the administration. Together with the special situation of the vineyard, the very different and very French method of wine making, it will be fascinating to see how the wine from the Woltner Estate turns out.

FRIDAY, 20 JUNE

Albert Givton, the editor of the *Wine Consumer* in Vancouver, B.C. drove me to Napanook, the winery close to Yountville where Christian Moueix and Robin Lail are producing the exciting new wine called Dominus.

The general manager is Daniel Baron who trained at Davis, has also spent some years first of all in the Médoc and later with the Moueix family in Libourne. He introduced us to Joe Baronzini who, although now retired, has managed this property since 1964 and is well versed in its history. There have been vines at Napanook for a hundred years and the vineyard was purchased by the late John Daniel in 1946 as an addition to his already famous Inglenook Winery. At that time, according to Joe Baronzini, only horses were used to do the work. This is not unlike the story of Château Latour for, when the *domaine* changed hands in 1963, there were no tractors at all, only Percheron horses, mules and even oxen, all of course sadly out of date. When John Daniel sold the Inglenook Winery in 1964, he retained Napanook but after his death in 1970 the grapes were sold to other wineries.

So great has become the renown of the California vineyards, that in common with other illustrious French wine producers, Christian Moueix, whose family owns many famous vineyards in

Pomerol and Saint Emilion in addition to half of Château Pétrus, became interested in producing a fine wine from the Napa Valley. As was only natural, he approached Robert Mondavi for advice and as it happened, Robin Lail, a daughter of the late John Daniel, was working as his assistant. The two were introduced, Christian inspected the vineyard and that is how the John Daniel Society came to life in 1981. In fact it is a partnership between Christian, Robin Lail and her sister Marcia. At the moment the area under vines is about 57 acres and these are planted with 75 per cent *cabernet sauvignon* with the rest a mixture of *cabernet franc, merlot, malbec* and some *petit verdot*. Many of these were planted in 1964 and I was told that the *cabernet franc* vines have a special character of their own.

In one respect the Napanook Vineyard is different from others in California – it is dry-farmed, whereas most vineyards have to use some form of irrigation. The soil is gravelly clay and the vines benefit from underground springs flowing off the nearby hills.

In order to obtain the best result, the maximum financial effort is being devoted to the vineyard and the making of the wine, so the construction of a winery is a luxury that will come later. Meanwhile, the wine is made and then matured in cask at the Rombauer Winery on the Silverado Trail, near St Helena. Mr and Mrs Koerner Rombauer are an attractive couple, who in order to establish their own winery, share their facility with a number of other growers. This is an admirable arrangement for the John Daniel Society whose wine is made and matured under ideal conditions and entirely under their own management.

After a walk through the vines at Napanook, Daniel Baron drove us to the Rombauer Winery in order to taste the vintages which so far have been made. All the casks in which Dominus is matured have come from Cheval-Blanc in Saint Emilion and have been used there for one vintage only. The 1983 vintage was matured entirely in these casks, but the subsequent one of 1984 and 1985 although matured in similar casks have also had 20 per cent new oak.

1985 Dominus, from the cask

Very dark colour, a distinguished bouquet with a hint of oak and vanilla. Still very immature, but what a potential this has. Great depth of fruit and flavour. Although this has been made mainly from the *cabernet sauvignon* grape, the taste reminded me more of a fine pomerol. A remarkable wine

1984 Dominus, from the cask

Similar colour, a concentrated bouquet, more mature of course, fine quality with a lovely style

1983 Dominus, after six months in bottle
A lovely ruby colour, the bouquet still somewhat subdued, a lovely concentration of ripe fruit. This also seemed somewhat French in style

These three vintages had a consistency of style and quality and they should turn out extremely well. When the 1983 has been released on the market, I must try to obtain at least a few bottles for the Zinfandel Club in London.

Tawfiq and Richel Khoury arrived from San Diego. A builder by trade, in 1984 Tawfiq received the award of the Professional Builder of the Year and recently was given the title of Mr Gourmet of 1986. We all went to dine at an excellent restaurant in St Helena, called Rose & Le Favour, where the proprietor/chef specialises in Thai cooking. The food was indeed remarkable.

For my first course, I chose oysters in a delicious cream of leek sauce while my neighbour had finely sliced raw beef and raw tuna also with a tempting sauce. With this we compared two chardonnays:

1983 Sonoma Cutrer
This has already been described in these notes, but this time it did not seem quite so good. I think we all preferred the regular 1981 from Robert Mondavi

My main course consisted of some delectable Muskovy duck with equally delicious vegetables, finely sliced and cooked in the Thai fashion. With this we compared two cabernets:

1981 Steltzer
A new name for me, but a nice wine with what I can only describe as an exciting taste

1981 Opus One
Excellent but this too has already been described in these notes

SATURDAY, 21 JUNE

Another delicious lunch at Mustard's on Highway 29 and it was packed as usual. We compared two more chardonnays with names entirely new to me.

1983 Perret, Carneros
Medium body with a very nice flavour

1984 Nyers

A fresh wine, lighter in style with a more lemony character. I personally preferred the Perret

The weather had become warmer than I like, it must have been well over 38°C and made me thankful for air-conditioning. That evening we drove into San Francisco for a major tasting of Château Lafite at the extremely nice Stanford Court Hotel. The tasting had been organised by Dr Haskell Norman, the brilliant director of the Marin County Chapter of the International Wine & Food Society, and was monitored by Michael Broadbent, that apostle of Lafite. It proved a remarkable evening.

Altogether there were 13 vintages and, *mirabile dictu*, everyone of them from a magnum. The vintages I liked best were 1966, 1961 (a marvellous wine) and, as expected, the 1953 was a delight. The 1949 was also excellent. The surprise for me was the 1947, a vintage which because of very hot weather at the time of the harvest, produced wines with volatile acidity, many of them with famous names. This Lafite 1947 was sweet and charming and much better, dare I say it, than our Latour of that year. The evening ended on a high note with the Lafite 1945, a splendid wine. Three months before in Los Angeles, Bipin Desai had organised a magnificent tasting of the 1945 vintage, but on that occasion neither of the two bottles was nearly as good as this magnum, but that perhaps is to be expected.

SUNDAY, 22 JUNE

As is only right and proper this visit to the United States was to culminate fittingly. It might be considered difficult to match a tasting of magnums of great vintages of Château Lafite, but now in a different field Haskell Norman had produced something equally interesting, a tasting of some of the fabled old vintages of Inglenook.

It has been my good fortune to have had a long association with the wines of California, indeed it goes back to the summer of 1964 when, as a guest of Dr Bill Dickerson, I attended a picnic of the Berkeley Wine & Food Society at the Heitz Winery in Spring Valley where Joe and Alice Heitz had established themselves a few months before. It was on that occasion that I met Barney and Belle Rhodes, who a year or so later, introduced me to the chardonnays made by Brad Webb for the Hanzell Winery. I believe Brad was the first Californian to use small oak casks from France and his success was phenomenal. The Rhodes also took me to the small Souverain Winery (now known as Burgess) where Lee Stewart was producing such fine results. Until then the wines

I had tasted from California had not stirred any enthusiasm, but these from Hanzell and Souverain were a revelation and opened my eyes to the potential of California. In a diary published a year or so later, I wrote the potential was so great that I would like to be around in 20 years' time to see what would happen. As it transpired the transformation was to take place within about seven years and was coupled with the mushrooming of all the boutique wineries.

With all due respect to the other fine establishments then existing in the Napa Valley, the vineyards of Beaulieu and Inglenook were regarded more or less in the same light as Lafite and Latour from Bordeaux. The names of their proprietors, George de Latour, the Marquis de Pins and John Daniel father and son, were spoken of with bated breath.

Dr George Linton, was, I believe, one of the first men to recognise the merits of the older vintages of California and I can remember an extraordinary event some 15 years ago at his house. On that evening he opened some unforgettable bottles of the decade of the 1940s from wineries such as Louis M. Martini, Charles Krug, B.V. and Inglenook. At 20 or more years old, those wines had all kept very well; but it is now said, and this is a much debated point, that as far as longevity is concerned, the more recent vintages from California have not been of the same calibre.

Inglenook is now a far more attractive place to visit than it was when I last went there many years ago. Under the guidance of the managing director, Dennis Fife, we made a tour of the premises and I was amazed by the wealth of the vintages in the Wine Library. There seemed to be all the vintages as far back as the repeal of Prohibition and some even as far as the 1880s. I was also surprised by the way the casks of maturing wine are stored. In France they are seldom more than three high, but at Inglenook the tiers are eight high. The difference of course was that here there was air-conditioning, an expense which fortunately is not necessary either in Bordeaux or Burgundy.

It would appear that the production of really fine quality at Inglenook has been difficult during recent years. When the Winery was sold in 1964, the three particular vineyards from which the late John Daniel had produced such splendid cabernets in the 1940s were disposed of separately and it is only during the past few years they have again become available. So from now onwards all should be well.

During his account of the history of Inglenook, Dennis Fife pointed out that, generally speaking, the quality of the wines of the decade of the 1940s was exceptional, that of the 1950s was regarded with mixed emotions and more or less the same with the 1960s. It had improved during the 1970s, the 1970 extremely good, the 1974 good and better still the 1977. All of this we were to discover for ourselves at the tasting and, even better, the new era which is blossoming for Inglenook in the 1980s.

The wines were of course all cabernet sauvignon and since they might have been overwhelmed by the vigour of the younger vintages, the older ones were served first.

1949
A fine dark colour, this had remarkable fruit and considerable vinosity and there was still some tannin. Definitely impressive

1946
A dark colour, another extraordinary wine, with less tannin, but it had lovely fruit

1943
Very dark colour, rich and full-bodied with marvellous balance, great quality

1941
Very dark colour, a high rich wine with a lovely depth of flavour. It was alive and vibrant with a charming sweetness. Truly an extraordinary wine

These four vintages were a revelation. With the exception of 1945, my recollection of the wartime vintages from Bordeaux seems that they may not have lasted so well. In their defence, of course, during those years all the vineyard workers had been called up for the armed forces during the summer of 1939.

1955
Good colour, pleasant flavour but with less depth than any of the preceding wines and there was a hint of acidity. I felt this needed drinking

1958
Good colour, very good fruit with a nice long finish, this had more depth than the 1955 and was better

1959
Good colour, medium body, some depth and a pleasant flavour. N.B. Of the 1950s I like the 1958 best and then the 1959

1961
Good colour, a pleasant full-bodied wine with plenty of fruit and a little tannin

1963

Although the flavour was good, this lacked depth and needed drinking

1966

Good colour, very good fruit and flavour, with a nice finish, a fine wine

1970

Dark colour, lovely fruit with delightful depth of flavour, for me the best of the 1970s

1974

Very good colour, a pleasant flavour etc. but disappointing for such a good vintage

1978

Dark colour, heaps of flavour, a powerful wine with a good future

1980

Good fruit and flavour and nicely balanced

1981, Cask Reserve Selection

A lovely deep colour, heaps of fruit, leaving a nice taste in the mouth

1983, Barrel Blend Reserve Cask 'Reunion'

A wine made from the three vineyards from which John Daniel used to produce the Inglenook classics of the 1940s. This was first rate

The winemaker John Richburg predicted this 1983 will become the most outstanding cabernet made during his ten years at Inglenook. It was still very young, of course, but certainly it showed considerable promise. From wines such as this, and from the excellent 1981 vintage, it would appear that Inglenook is back on the right lines and that henceforth much more can be expected from this vineyard. It was a privilege to be present on such an auspicious occasion. It provided a high note to end this visit to California.

20
PLEASURE TO COME

What will we be drinking in 1987? This is only a rough forecast, but it looks as though there will be some very good wine around in the near future and especially from France. Indeed, we wine lovers should be counting our blessings, for I cannot remember a period when there has been such an abundance of attractive wines waiting for us to drink.

Although the 1984 vintage produced nothing very special either for red or white wine, the remarkable vintages of 1983 and 1985 have bent over backwards to provide us with a profusion of good things and from a number of different districts. There have of course been combinations of good vintages in the past, but in days gone by the methods of viticulture and the art of vinification were not nearly so good as they are today.

From long experience I have learnt that good times do not last for ever and that unfavourable conditions will surely return. For the time being, therefore, we must take full advantage of the blessings that lie before us.

Let us begin with white wine, for by 1987 some of the success-ful 1985s should be ready to drink although at the moment of writing it is too early to predict precisely how they are going to turn out.

The 1983 vintage was excellent for both the Rhine and the Moselle, as good as, if not better than, 1976. Vintages as good as this and 1985 do not occur too often in these northern wine districts so the opportunity to snap up some of the good 1983s and 1985s is not to be missed.

The situation in Alsace is similar, there also the 1983 vintage was unusually good, the best since 1976 and perhaps even finer. The regular wines of 1983 such as riesling and gewurztraminer have been delightful to drink during 1985 and with the extra time to develop in bottle, they should be even better by 1987. By then the new category of fine wines labelled *vendange tardive*, which takes longer to mature, should be ready to drink. The 1985 vintage for the wines of Alsace was also 'manna from heaven', so if by 1987 many of the good 1983s have disappeared from the market, there will be the younger and perhaps equally good 1985 vintage to fall back upon.

Not to be outdone, the Loire Valley produced some attractive wines in both 1983 and 1985, especially the latter, so this is good news for those whose taste is for wines such as Sancerre, Pouilly Fumé and Muscadet.

The prospect for white burgundy is equally good. There may still remain some of the two good vintages of 1982 and 1983 to draw upon, and some of the 1984s, although leaner and not so immediately attractive, are not too bad. Better still will be the 1985s and these should be available in 1987. Owing to the strong demand, the price of Pouilly Fuissé will probably be too expensive, likewise that of Chablis, but for other reasons. The production of Chablis has been severely curtailed because of frost to which this district is so prone. For less expensive wines, it will be better to concentrate on Mâcon Blanc, Mercurey Blanc and Rully.

As to red wine, one of the most exciting sources of enjoyment will be the 1985 vintage from the Beaujolais, the finest it is claimed for 40 years. Being no fan of 'Beaujolais Nouveau', a cult I consider overdone, I have to admit some of the 'beaujolais nouveau' of 1985 was very good. By 1987 the better wines from the Beaujolais of 1985 such as Fleurie, Morgon, and Brouilly should be approaching their best.

Although somewhat irregular, a number of the red wines of the 1983 vintage from the Côte d'Or are very good, but these will be for buying with a view to the future. In this case the selection will depend on the ability of your supplier, who may have sold his best wines if you wait too long.

If not great, the 1982 vintage is proving very useful for the wines of the Côte d'Or and some of the 1980s are better still. At the moment I am not touching the good 1978s in my own cellar, but perhaps by 1987 they may have become more agreeable to drink.

Red bordeaux is easier to buy than red burgundy, because a specialised knowledge is not so necessary, and the prospects for the former are every bit as exciting as they are for the 1985 beaujolais. For example, for everyday drinking, some of the *petits châteaux* and the *crus bourgeois* of 1982 are some of the most attractive inexpensive wines the writer has ever known. Some of them have been enjoyable to drink since they were very young and in this case infanticide has been no bad thing. Thanks to all the publicity and all the hoopla over the 1982 vintage, the prices of the finer clarets have doubled and even trebled, but so far, that is in February 1986, the price of these excellent lesser wines has remained stable. At a pinch, it may be possible to drink some of the lesser wines of 1981 while many of the finer wines of 1980 have been agreeable for some time.

A veritable feast of good things lies before us.

INDEX

Index